IMAGES
of America

CHIRICAHUA NATIONAL MONUMENT

On the Cover: One of the many remarkable pinnacles in southern Arizona's Chiricahua National Monument drew the close attention of this 1930s-era hiker. (Courtesy of the Western Archeological Conservation Center, Tucson, Arizona.)

IMAGES
of America

CHIRICAHUA NATIONAL MONUMENT

Cindy Hayostek

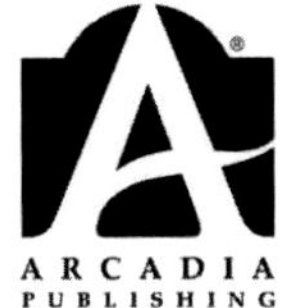

Copyright © 2018 by Cindy Hayostek
ISBN 978-1-4671-2849-0

Published by Arcadia Publishing
Charleston, South Carolina

Printed in the United States of America

Library of Congress Control Number: 2018932490

For all general information, please contact Arcadia Publishing:
Telephone 843-853-2070
Fax 843-853-0044
E-mail sales@arcadiapublishing.com
For customer service and orders:
Toll-Free 1-888-313-2665

Visit us on the Internet at www.arcadiapublishing.com

Dedicated in honor of National Park Service rangers Paul Fugate and Karen Gonzales for their efforts to preserve Chiricahua National Monument's natural and cultural resources

CONTENTS

ACKNOWLEDGMENTS

My first acknowledgement is to my father, John H. Davis Jr. His father arranged to have my dad learn ranching skills shortly before he turned 10 years old. My dad arranged the same thing for me by taking me to Faraway Ranch at about the same age. It's where I learned to ride horseback for miles and miles and never slump in the saddle, where I learned to work range cattle, and where I learned to appreciate the spectacular beauty that is Cochise County.

Thanks also go to five people who helped me in numerous ways. They are Suzanne Moody, Chiricahua National Monument park ranger; Khaleel Saba and Veronica Furlong, both of the Western Archaeological and Conservation Center; Robin Pinto, National Park Service consultant; and Andres Rivera, borderlands techie and teacher.

Except as noted, all photographs are courtesy of the Western Archeological Conservation Center in Tucson, Arizona.

Introduction

Chiricahua National Monument, in Arizona's southeast corner, is famous for its scenic and biological richness. Set in the Chiricahua Mountains' northern end, the monument overflows with fancifully named rock formations and pinnacles interlaced with hiking trails. The Chiricahuas (Cheery-ca-wahs) are the largest of the "sky island" mountain ranges, renowned for their variety of distinctive plants and animals.

Chiricahua National Monument also receives recognition for its cultural history that links Chiricahua Apaches, buffalo soldiers, ranchers and homesteaders, indomitable females who were guest ranch entrepreneurs, National Park Service employees, and thousands of visitors who appreciate the marvels of a special place.

Chiricahua National Monument, including its Bonita Canyon entrance, encompasses 12,025 acres; 86 percent is federally classified wilderness. It lies 37 miles southeast of Willcox, Arizona, and 70 miles north of Douglas, Arizona. Both are in Cochise County, which also hosts Tombstone, "The Town Too Tough to Die," and Bisbee, voted one of the best small towns in America.

The Chiricahua Mountains trend northwest–southeast. They rise above the grassy Sulphur Springs, San Bernardino, and San Simon Valleys as part of the basin-range structure that dominates Arizona and much of northern Mexico.

Favored with mild temperatures, the Chiricahuas receive around 19 inches of moisture each year. About two-thirds falls during July and August and the rest in January and February.

The Chiricahuas, approximately 40 miles long and 4 to 20 miles wide, are southern Arizona's largest single mountain range. In certain spots, they rise from about 4,000 feet to almost 10,000—over a vertical mile—in less than three horizontal miles.

This means five of North America's seven biological life zones occur in the Chiricahuas. Additionally, the "Cheery Cows" lie within the intersection of the Chihuahuan and Sonoran Deserts and the Sierra Madre and Rocky Mountains, thus supporting a vast biological diversity.

The Chiricahuas host North America's southernmost stand of Engelmann spruce and northernmost extensions of three Mexican oak species. Chiricahua fox squirrels enliven the mountain slopes, as do groups of long-nosed coatis foraging for food with their striped tails held erect. Brightly colored trogons, birds most often seen in tropical climes, frequent the Chiricahuas in the summer.

An abundance of Coues deer, one of North America's smallest whitetail deer, perhaps attracted prehistoric Native Americans who inhabited the monument. By the time Spanish conquistadors marched past Bonita Canyon in the 1540s, Chiricahua Apaches lived in the area.

Highly mobile and skilled in utilizing the land, Apaches dominated Cochise County for the next 300 years. In the 1850s, US citizens began arriving in Arizona to prospect, ranch, or otherwise try to wrest a living from the territory.

Clashes between Apaches and Americans led inevitably to a US military presence. In his 1885–1886 campaign, Gen. George Crook's tactics involved units that used Apache scouts and the 10th Cavalry, a regiment of buffalo soldiers.

One unit with Apache scouts was the 4th Cavalry. It also included a Swedish immigrant, Sgt. Neil Erickson. At the time, he was courting another Swedish immigrant, Emma Peterson. She managed a boardinghouse at Fort Bowie, a few miles north of Bonita Canyon.

Peterson visited Bonita Canyon when the buffalo soldiers were stationed there. Their duties were to prevent Apaches from using Bonita Canyon's water and to protect the families of farmer Ja Hu Stafford and ranchers Louis Prue and Brannick Riggs.

The buffalo soldiers never saw any Apaches in Bonita Canyon. To pass the time, they carved local stones into personalized blocks that they assembled into a monument honoring Pres. James A. Garfield. Their one-of-a-kind effort still exists at Faraway, although in a different form than the original.

Neil and Emma married in 1887. They moved to Bonita Canyon in 1888 and into a cabin that had housed 10th Cavalry officers. They arrived soon after Lillian, their first child, was born. Ben and Hildegard followed her.

In 1890, the Ericksons survived an Apache scare. Two renegades, believed to be a man and a woman, fled through Bonita Canyon. Neil and Prue trailed the pair eastward and thus were the first American settlers documented to enter what became Chiricahua National Monument.

The Ericksons made a living in Bonita Canyon, but only because Neil worked in Bisbee. In 1903, Neil got a job with the US Forest Service and worked from home. In 1917, the Forest Service transferred Neil away from Bonita Canyon.

Then Lillian and Hildegard took over the family ranch's operation. Hildegard solicited friends and acquaintances to meals and overnight stays at the ranch. An initially reluctant Lillian soon saw the business possibilities and quit her teaching job to help run what she named Faraway Ranch. The sisters developed it into one of Arizona's first guest ranches, which Lillian managed by herself after Hildegard married in 1920 and moved away.

The Riggs family, who were the Ericksons' neighbors, raised cattle in the Sulphur Springs Valley, west of Bonita Canyon. Brannick and Mary Riggs had arrived in Cochise County about 1879.

One of their grandsons, Ed Riggs, married Lillian in 1923. The couple ran some cattle and promoted Faraway. They did this by publicizing what they called the Wonderland of Rocks. Ed took photographs that grabbed the attention of two Douglas men, who took more photographs and displayed them. Other Douglasites contacted Arizona governor George W.P. Hunt.

Ed and Lillian had started clearing trails in the Wonderland, so when Hunt visited Faraway in 1923, he could ride into the area on a burro. What he saw convinced him to lobby Pres. Calvin Coolidge, who established Chiricahua National Monument with a 1924 presidential proclamation.

Ed continued trail-building under Forest Service contract and created pathways still used today. In 1933, the National Park Service assumed monument management and oversaw completion of a paved road through Bonita Canyon to Massai Point.

Members of the Civilian Conservation Corps (CCC), one of Pres. Franklin Roosevelt's programs designed to pull the United States out of the Great Depression, provided much of the labor. The CCC also constructed Ed's masterpiece, the Echo Canyon Trail, and connected it with other trails enjoyed today by monument visitors.

Following Ed's 1950 death, Lillian continued to run Faraway. But she struggled; she had depended on Ed because of a worsening hearing problem and the loss of her eyesight in 1942. Emma also died in 1950, and another guest ranch, the Silver Spur, operated nearby.

Despite all this, Lillian persevered. Faraway, although past its prime, still drew visitors because "only a congenital stuffed shirt could fail to melt under the relaxing informality of the place," wrote A.T. Steele in an article about Lillian and Faraway that appeared in a 1958 *Saturday Evening Post.*

In this, J.P. "Andy" Anderson, who became Faraway's manager in1960, assisted Lillian. He saw her and Faraway through their final years. Faraway closed in 1970, and Lillian died in 1977.

Ben and Hildegard approached the Park Service about buying Faraway. That happened in 1979. Park Service personnel restored Faraway's house to its 1950s heyday and added other displays. Faraway reopened in 1988 with a ceremony attended by family members and various dignitaries.

Today, the National Park Service welcomes visitors to Faraway and the monument so they can marvel at the rock formations Lillian named, appreciate its unique wildlife and plants, and learn the history of a remarkable family and remarkable place.

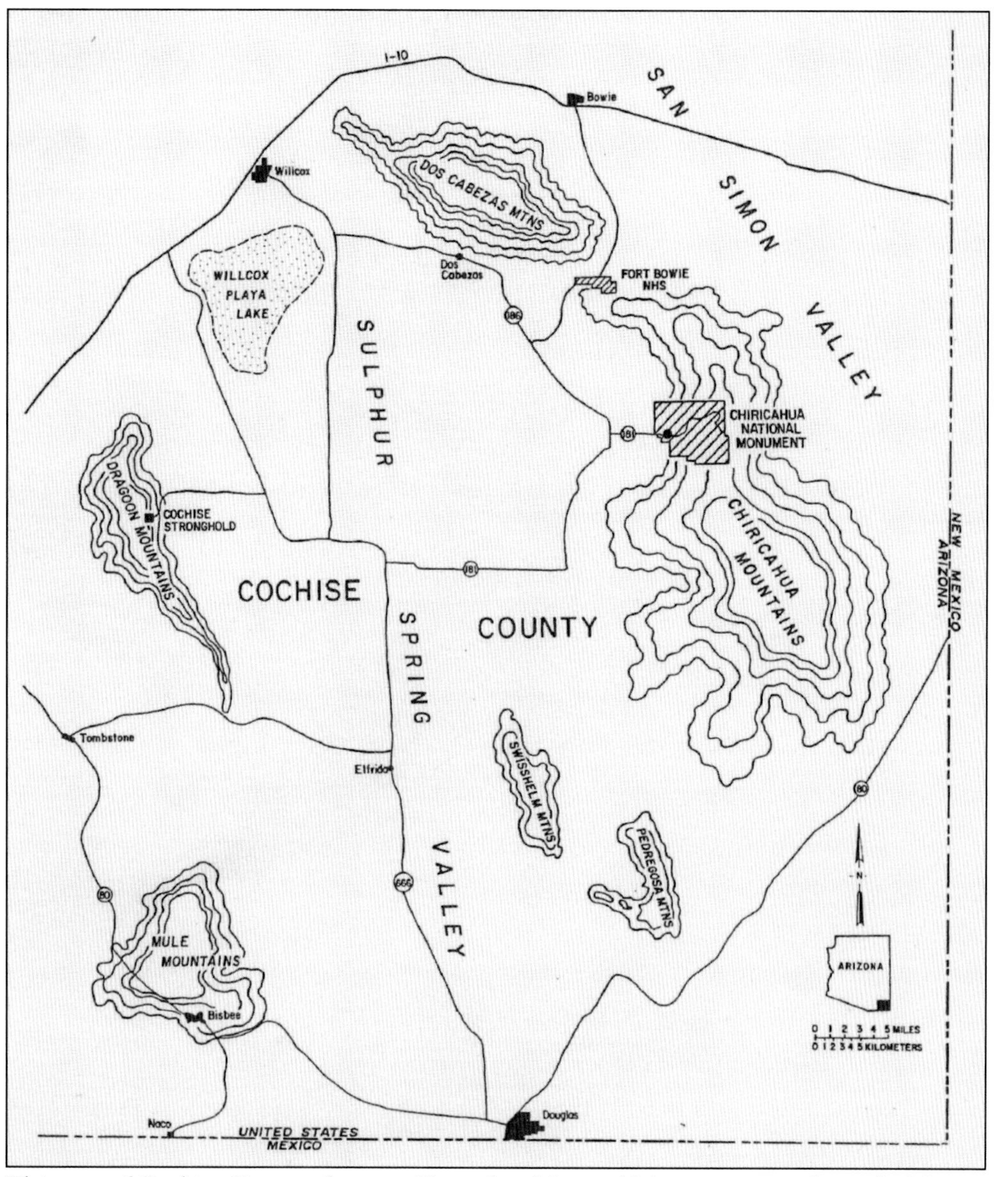

This map of Cochise County, showing Chiricahua National Monument, was drawn by Martyn D. Tagg of the Western Archeological and Conservation Center in Tucson, Arizona.

One

The Setting

In 1967, writer and naturalist Weldon Heald published *Sky Island*, a now classic book about the Chiricahua Mountains. Heald introduced them by describing a drive on the mountains' east side beginning in the Lower Sonoran Zone of grass and mesquite, going through the Upper Sonoran Zone's chaparral and into the ponderosa pines of the Transition Zone.

Visitors approaching Chiricahua National Monument from the west experience the same effect. They drive through lush grassland dotted with light green mesquites and edged with dark green ribbons of oaks. Once within the monument, piñons, junipers, and other chaparral plants cascade down the hills. Those who continue up Bonita Canyon eight miles to Massai Point see Douglas firs and ponderosa pines, including one that forms the eyelash on the famous Cochise Head rock formation. It is just one of thousands of rocks eroded into evocative shapes or slim spires throughout the area.

From Massai Point, visitors gazing westward see a vast vista widening 30 to 40 miles across the grassy Sulphur Springs Valley to the Dragoon and Dos Cabezas Mountains. The view eastward is equally impressive, since it extends the same distance across the San Simon Valley past the New Mexico state line.

Massai Point's panorama makes it easy to understand exactly what a sky island is all about: an upward sweep of stacked life zones in one vertical mile. What is not as obvious is that the Chiricahuas are at the intersection of four biomes: the Sonoran and Chihuahua Deserts and the Rocky Mountains and Mexico's Sierra Madre. All contribute unique flora and fauna found nowhere else in the United States.

It is easy to admire all this because, as Rick Taylor, another author writing about the mountain range, puts it: "The Chiricahuas are largely unmolested by the hand of man. There are no ski bowls, no open pit mines, no hydro-electric storage reservoirs. There is only the mountain."

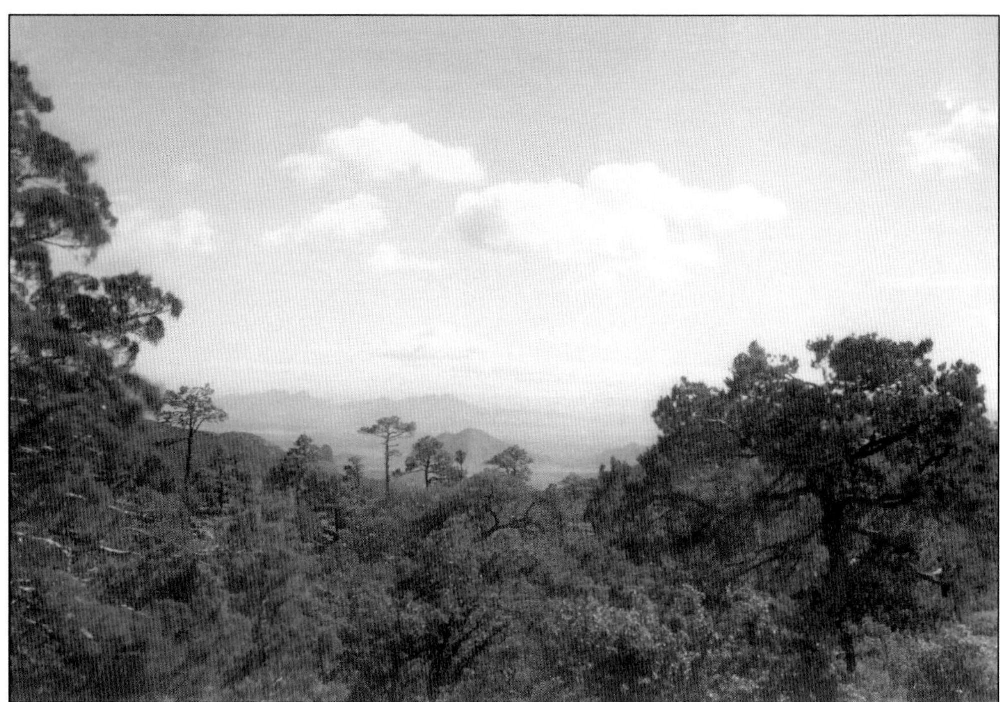

These east and west vistas seen from Chiricahua National Monument high points show how the Chiricahua Mountains rise thousands of feet up from valley floors. The view in the photograph above looks northeast from Massai Point across the San Simon Valley to the Animas Mountains on the other side of the New Mexico state line. The view below looks northwest from Heart of Rocks down Rhyolite Canyon toward the Dos Cabezas Mountains. The two (*dos*) knobs that resemble heads (*cabezas*) combine into the tallest point on the left. The Dos Cabezas dominate an area of the same name, which contains one of Cochise County's well-known ghost towns.

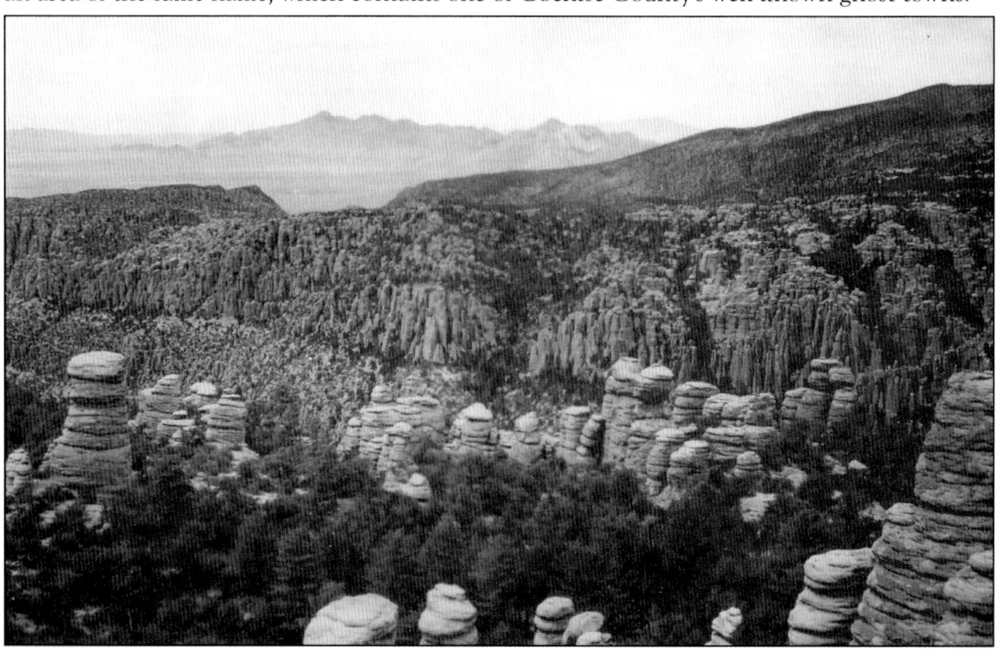

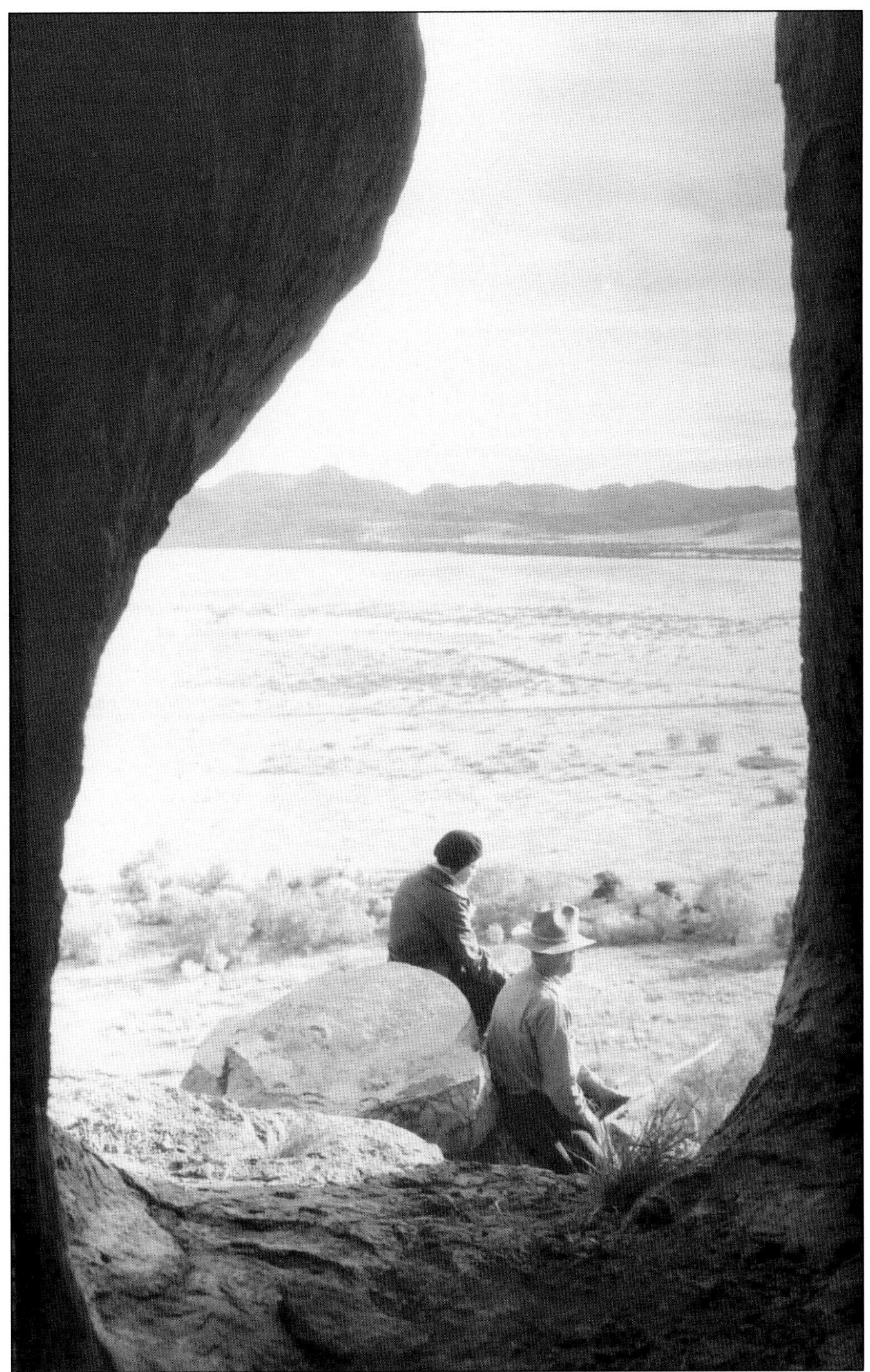

The pleasure of viewing 30 to 40 miles of the grassy Sulphur Springs Valley sweeping north, south, and west toward the Dragoon Mountains attracted this 1930s-era couple to the Chiricahua Mountains. Such a reminder of humans' speck of existence in a vast world continues to attract visitors to Chiricahua National Monument today. About 55,000 people visit Chiricahua National Monument every year.

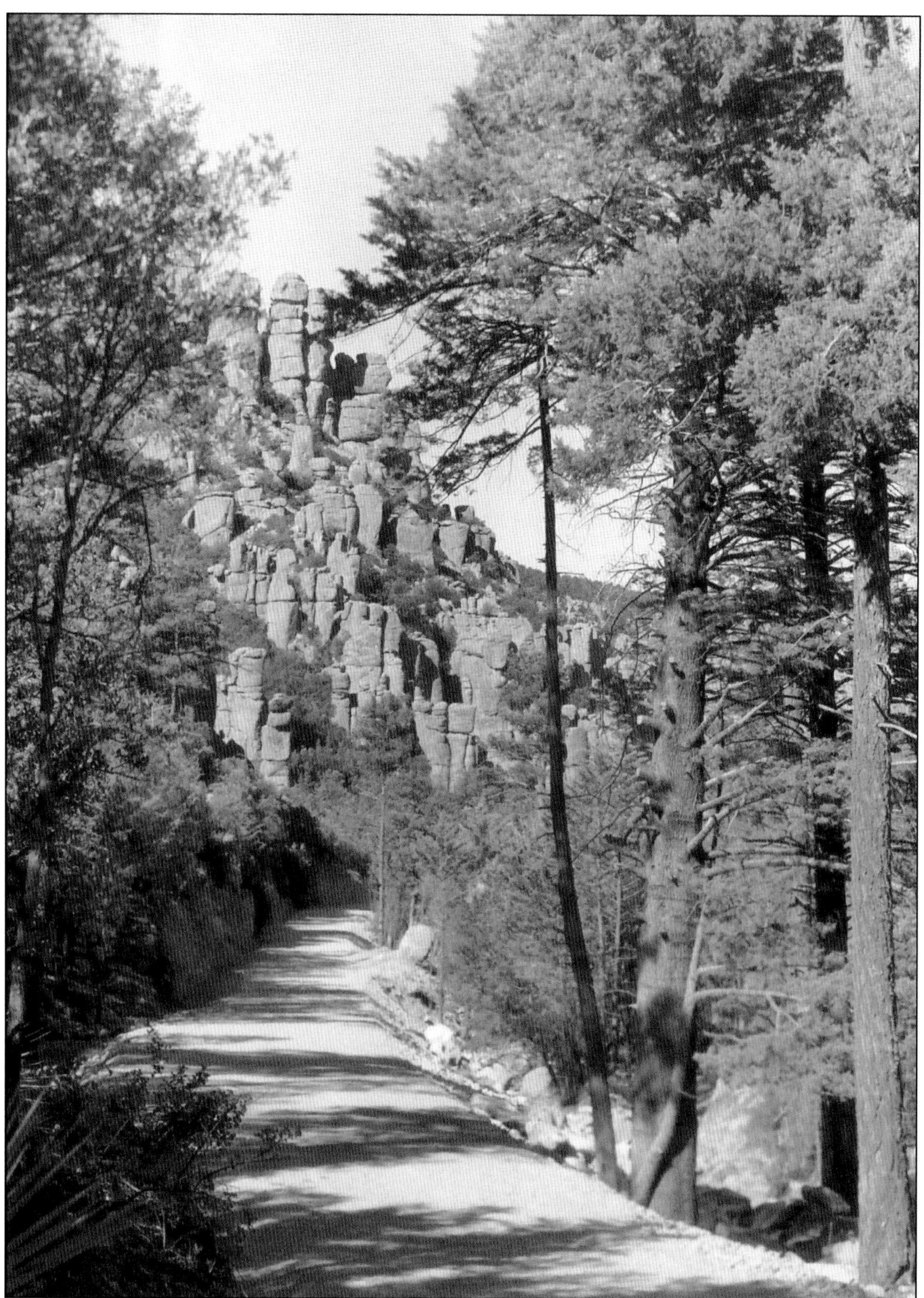

The sky islands' fascinating biological diversity and captivating beauty, which Weldon Heald writes about in the 1967 book *Sky Island*, is shown here with a road winding past ponderosa pines toward amazing rock columns. The photograph typifies the attraction of Chiricahua National Monument, established in a 1924 proclamation by Pres. Calvin Coolidge. Chiricahua was one of eight monuments Coolidge created that year, tying a record set by Theodore Roosevelt in 1908.

Two

Plants and Animals

Over 1,000 plant species grow in the Chiricahuas, many within monument boundaries. This includes *Apacheria chiricahuensis*, a woody perennial discovered in 1973 on the monument. Visitors entering the monument from the west drive past more than 50 different grasses, seven types of oaks, 11 cactus and two agave species, and nine species of conifers.

The monument's diversity of habitats insures a variety of animal species. There are 71 mammal, 46 reptile, 8 amphibian, and 171 bird species documented. The avian number does not include those seen during migratory periods; the count jumps to 200 then.

For quite a few of these critters, the sky islands are the northernmost tip of the animals' range. White-nosed coatis, raccoon relatives that ramble about in female-led family units, are also common in northern Mexico. Endemic mammals, such Chiricahua fox squirrels, were isolated millennia ago in the Chiricahuas' mountain forests by encircling grassland.

So was one of Arizona's three protected rattlesnake species, the banded rock. Other reptiles with limited US range, such as green rat snakes, Yarrow's spiny lizards, and bunch grass lizards, also live within monument boundaries.

But it is birds that draw the most attention at the monument and in the Chiricahuas. Mexican chickadees, brown creepers, and nuthatches flow through the mountains, flitting and foraging in always-on-the-move gangs. Yellow-eyed juncos scour the monument's forest floor above 6,000 feet.

Birders have seen 13 hummingbird species on the monument, including nesting violet-crowned and beryllines. Other hummers, such as Lucifer and broad-billed, drift in from Mexico. So do elegant trogons, brightly colored tropical birds that nest in the Chiricahuas each summer.

Other sought-after birds for life lists that can be seen within the Chiricahuas are red-faced and olive warblers, sulphur-bellied flycatchers, Mexican jays, and band-tailed pigeons. The monument is one place where Gould's turkeys have been reintroduced.

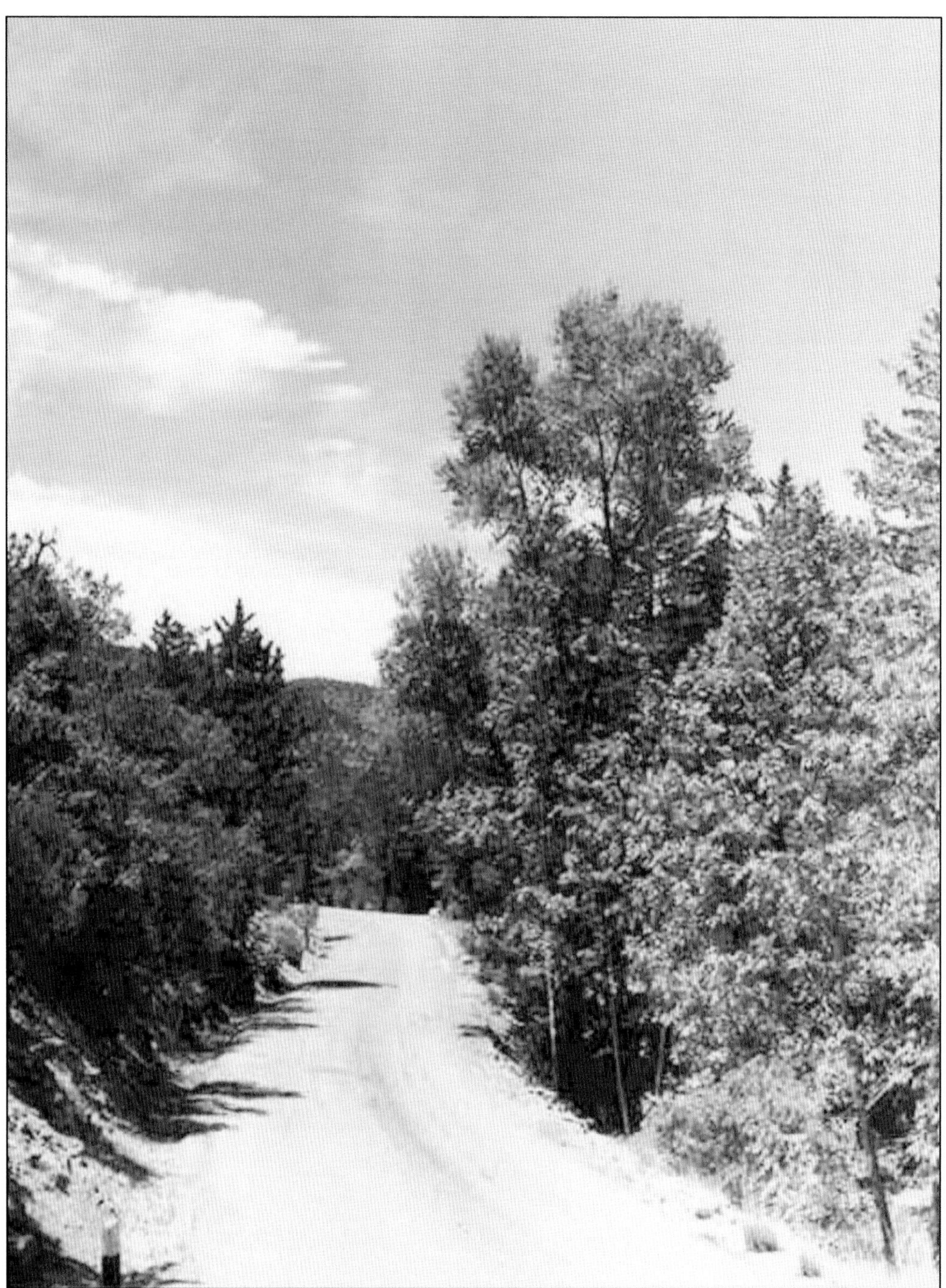

The Chiricahua Mountains' vertical span within just Bonita Canyon produces the plant variety shown in this photograph. Among the plants visible are Mexican piñon, Arizona white oak, willow, madrone, cottonwood, sycamore, Arizona cypress, and silk tassel. The cottonwood and sycamore are riparian species, while the others grow through chaparral elevations into the Transition Zone, which hosts three species of pine—Chihuahua, Apache, and five-needle ponderosa—that are all at the limit of their ranges.

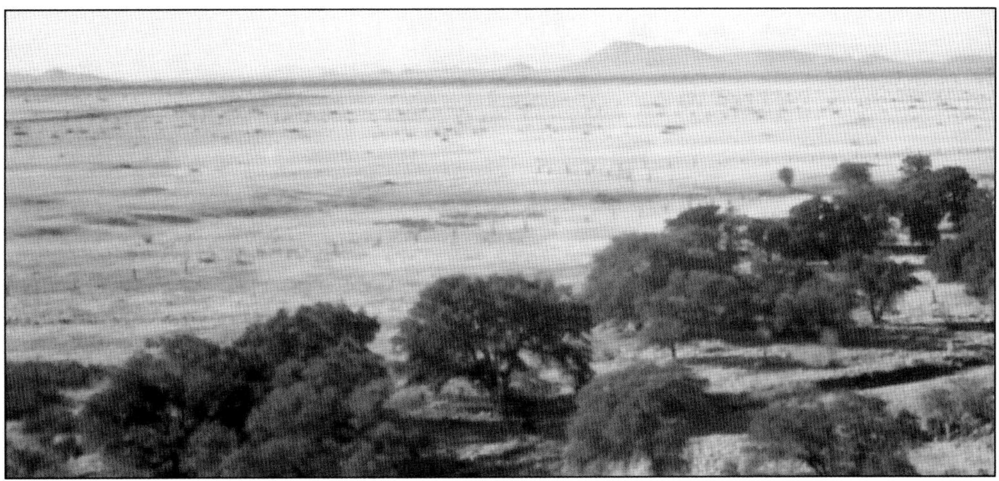

The plants in these two photographs typify lower-elevation vegetation at the entrance to Bonita Canyon. Above, water flowing out of Bonita Canyon runs in a stream bordered by oak trees. Three oak species—Arizona white, Emory, and silverleaf—reach their northern limits in the Chiricahuas. Often seen next to oak trees is a plant some people call bear grass (below); others call it sacahuista. In the past, its tough, bladelike leaves were shredded and used to weave baskets. Today, the leaves are harvested and made into brooms.

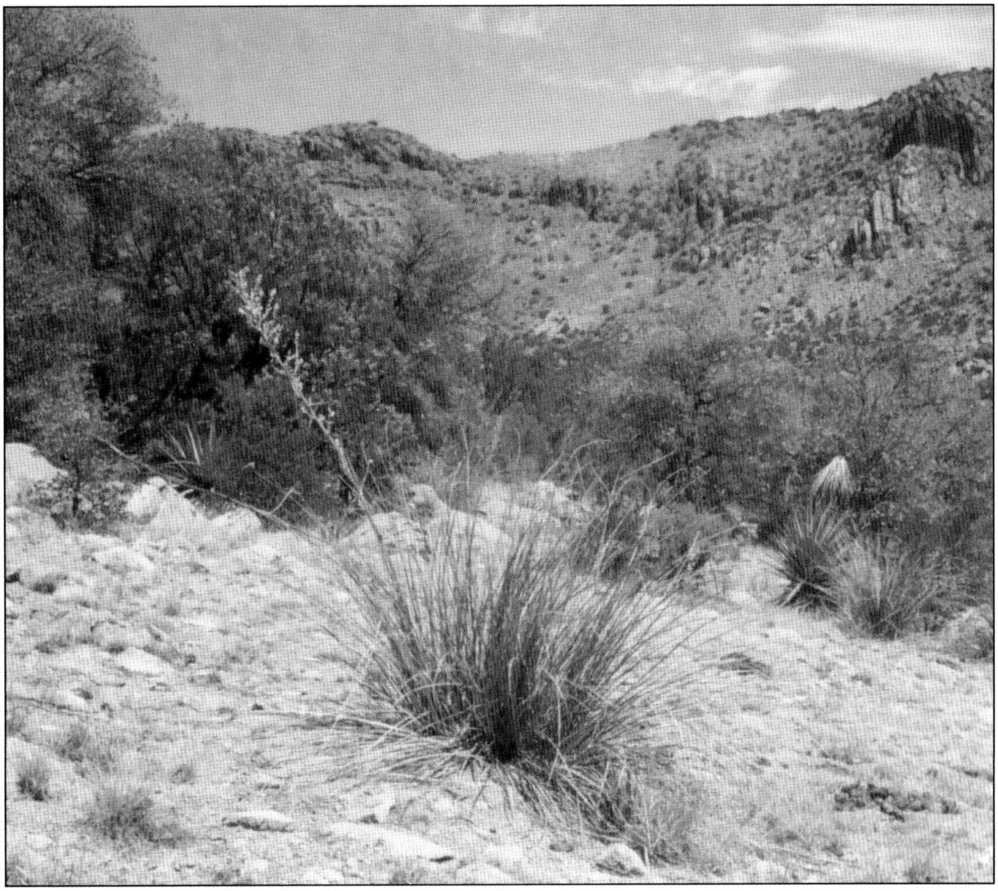

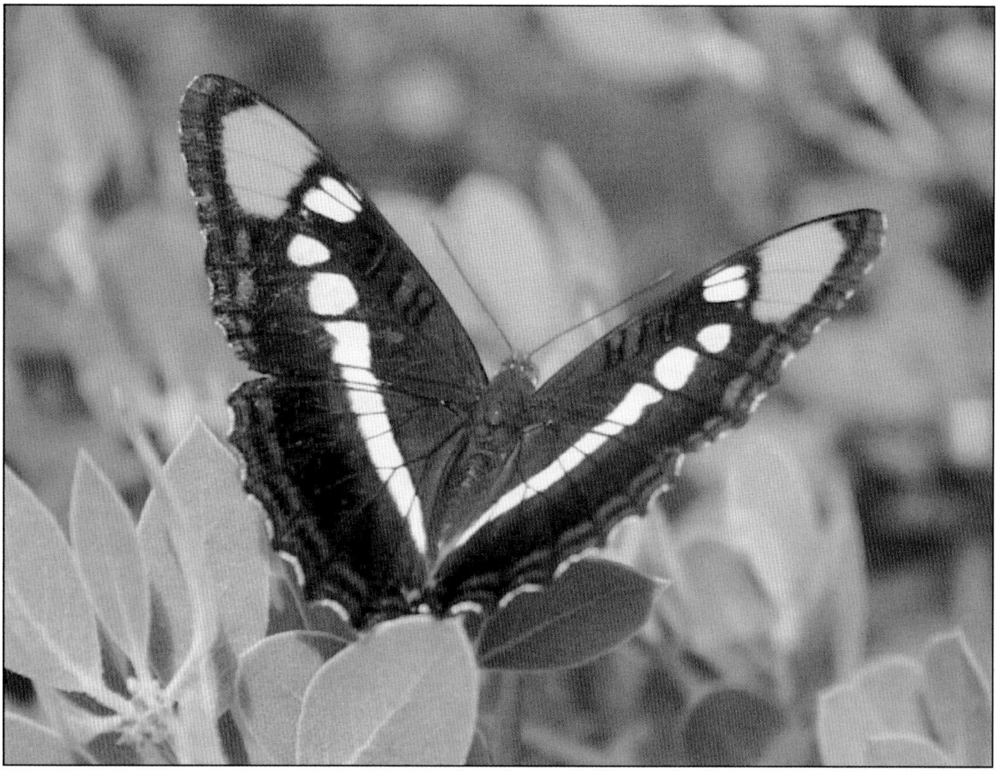

The top wing surface of Arizona sister butterflies is dark chocolate brown embellished with white splashes, orange blobs, and blue accents. This color scheme indicates *Adelpha eulalia* is unpalatable to predators. Scientific studies declared the Arizona sister a separate species found only in the southwestern United States and south into Mexico. The butterflies are a common sight in the monument's oak woodlands. (Photograph by Suzanne Moody.)

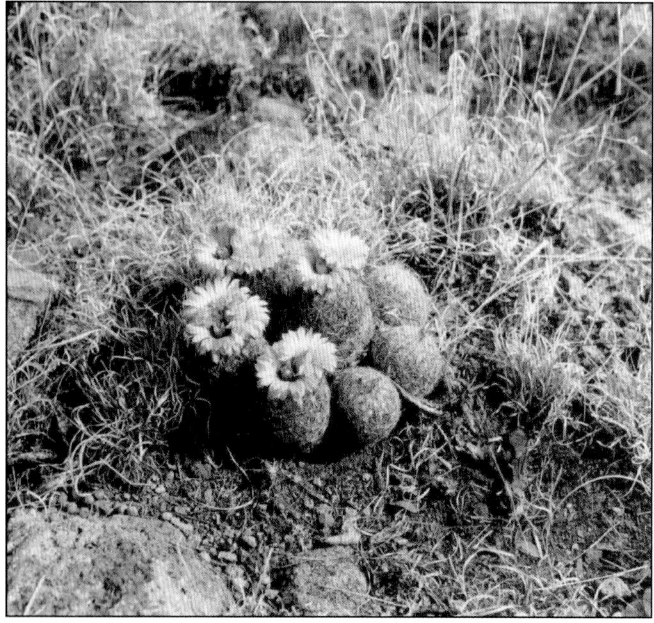

The *Coryphantha* genus of cactus, such as this one photographed at the monument's western entrance, are small- to mid-sized plants that blossom on top. With 57 species found in arid areas of the American Southwest down through Mexico to Central America, it is one of the largest cactus families in the world. The monument's many microhabitats mean cacti like this one can be found in unexpected places, such as underneath a pine-oak canopy.

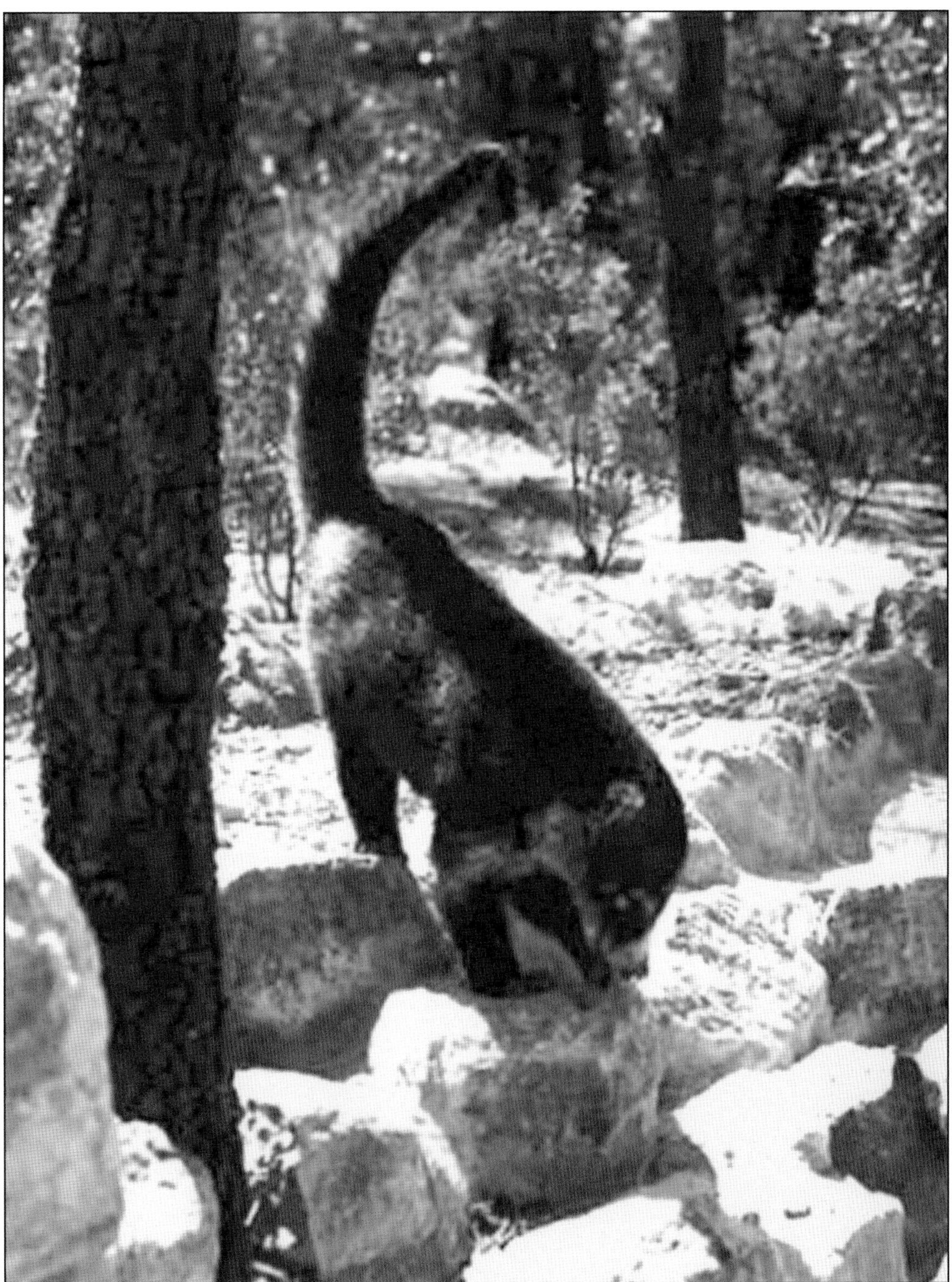

They are officially known as white-nosed coatimundis, but many locals call them *chulas*, Mexican slang for "cute." The nickname carries a typical borderlands touch of humorous sarcasm. Coatis are raccoon relatives with similar behaviors; they are omnivorous foragers who paw through their woodland home digging for grubs and tubers and gobbling up nuts, birds and eggs, insects, and small reptiles. *Nasua narica* holds its ringed tail erect and keeps its long snout in constant action. Female-led groups of one to two dozen chulas converse as they ramble through forested areas of Arizona's sky islands; they are more common south of the border.

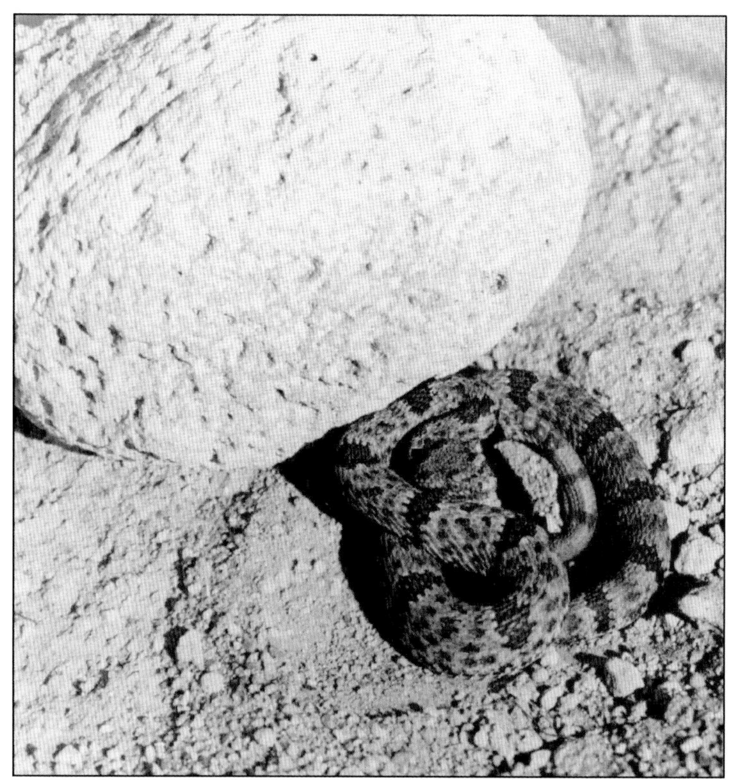

Banded rock rattlesnakes are the smallest of several rattlers found on the monument, but they are not often seen, since they are usually shy. Clad in gray tones, the banded rock rattlesnake sometimes has a greenish cast that led to its local nickname of green rock rattlesnake. Officially known as *Crotalus lepidus klauberi* in honor of American herpetologist Laurence M. Klauber, this species is one of three rattlers listed by the State of Arizona as endangered. It is against the law to harm them in any way.

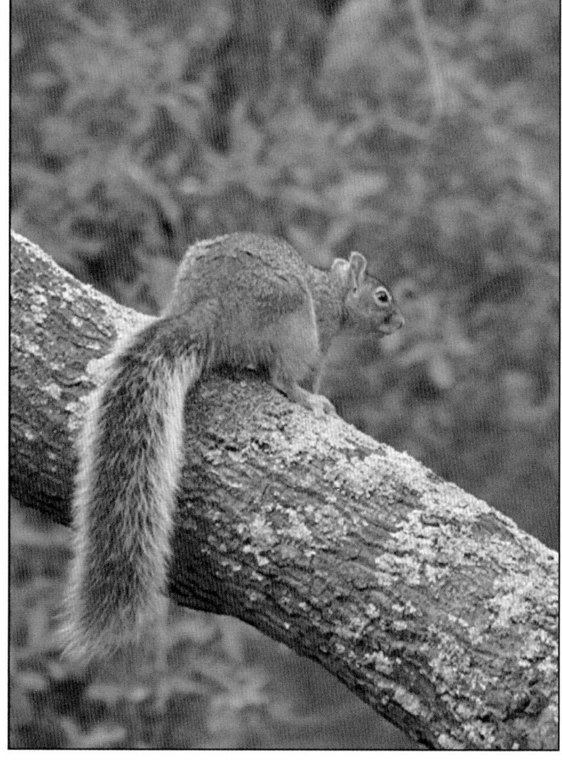

Scientific studies have shown that Chiricahua fox squirrels are genetically unique due to their isolation from the rest of the world, a condition imposed by southern Arizona's basin-range topography. *Sciurus chiricahuae* is protected by Arizona law as an endangered species. It is a large squirrel with a gray coat enlivened by a russet underbelly. They eat seeds and nuts, which they also hide under soil and leaves. Unlike other squirrels, they do not frequent campgrounds and are not easily seen in their thick-growth forest habitat. (Photograph by Suzanne Moody.)

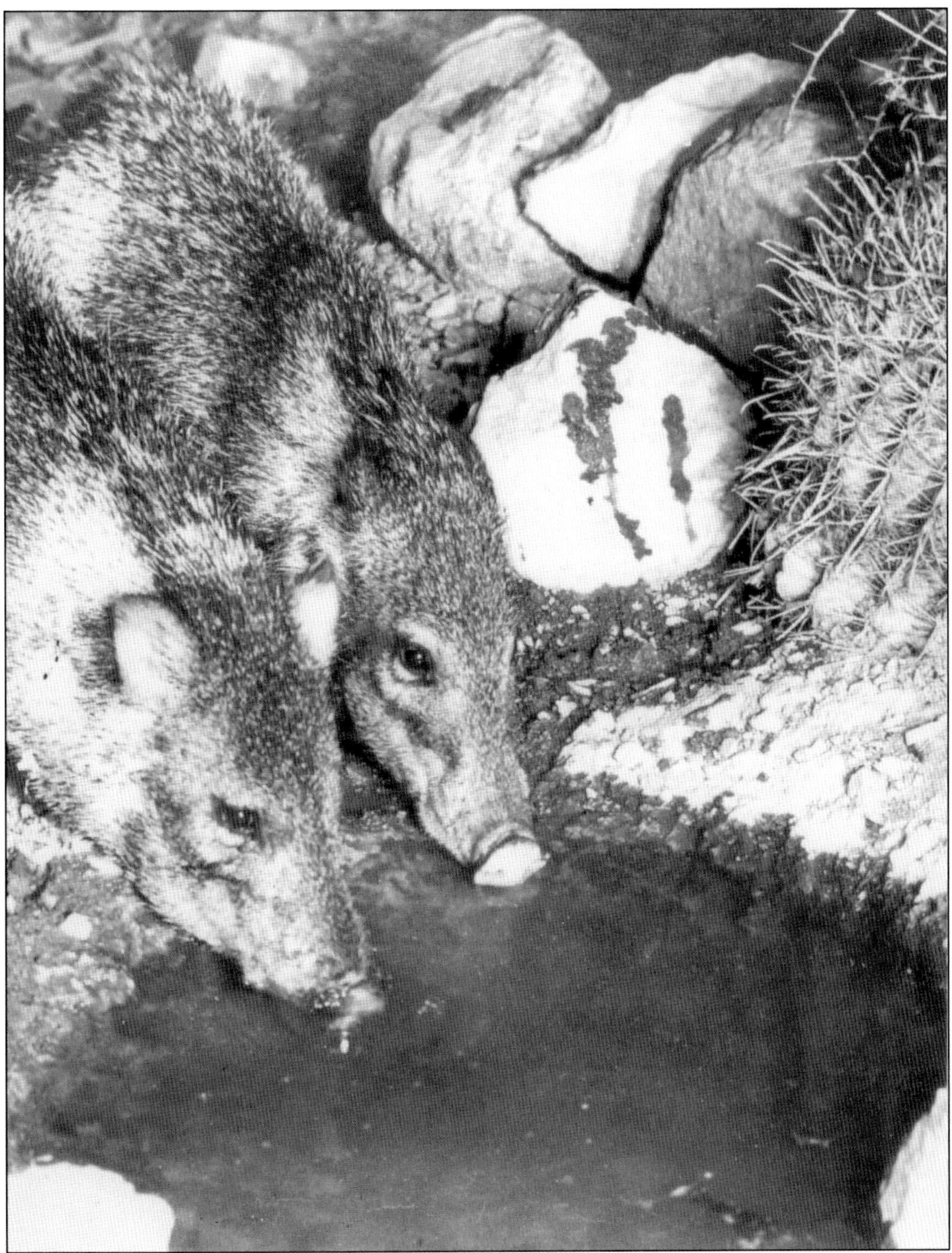

Javelinas, shown here drinking at a monument watering hole, are also known as white-collared peccaries or *Pecari tajacu*. They are medium-sized, piglike animals with coarse, grizzled hair; youngsters are more brown-toned. Javelinas are notoriously near-sighted and compensate by congregating in herds of a half dozen or more. Javelinas do not tolerate cold weather well and so are confined to the monument's lower elevations, where they dine on prickly pears, mesquite beans, tubers, and other delicacies found while rutting through their territory.

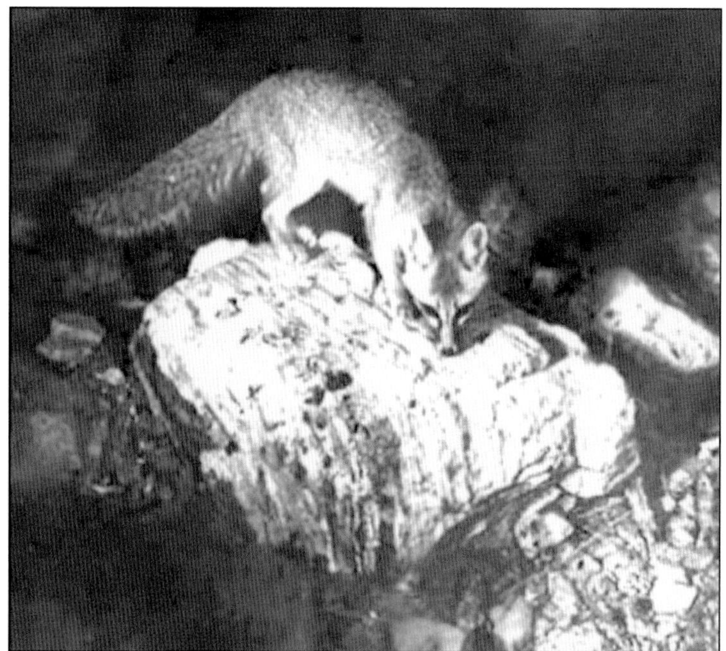

The gray fox has grizzled fur with light tan and rusty accents. It is a nimble climber and is the only member of its family that ascends trees. Cottontails and jackrabbits make up a large portion of *Urocyon cinereoargenteus*'s diet, but it also hunts small rodents and birds. Because they climb trees, gray foxes eat a lot of fruit. They are so fond of hackberries, a desert shrub, that some people call the small scarlet fruit "foxberries."

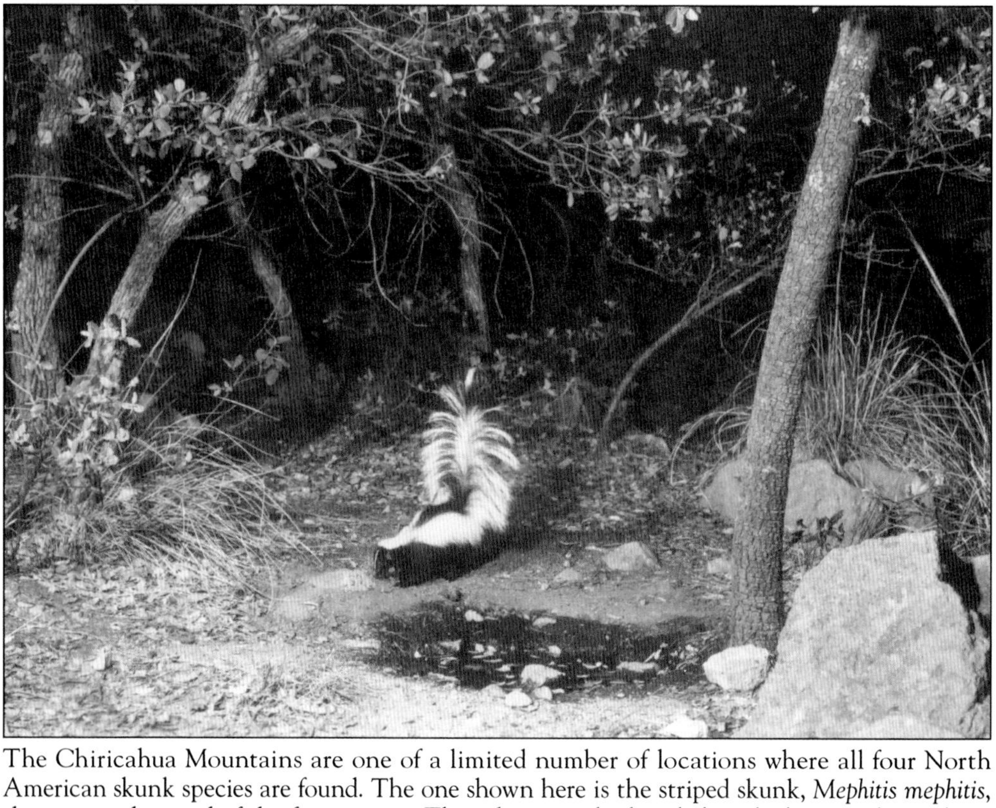

The Chiricahua Mountains are one of a limited number of locations where all four North American skunk species are found. The one shown here is the striped skunk, *Mephitis mephitis*, the most widespread of the four species. The others are the hooded, with the most limited US range; hognose, wearer of the most white fur; and spotted, the smallest skunk. All four species are primarily or entirely nocturnal and are voracious consumers of insects and small rodents.

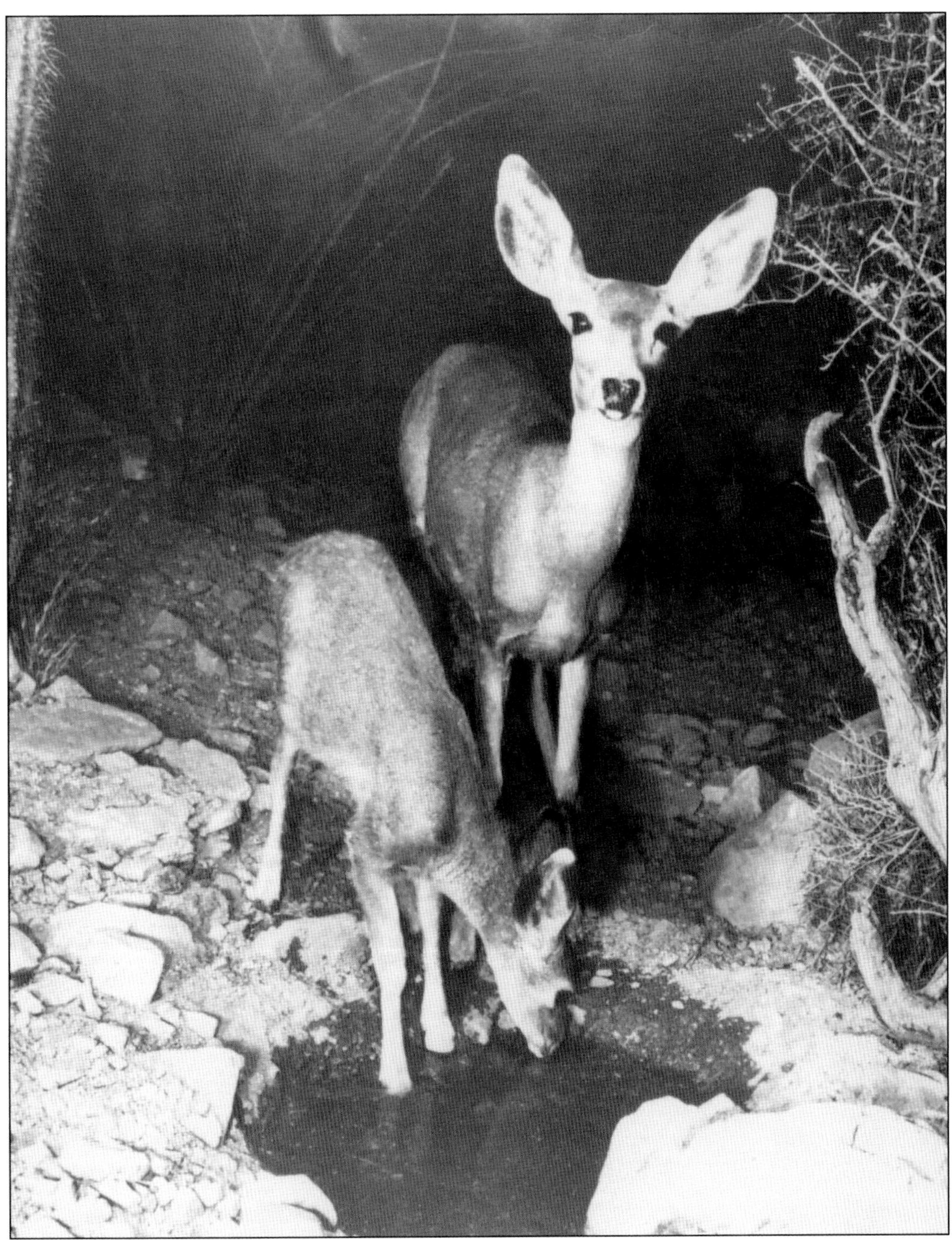

Mule deer, such as this mother and offspring at a monument watering hole, are one of the area's two deer species. Mule deer, *Odocoileus hemionus*, tend to live in lower elevations, while white-tailed deer, *Odocoileus virginianus couesi*, live at higher elevations. The monument's white-tails are a subspecies named for Elliott Coues, an early American naturalist. Coues deer are one of the smallest deer found in North America; males seldom weigh over 100 pounds. Both mule and Coues deer eat grasses, forbs, nuts, and twigs from plants such as junipers, mountain mahogany, and oaks.

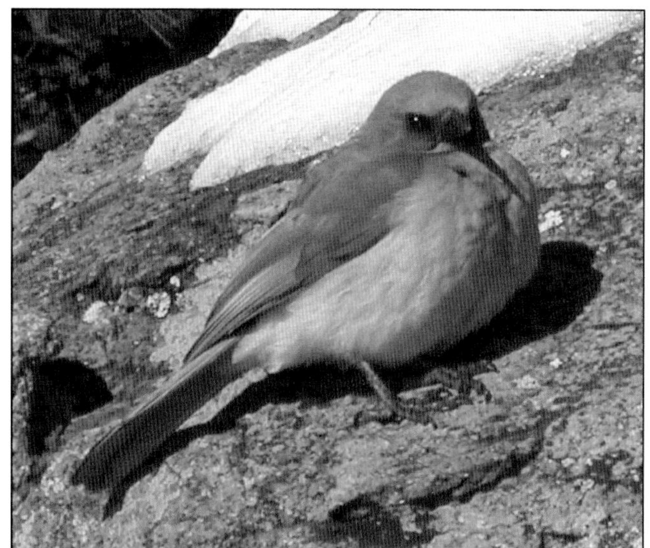

The Mexican jay, blue on top and gray underneath, is commonly seen on the monument. It is the largest and palest of a subspecies found only in sky islands of the United States and Mexico. Given the Latin name *Aphelocoma wollweberi arizonae*, Mexican jays eat acorns and pine nuts and, occasionally, small animals. Mexican jays raise youngsters cooperatively—other birds in a flock besides the parents feed nestlings and fledglings. (Photograph by Suzanne Moody.)

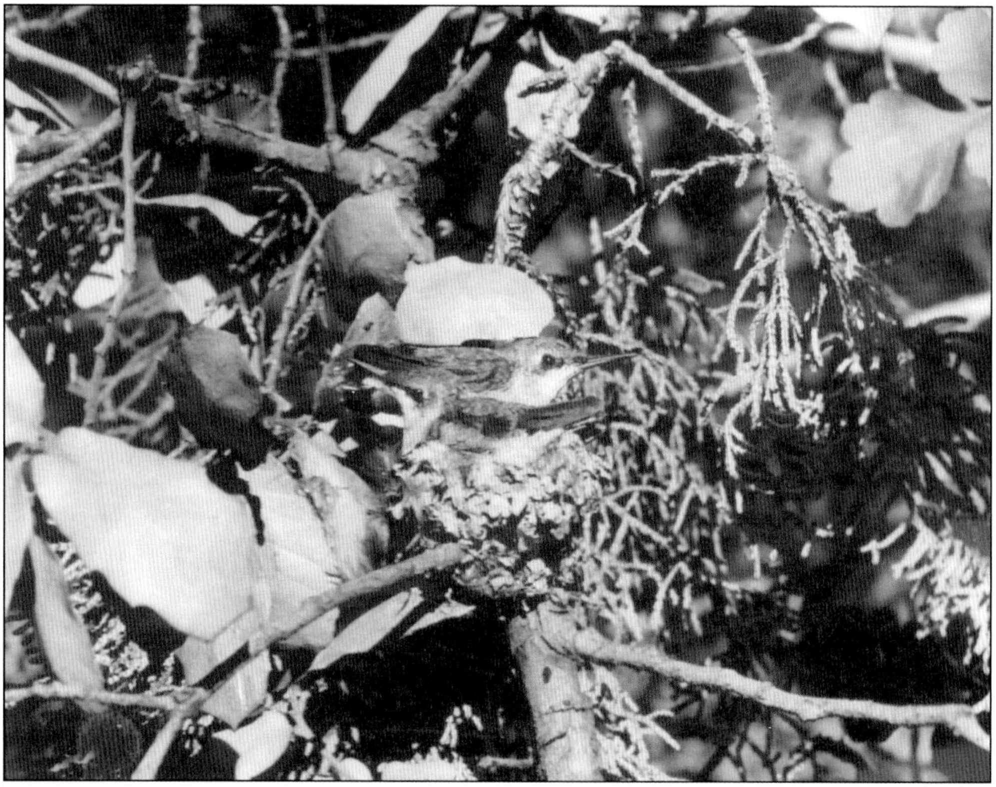

These two broad-tailed hummingbird youngsters represent one of 13 hummer species seen on Chiricahua National Monument. Broad-tails are a widespread western species, but there are also many uncommon species on the monument. These include nesting violet-crowned and berylline as well as Lucifer and broad-billed hummers. Blue-throated, magnificent, and black-chinned hummers are common. Other Chiricahua birds that can be added to life lists include red-faced and olive warblers, sulphur-bellied flycatchers, Mexican chickadees, band-tailed pigeons, and elegant trogons.

The canyon wren, *Catherpes mexicanus*, is a small songbird found throughout the West. Given the wren's preference for rocky cliffs, outcrops, and canyons, and the monument's abundance of such things, it is no surprise that the canyon wren's distinctive song of loud notes decelerating and descending is something monument visitors often hear.

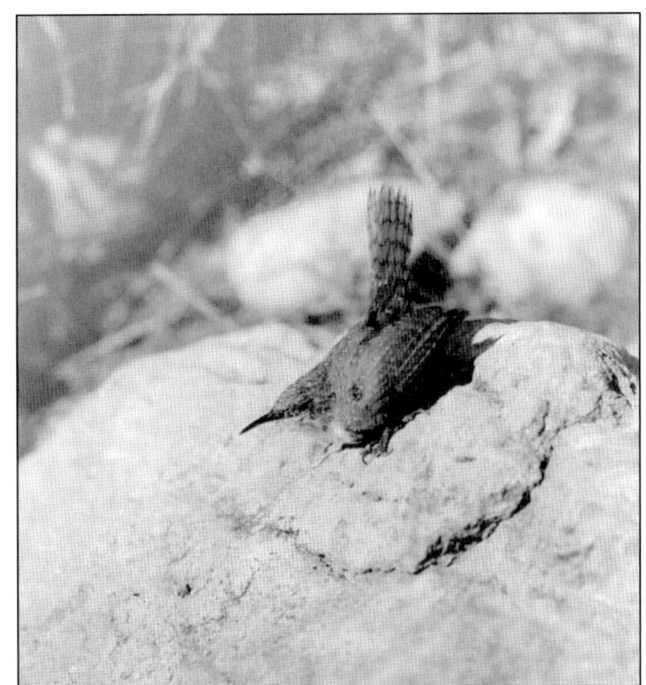

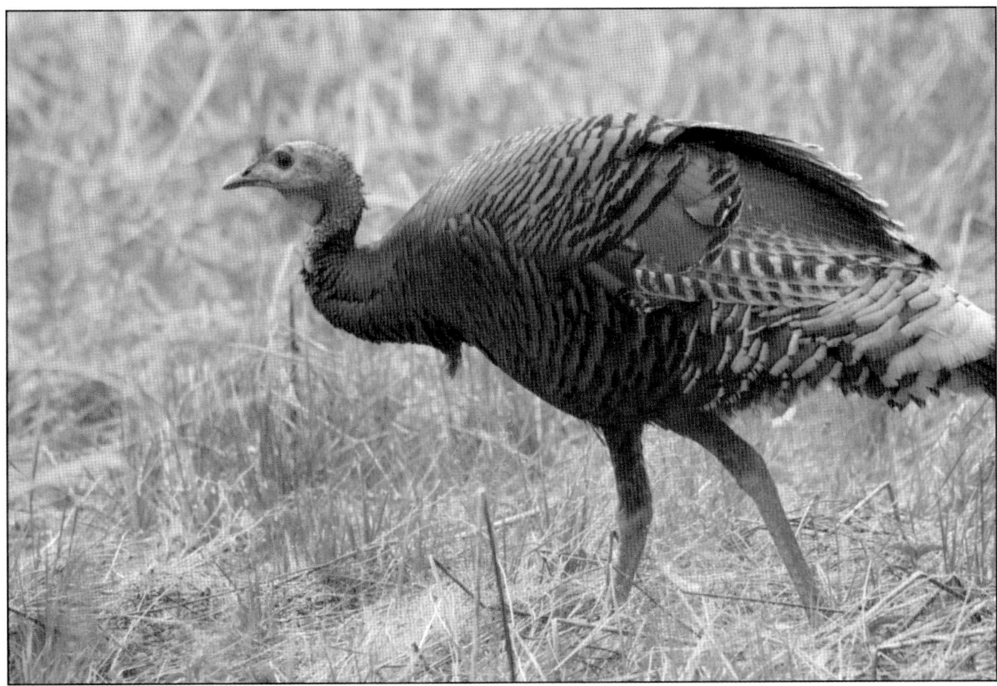

Chiricahua National Monument was one of several southern Arizona locations selected to host reintroduced Gould's turkeys. *Meleagris gallopavo mexicana*, one of Arizona's two native turkeys, is slightly larger than the Merriam's subspecies. Gould's were all but eliminated from Arizona by overhunting and habitat destruction during the 20th century. In 2003 and 2004, Gould's turkeys captured in Mexico and released in the Chiricahuas were the vanguard of an ongoing comeback of the species in Arizona. (Photograph by Suzanne Moody.)

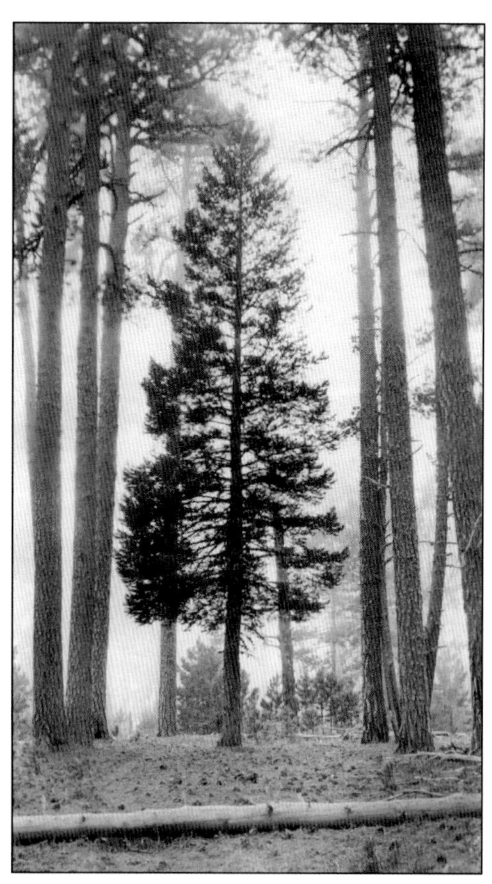

The diversity of natural life in the Chiricahua Mountains is typified by these two photographs taken within a few miles of each other. The image at left shows a young ponderosa pine in an early summer morning fog left over from a rainstorm the night before in the upper reaches of the mountains. The sentry-like yucca below guards Bonita Canyon's western entry through high desert grassland.

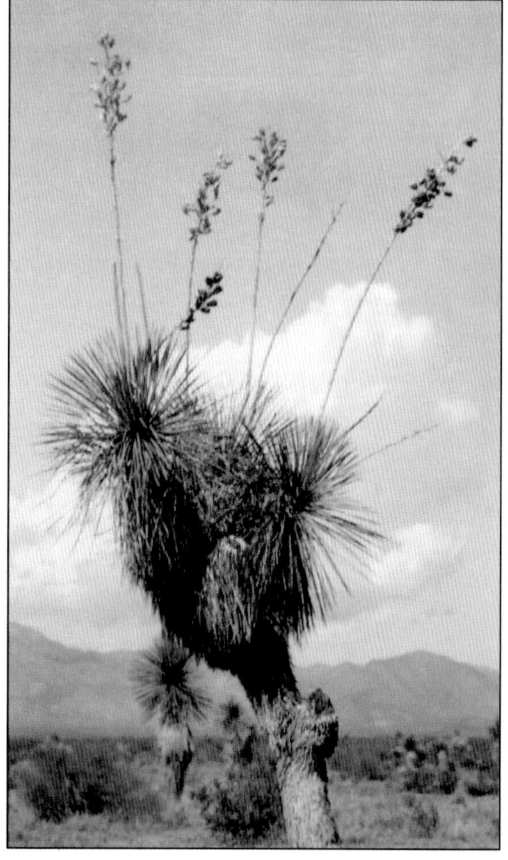

Three

Rock Formations

Geologists believe the processes that formed today's Chiricahua National Monument began about 27 million years ago with a gigantic volcanic explosion. Estimated to be 1,000 times larger than the 1980 eruption of Mount St. Helens, the explosion created the Turkey Creek caldera, a basin-shaped depression 12 miles wide and 5,000 feet deep.

Further eruptions flung clouds of superhot ash and pumice over a 1,200-square-mile area. Once the ash and pumice settled and cooled, it fused into what is called tuff. As the tuff deposits cooled and solidified, they contracted, forming joints and cracks. Over the eons of geological time, water seeped into the cracks and infinitesimally began eroding out rock columns and formations, assisted by stream flow and wedging action caused by freezing water. Wind erosion and organic acids produced by lichens also contributed to the process.

Three types of igneous (volcanic) rocks dominate the monument. One is dacite, a rock made of 63 to 70 percent silica. It did not explode into ash, instead flowing as lava and solidifying into an erosion-resident rock. Sugarloaf Mountain's summit is dacite.

The other two rock types dominating the monument are rhyolite and Rhyolite Canyon tuff. Rhyolite is more than 70 percent silica, which sparkles when a specimen is freshly broken open. Rhyolite Canyon tuff is made of ash, pumice, crystals, and rock fragments welded together during creation of the Turkey Creek caldera.

Development of the monument's rock columns, also called spires, pinnacles, or hoodoos, into rows occurred because the tuff compacted and eroded at different rates. What visitors see today is an endless variety of formations still undergoing sculpting processes.

Many formations bear names received from Lillian Riggs. Some are fanciful—Kissing Rocks—and others descriptive—Old Maid. Dominating all is Cochise's Head, clearly a tribute to the Chiricahua leader.

Although Lillian's father, Neil Erickson, immigrated to the United States to avenge his father's death by Indians, Neil came to be, as he told his son, Ben, "more in sympathy with the Indians than I was with the white man. . . . Indians got a raw deal."

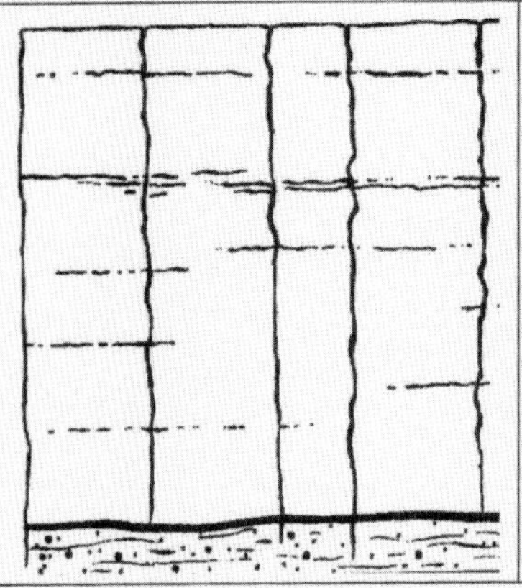

As the ash settled, the hot layers melted or welded together. This created the gray rock called Rhyolite Canyon Tuff. The rhyolite contracted, cracked, and formed joints as it cooled.

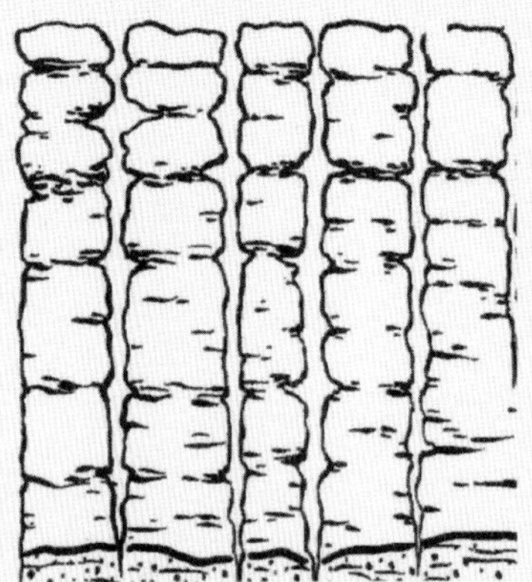

Frost wedging enlarged the joints when water seeped into them, froze and expanded. Some layers of the rhyolite were not welded together as tightly as other layers. The weaker material was washed away.

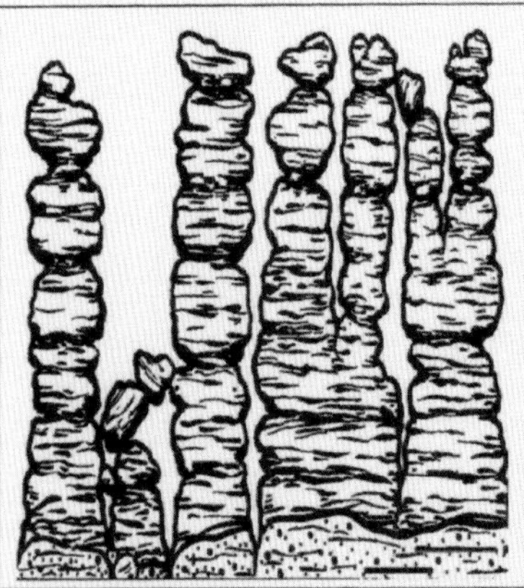

Wind, lichens and more water erosion smoothed and rounded the columns into the shapes we see today.

The landscape seen today at Chiricahua National Monument exists because the Turkey Creek volcano erupted an estimated 27 million years ago. Instead of lava flow, the volcano spewed ash and other debris that solidified into layers at least 2,000 feet deep. These layers underwent the geological progression illustrated here, resulting in the monument's fanciful formations.

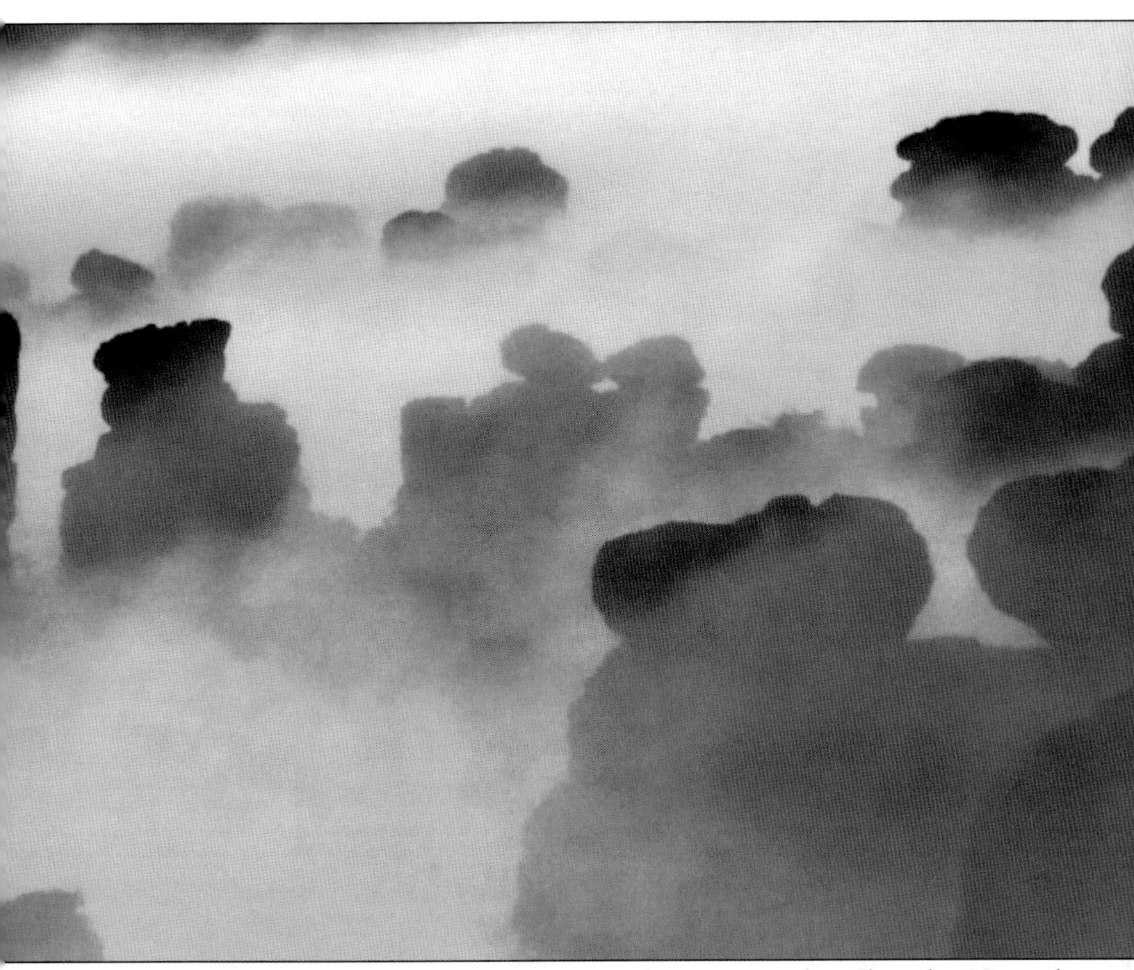

It was a rare foggy morning in normally clear, sunny southern Arizona when Chiricahua National Monument park ranger Suzanne Moody snapped this photograph of rock pillars at Massai Point. She found the mystical feeling the fog imparts to be most memorable. Massai was a Chiricahua Apache who served as a scout with US cavalry units that brought about the surrender of Geronimo in 1886. Despite this, Massai was stuffed into a railroad car taking Geronimo's followers to Florida. In Missouri, Massai escaped by squeezing out of a window and jumping off the train. He walked back to Arizona and apparently became part of a shadowy group of Apaches who lived as renegades in Sonora or who hid in plain sight on US government-designated reservations. Neil Erickson believed that Massai was one person he tracked in 1890 through Bonita Canyon into what is now Chiricahua National Monument. Erickson, a former US cavalryman, came to believe that Indians, including the Apaches he had pursued, had been treated unjustly. Toward the end of his life, he petitioned the National Park Service to name a scenic overlook in Chiricahua National Monument for Massai.

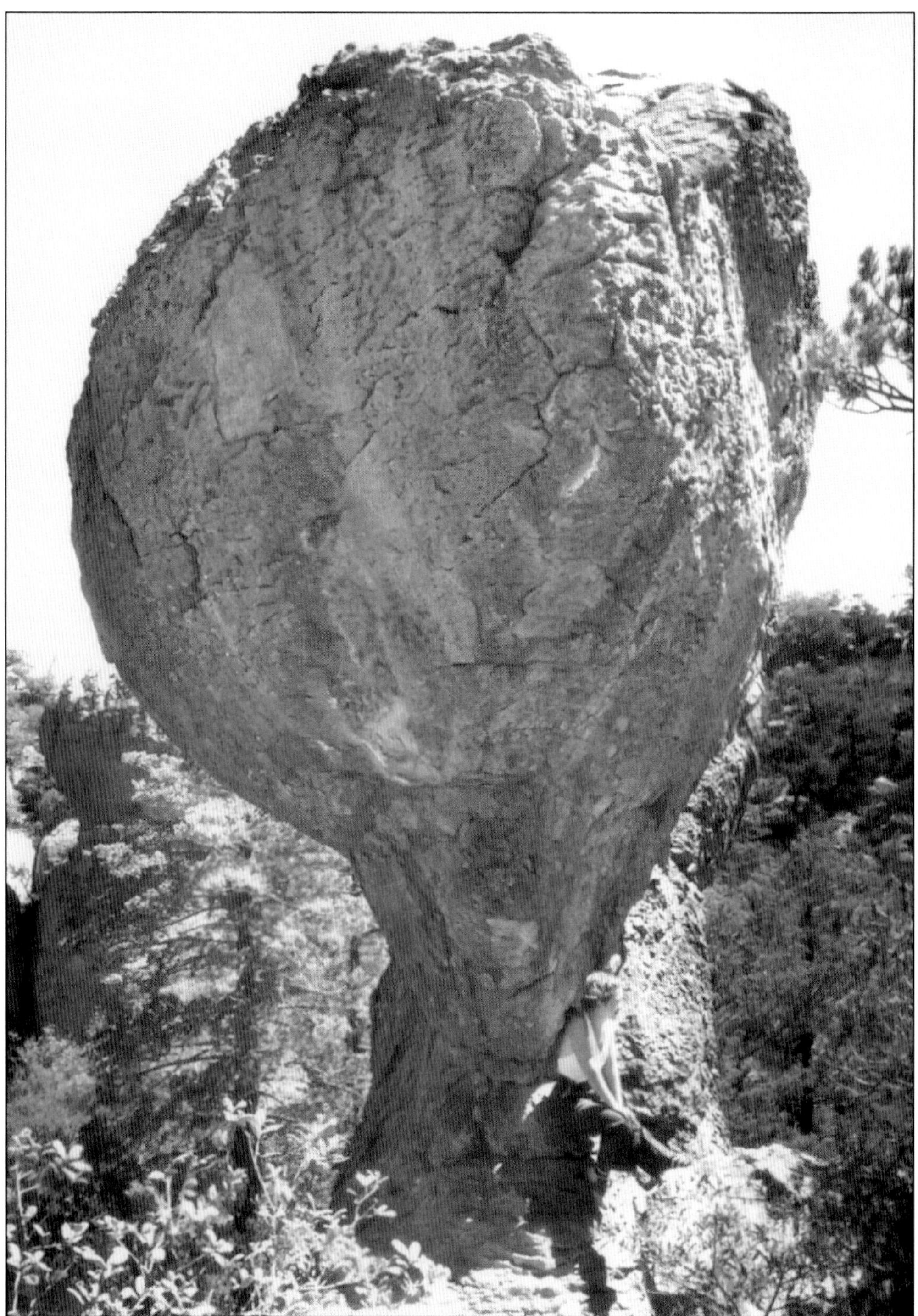

Chiricahua National Monument's rock formations became more widely enjoyed following World War II, as summer vacations became an American tradition. National Park Service statistics document an increase in monument visitations during the 1950s. That is when this unidentified woman was photographed seated beneath a balanced rock in Echo Canyon.

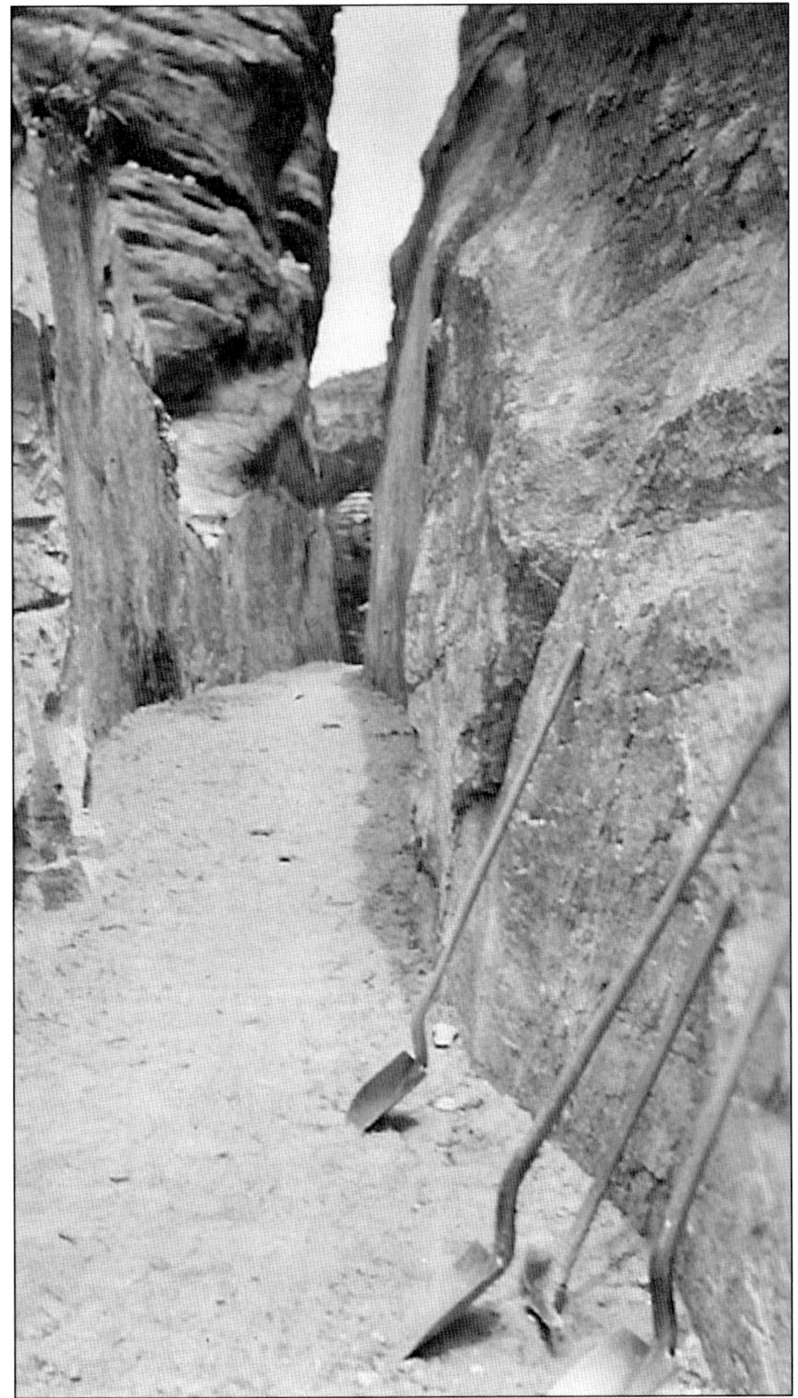

As Ed Riggs designed the Chiricahua National Monument trails system, he took advantage of the natural landscape, including this fault in Echo Canyon. In the 1930s, Civilian Conservation Corps members expanded the fault with shovel work as they built the Echo Canyon Trail. Hikers today who take the time to look carefully can spot drill holes and other evidence of CCC work along this section of the trail.

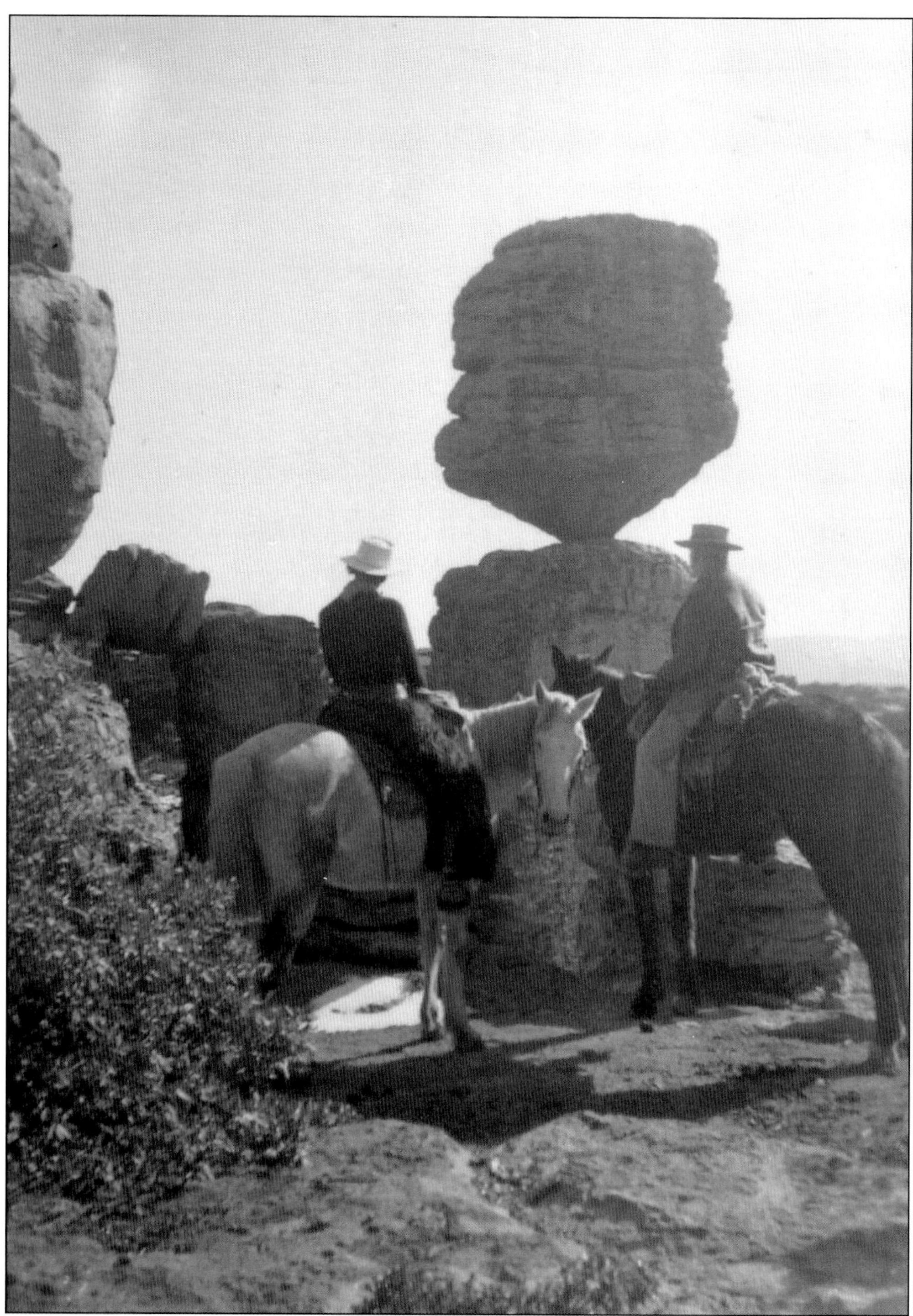

Big Balanced Rock, near the Heart of Rocks Loop entrance, has always been a favorite stopping point for hikers and horseback riders. Chiricahua National Monument still welcomes horseback riders who want to cover the trails the same way Faraway Ranch guests did for 50 years. There is a separate parking area for horse trailers near Faraway's main house.

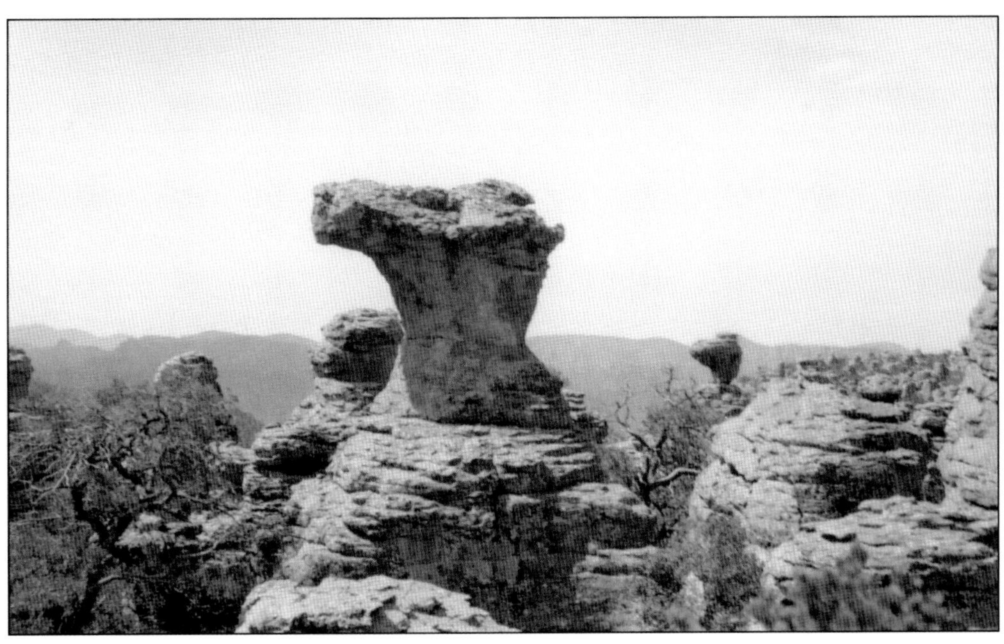

The variety of form and size of Chiricahua National Monument rock formations has always intrigued visitors. For instance, does the formation above look like a camel's head or something else? The cowboy standing next to Mushroom Rock, below, provides a sense of the massive size of most formations.

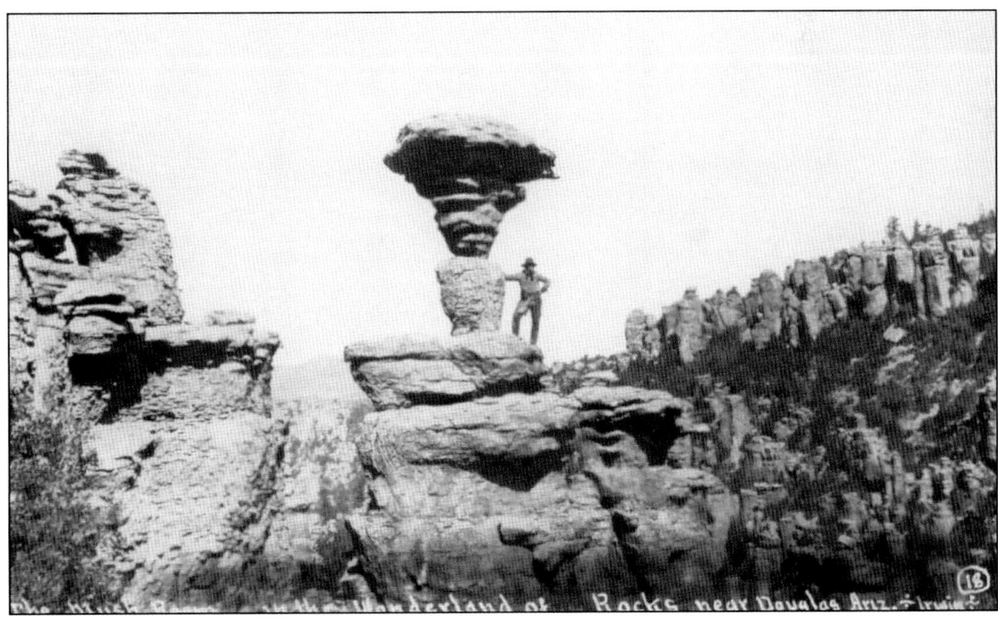

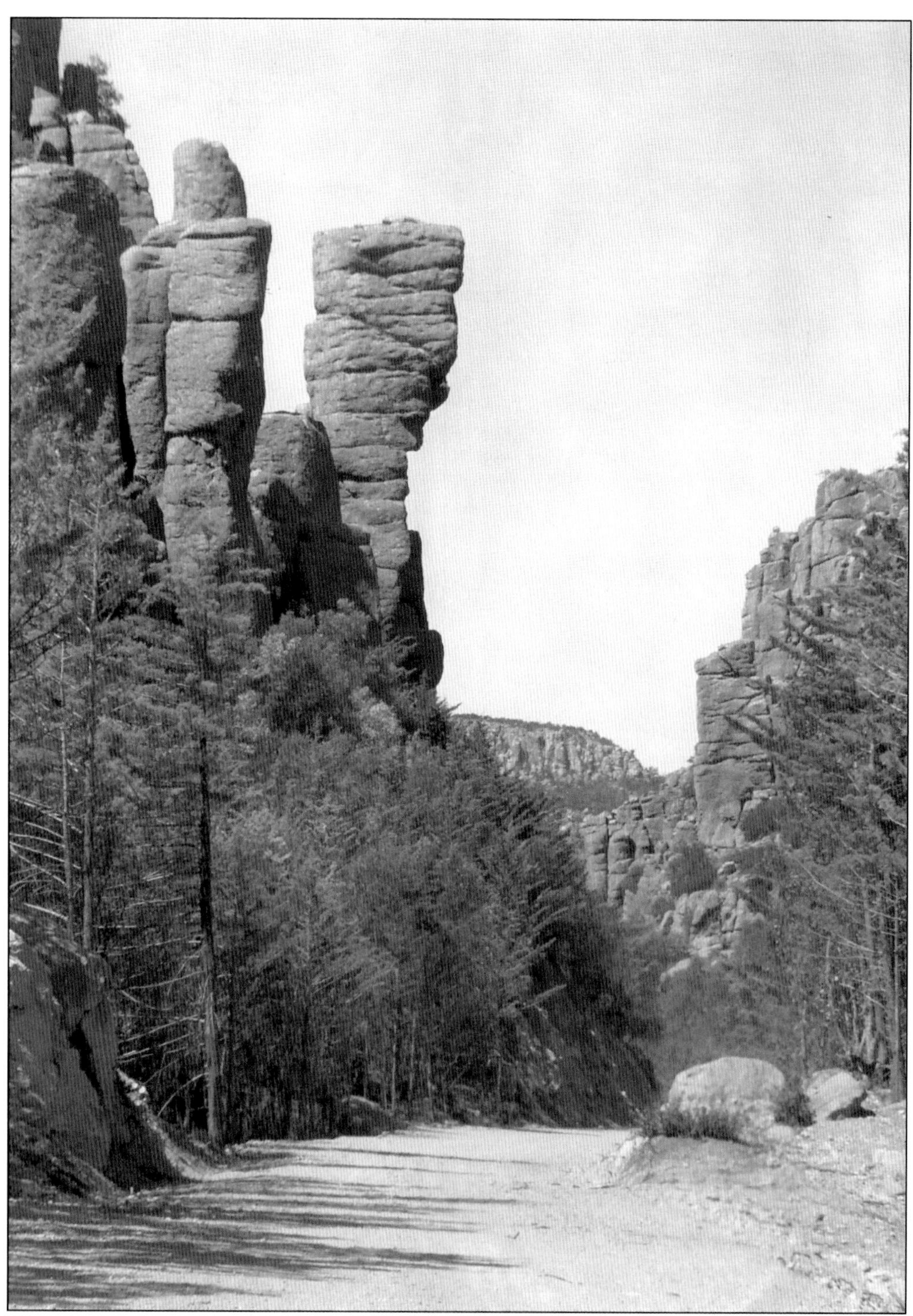

China Boy is one of several distinctive formations seen along Bonita Canyon Drive. The eight-mile road begins in the grasslands of Bonita Canyon's entrance and climbs 1,500 feet to end amongst conifer trees at Massai Point. Private vehicles longer than 29 feet are not permitted on Bonita Canyon Drive past the visitor center due to its narrowness and many curves.

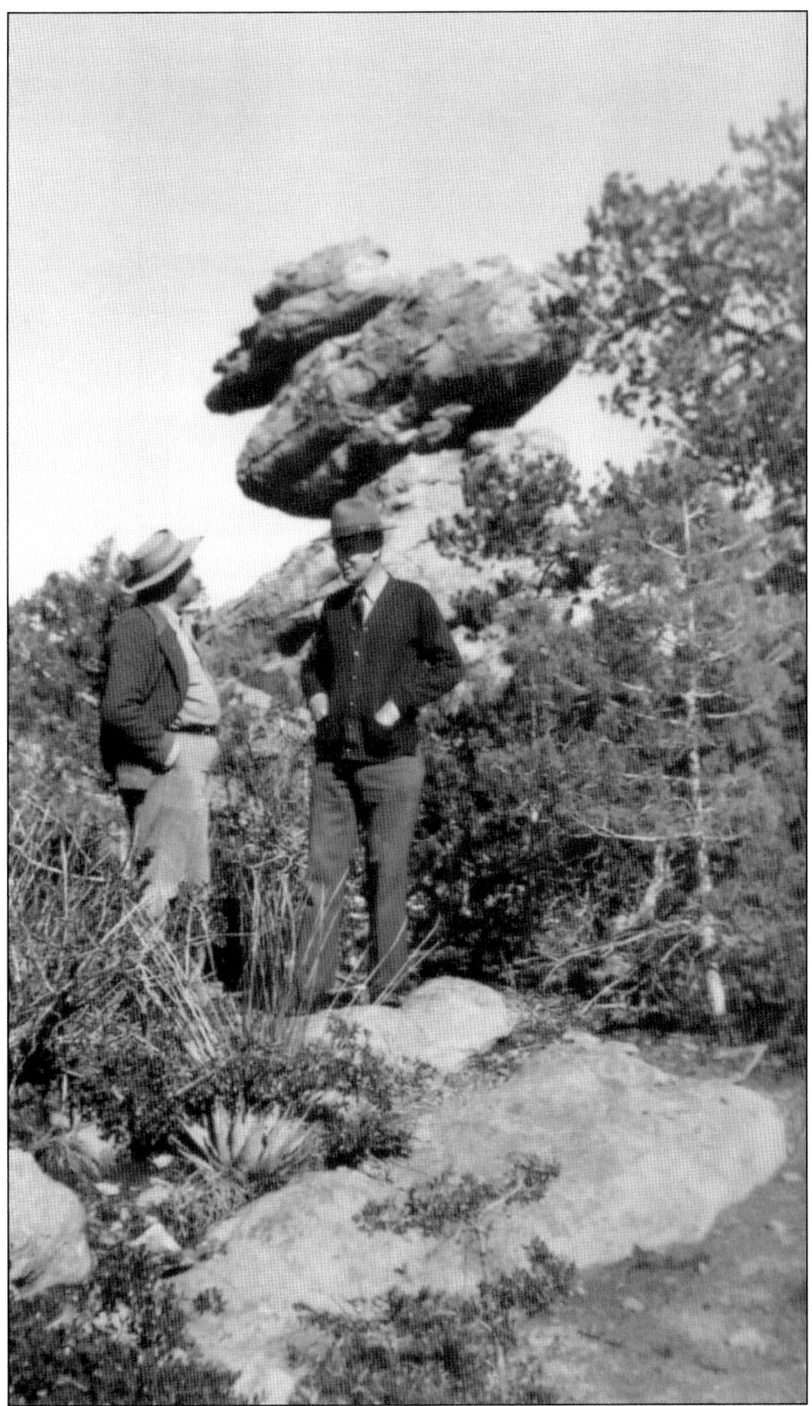

Perhaps the two men in this photograph are wondering exactly where Duck on a Rock is. The answer is on the one-mile-long Heart of Rocks Loop. Visitors reach the loop via the Sarah Deming or Big Balanced Rock Trails. Both require 2- to 3-mile approaches, so visitors need to be prepared with enough water, snacks, sunscreen, and clothing appropriate for the weather in order to complete the 7.3-mile round-trip comfortably.

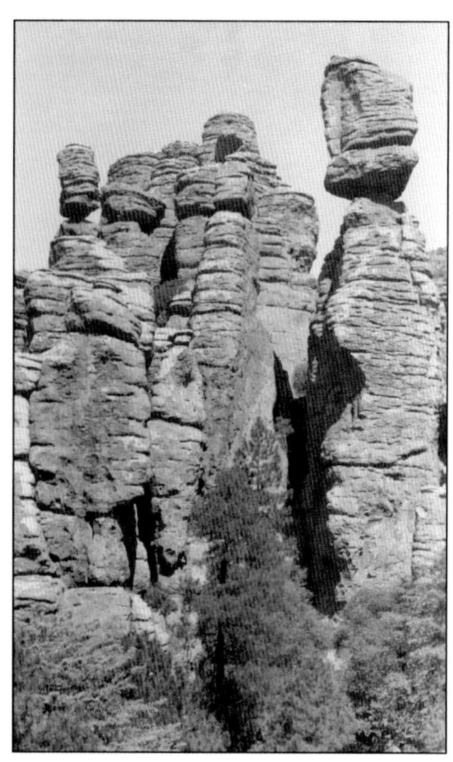

A safe and easy way for Chiricahua National Monument visitors to get an intimate view of monument formations is to hike the Echo Canyon Trail. It begins at a parking area off Bonita Canyon Drive, goes past pinnacles (left), and a half mile later reaches Echo Canyon Grotto (below). The grotto is not a cave but an undulating arms-width passageway through a series of smooth-walled columns.

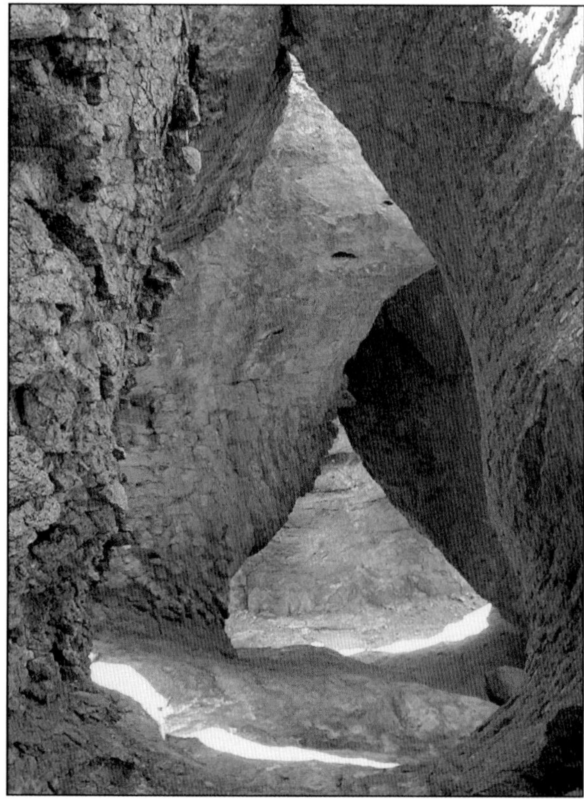

Visitors who hike the 3.3-mile Echo Canyon Loop will see cliffs and columns carved out from layers of rhyolite rock. The Hailstone and Ed Riggs Trails make up part of the loop and are good places to look for evidence of ancient volcanic activity. This includes fiamme, light-colored streaks found in darker rhyolite. *Fiamme* is a geological term that comes from the Italian word for "flames."

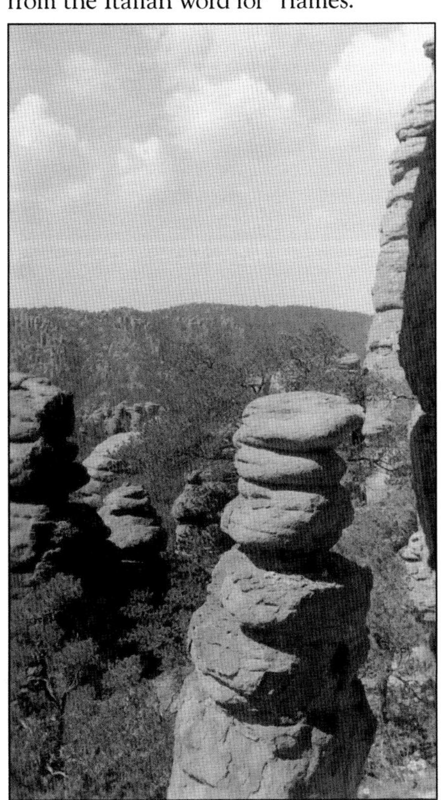

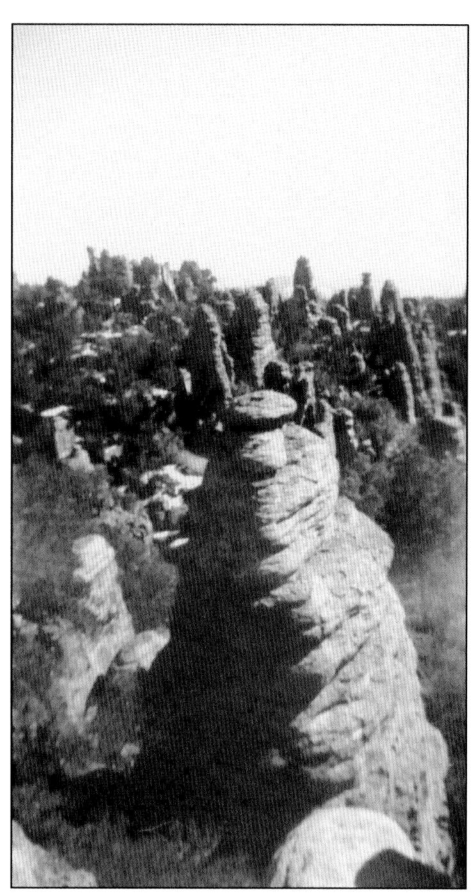

The Baby Shoe, atop the pinnacle at left, and the Lighthouse, below, were both photographed by Douglas resident Marvin E. Irvin during a two-week mule-pack trip in the Wonderland of Rocks in the early 1920s. As a 15-year-old in 1896 Oklahoma, Marvin paid 50¢ to Geronimo so he could take a photograph of the famous Apache leader. Irwin moved to Bisbee in 1901 with his brother William, also a photographer. Marvin established his own studio in Douglas about 1913. He took photographs of Cochise County scenery and people until his 1946 retirement.

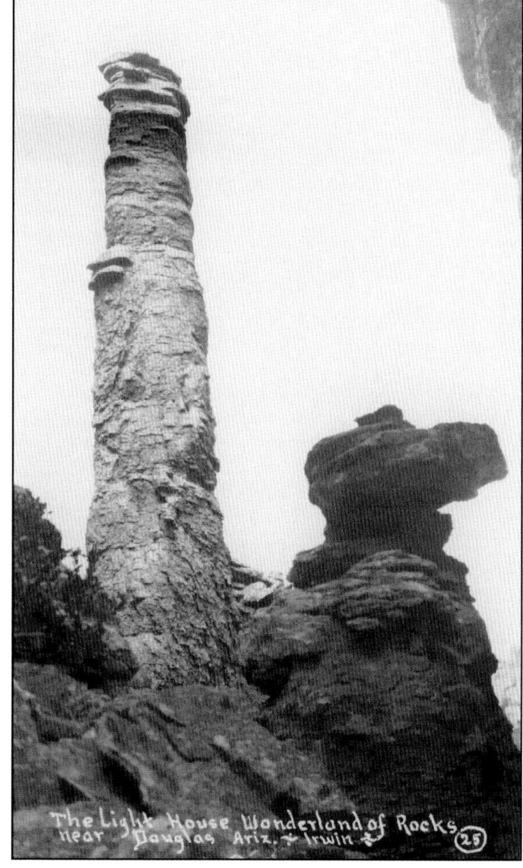

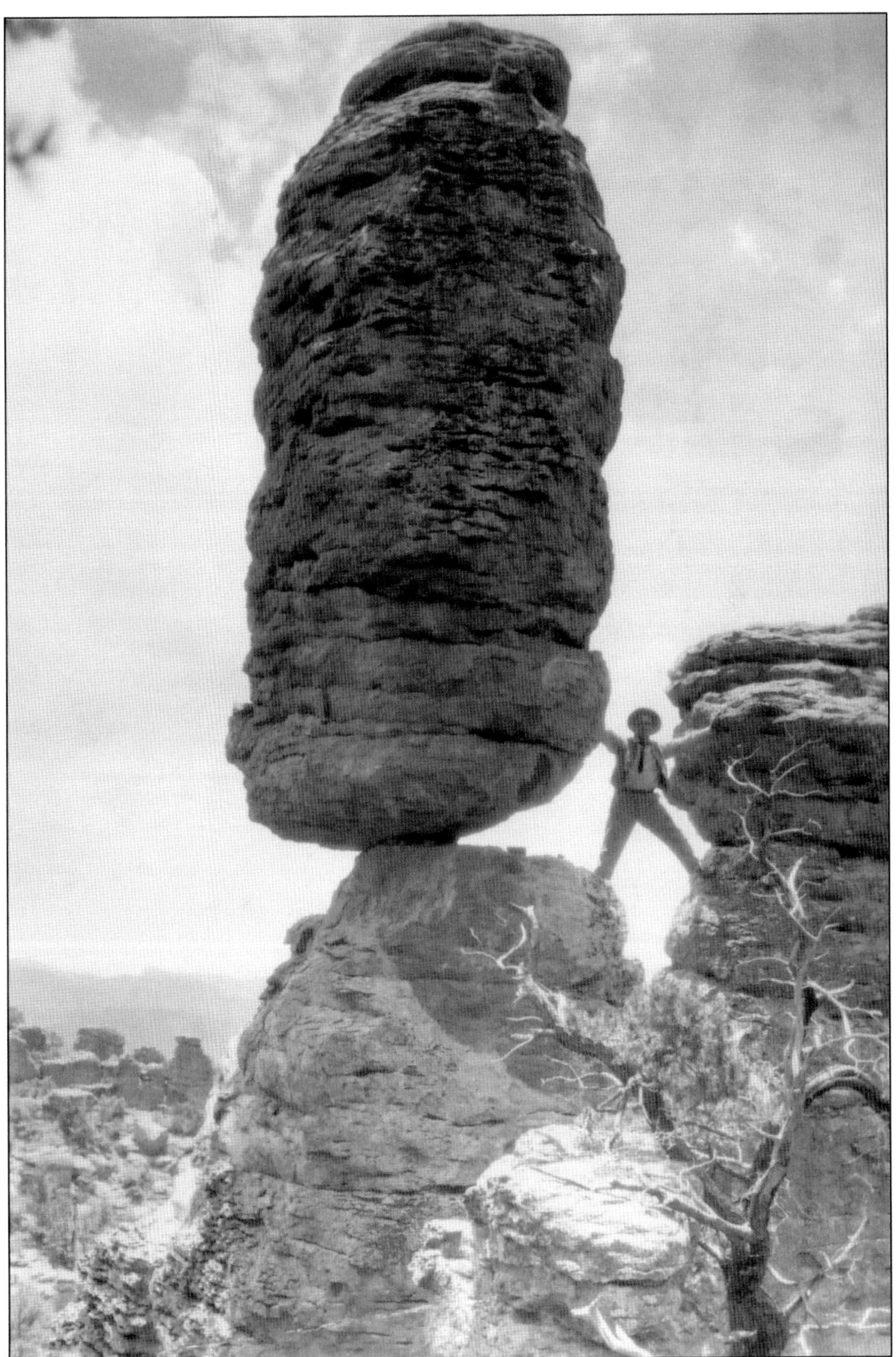

Chiricahua National Monument might look like a rock climber's paradise. Indeed, many historic photographs have people posed in precarious positions, such as this one with Ed Riggs next to Pinnacle Balanced Rock in the Heart of Rocks Loop. But technical rock climbing is not allowed in Chiricahua National Monument in order to protect visitors and preserve formations.

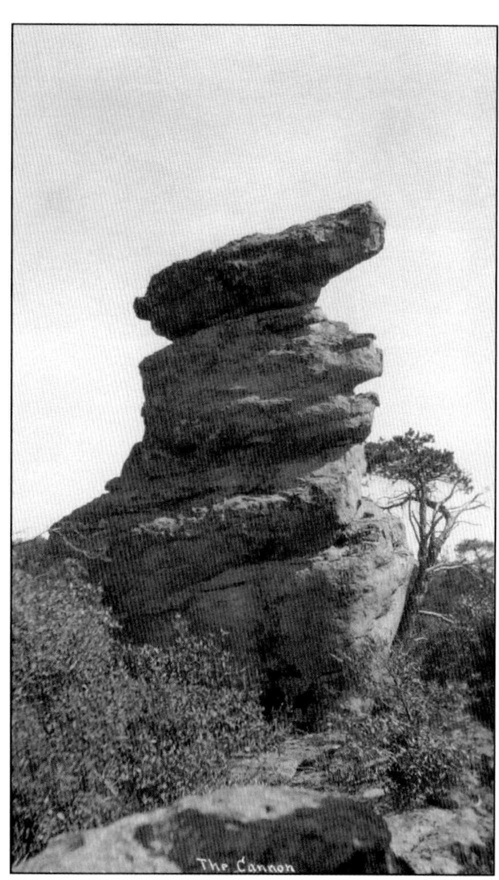

Decorating Chiricahua National Monument formations such as the Cannon, left, and the Doughnut Hole, below, are a variety of lichens in shades of bright green, orange, brown, or black. Lichens are organisms composed of a fungus paired in a symbiotic relationship with an alga. The fungi form a sheltering structure, while the algae produce food through photosynthesis. Lichens generate a weak acid that gradually scoops out indentations into rocks. Over millions of years, lichens helped form the Cannon and Doughnut Hole and other monument formations.

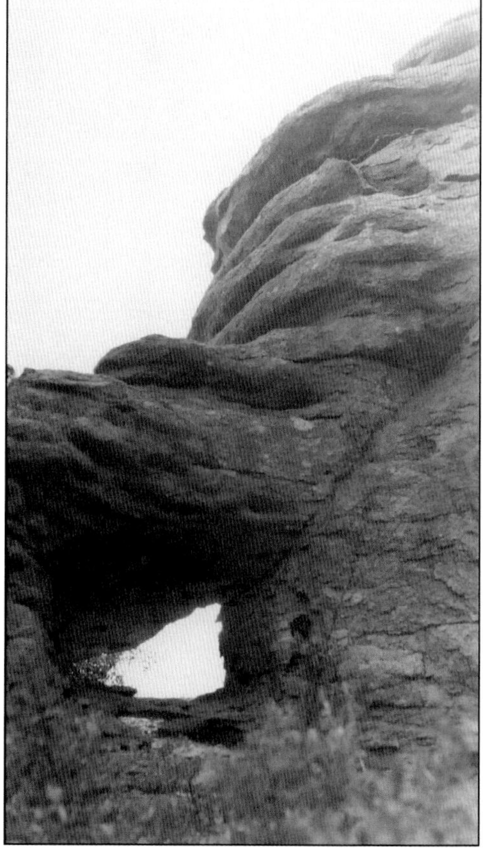

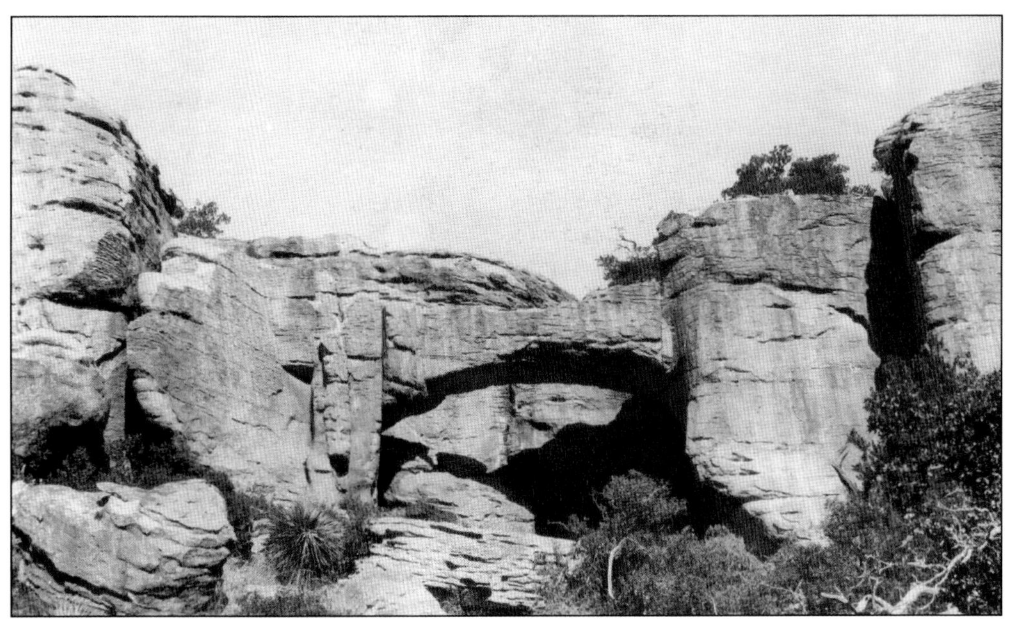

In the northern portion of Chiricahua National Monument is the Natural Bridge, above. It is reached by a 2.4-mile trail that goes through Pickett Park, below. The 30-foot bridge is a true water-carved span that can seem to disappear because of light changes and vegetation growth. A small parking area on Bonita Canyon Drive provides access to the 4.8-mile round-trip to the Natural Bridge.

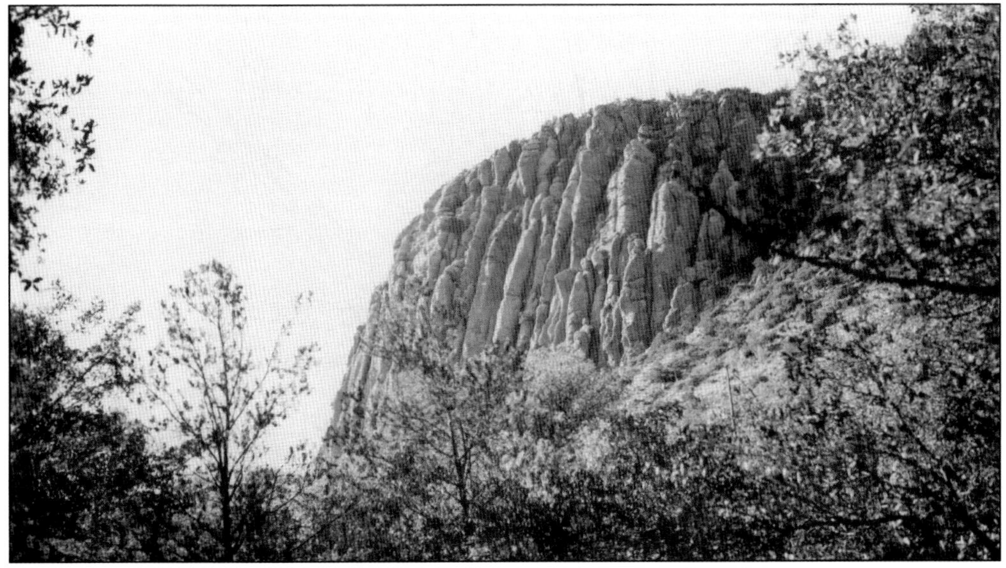

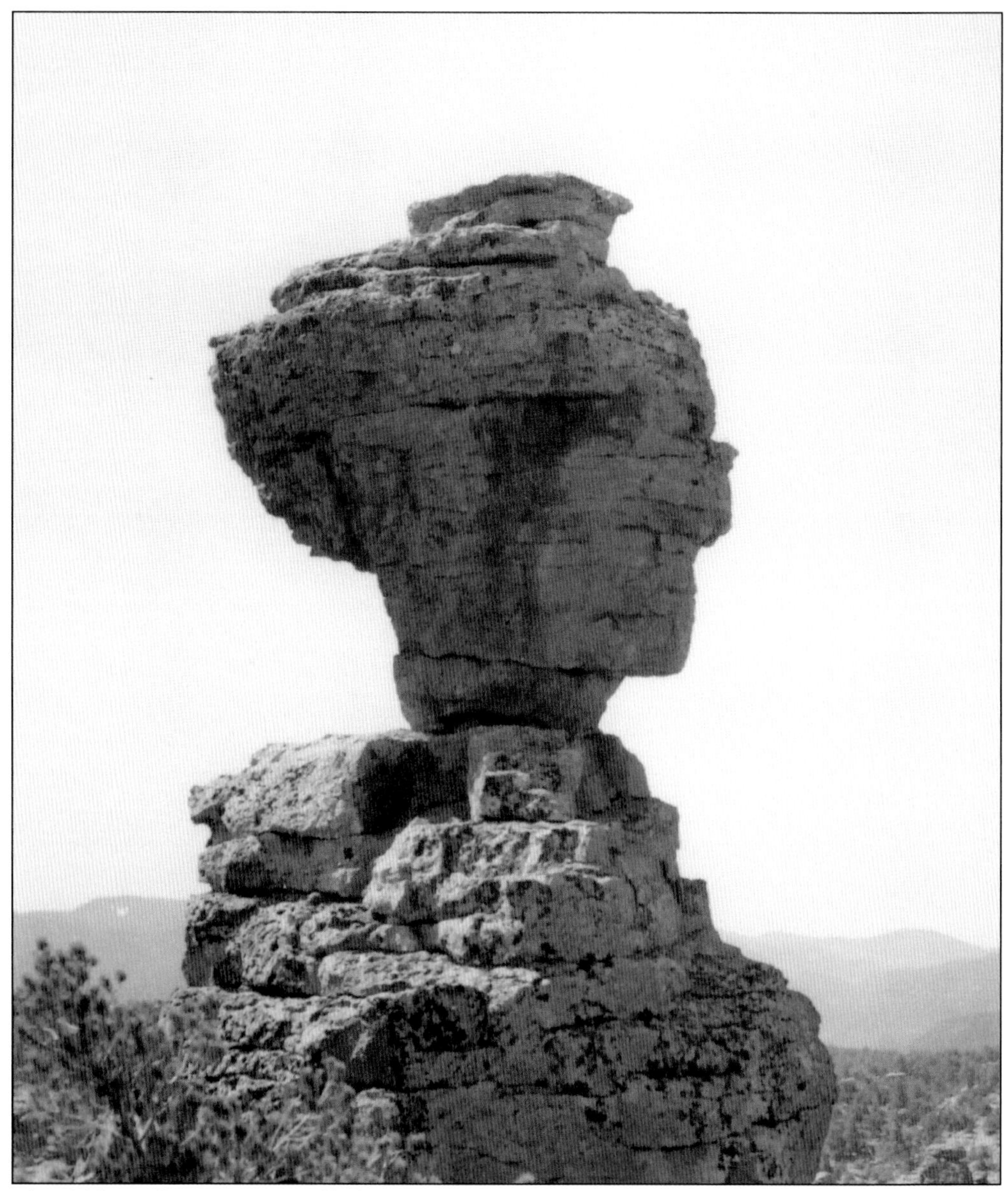

The Old Maid, sometimes called Queen Mary, is another of many named formations in the Heart of Rocks Loop. The Heart of Rocks area, but not individual formations such as Old Maid, can be seen from Massai Point. It was named by Ed and Lillian Riggs in the 1930s and is one of the appellations that sometimes confuses visitors today. Just what is an old maid? And who was Queen Mary?

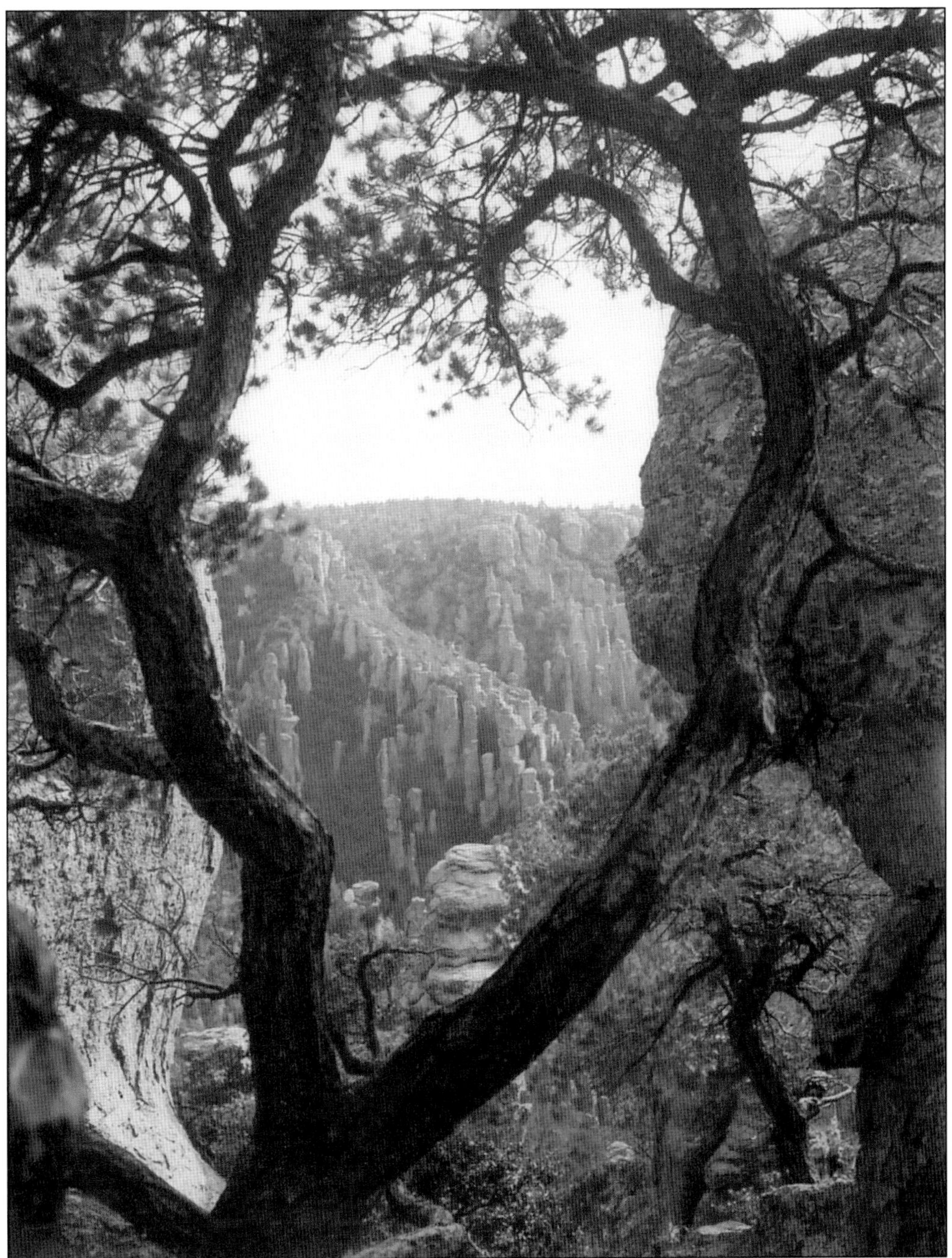

Publications such as *Arizona Highways* have printed photographs similar to this one of Chiricahua National Monument in their pages for many years. Lillian and Ed Riggs and other entrepreneurs involved in promoting southern Arizona as a vacation destination relied upon such publications for decades. Today, many people also use www.nps.gov/chir/index.htm.

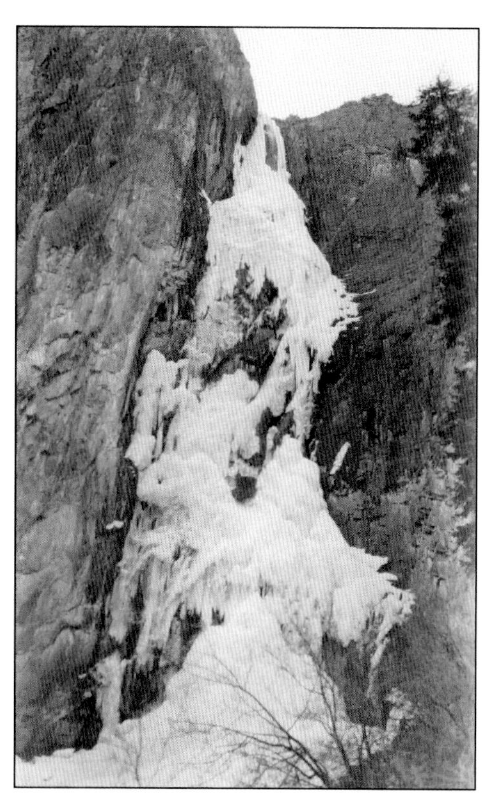

People visiting Chiricahua National Monument in December or January might be surprised to find a winter wonderland. A Massai Point icefall is on the left, and the monument headquarters is below. Winter storms can bring two to six inches of snow to lower elevations of the Chiricahua Mountains, but that usually melts in a matter of days.

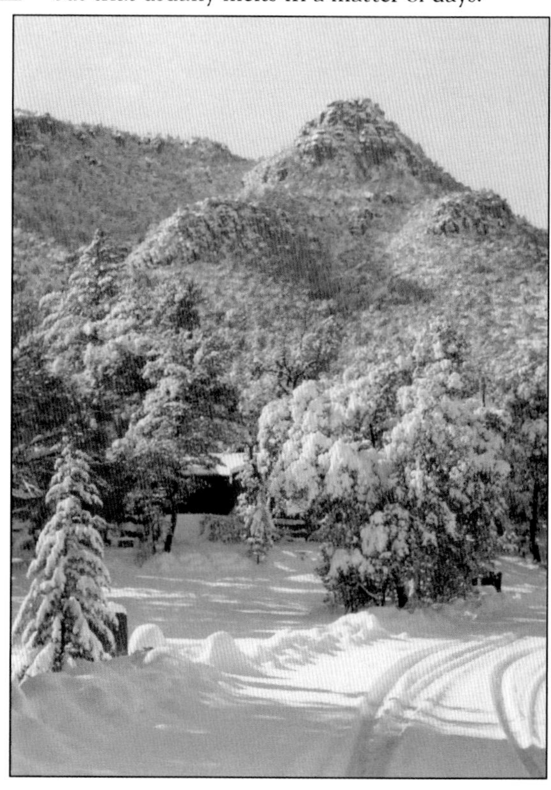

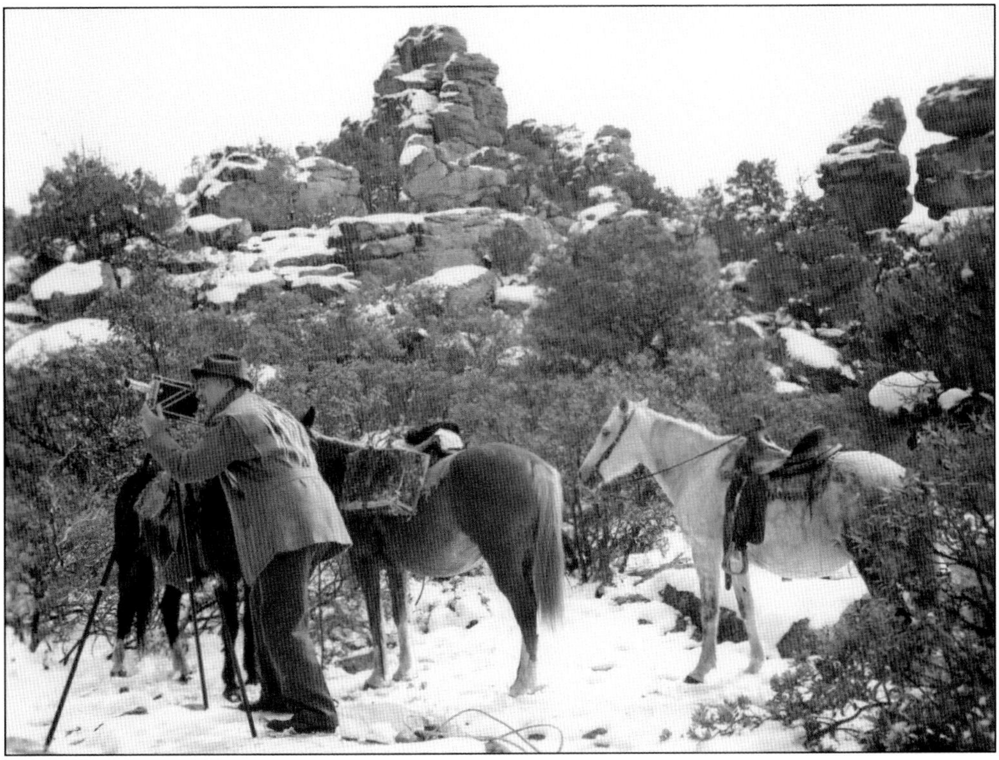

Although snow can close Bonita Canyon Drive until National Park Service crews clear accumulations, the monument's hiking trails are not restricted. Since snow brings a totally different feeling to the monument's landscape, photographers have always hurried to capture images like the one above of places such as Big Balanced Rock, below, when there is snow.

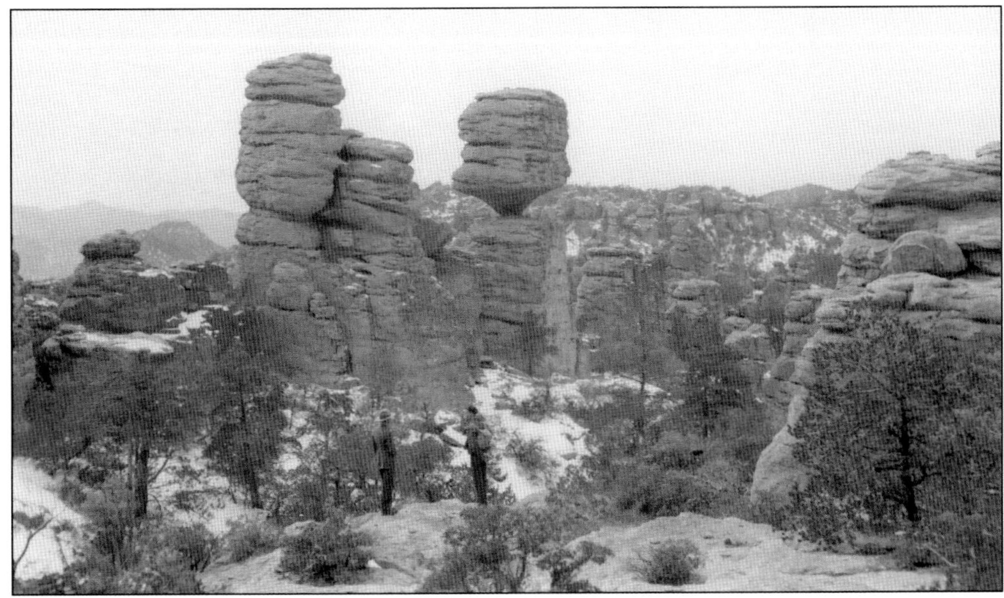

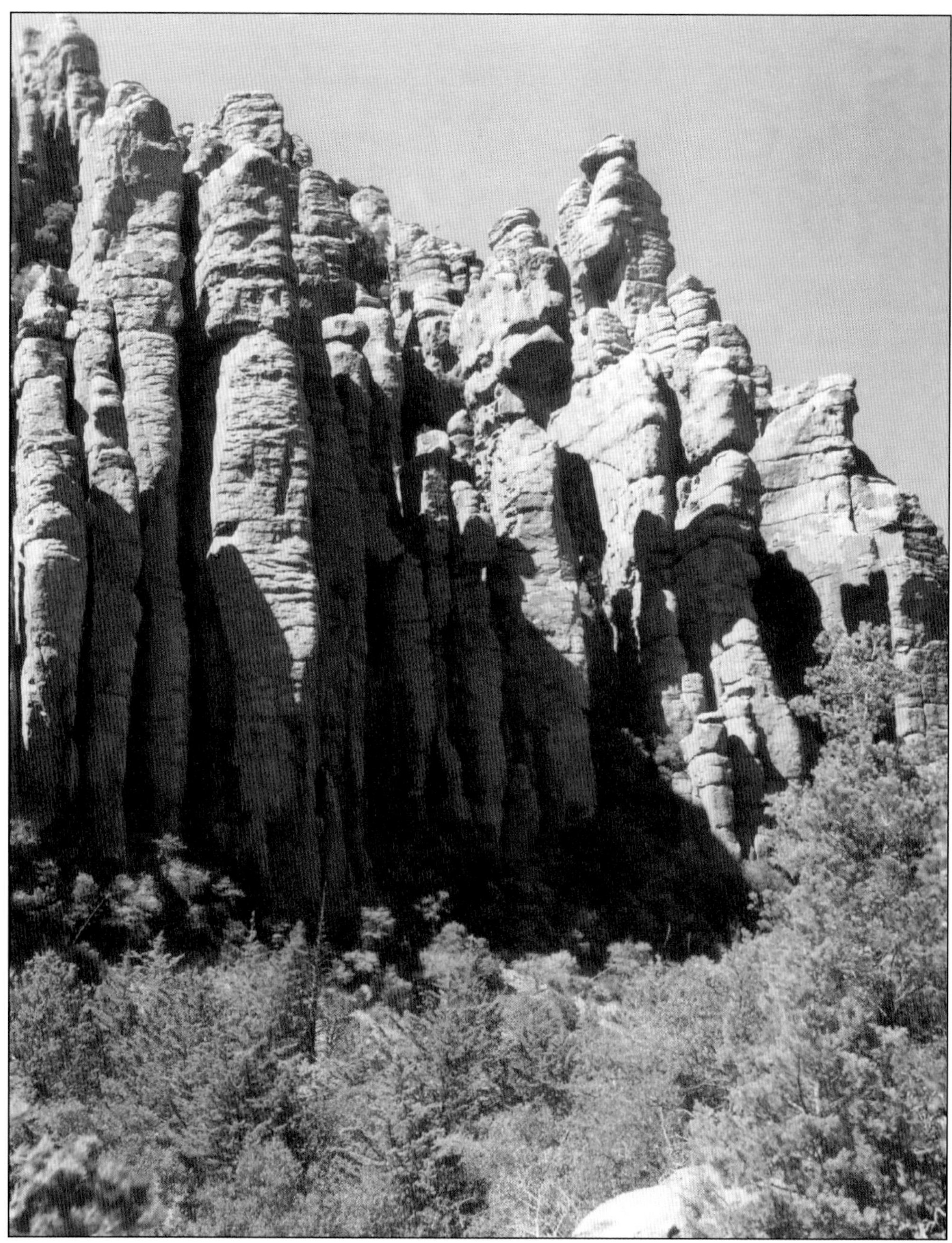

The Organ Pipe formation is visible from Bonita Canyon Drive. There is a pull-out space on the north side of Bonita Canyon Drive so visitors can stop and look for the Praying Padre. He is in the upper right of this photograph, but he is one of the formations that takes more imagination to find than most others.

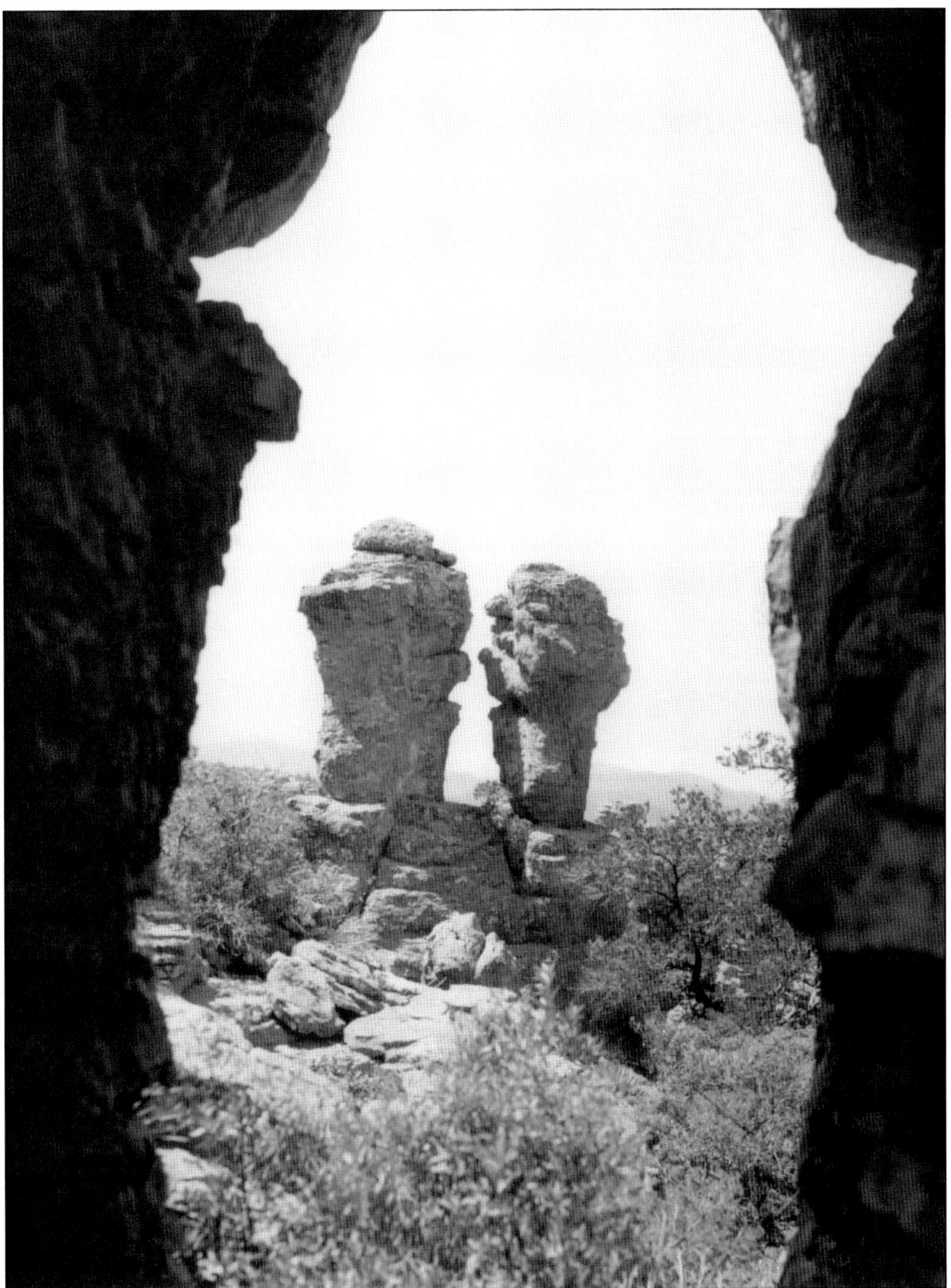

Punch and Judy, located in the Heart of Rocks, is a formation that requires no imagination to see. Punch and Judy are puppet show characters invented in 17th-century Italy. Known for their bickering and physical comedy, Punch and Judy remain popular characters.

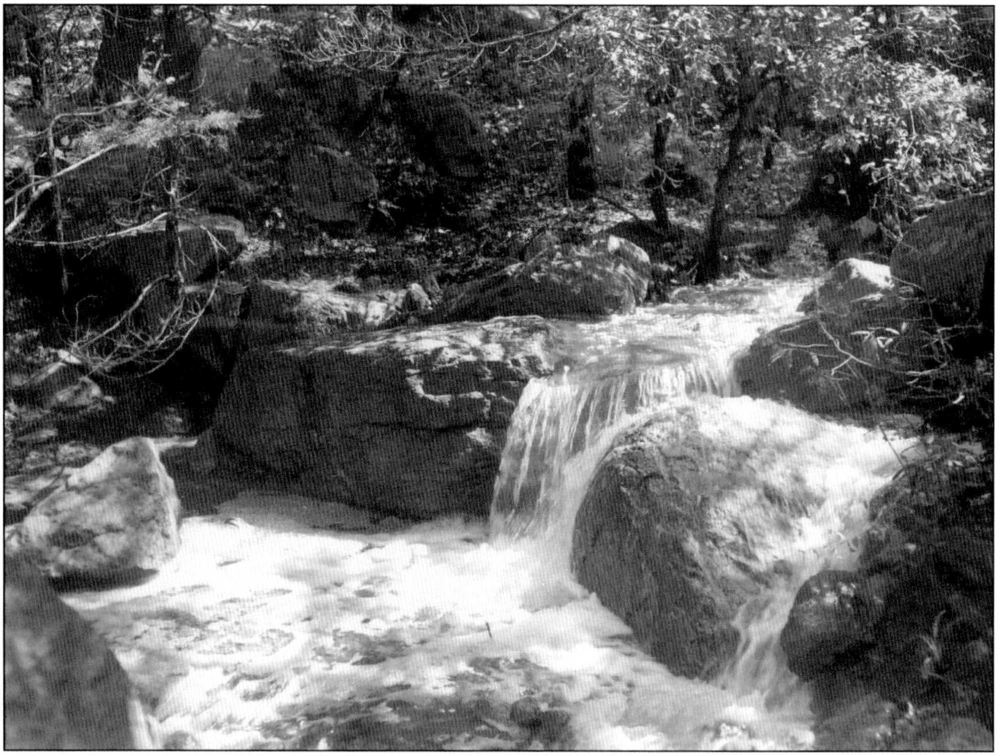

The majority of the almost 20 inches of rain that falls annually on Chiricahua National Monument arrives during the summer monsoon season from July into September. Runoff flows down Bonita Canyon, past the ranger station and Faraway Ranch. Although flash flooding can temporarily limit vehicular travel, the rainfall brightens grass to a vivid green and causes wildflowers to bloom and decorate the monument with splashes of color.

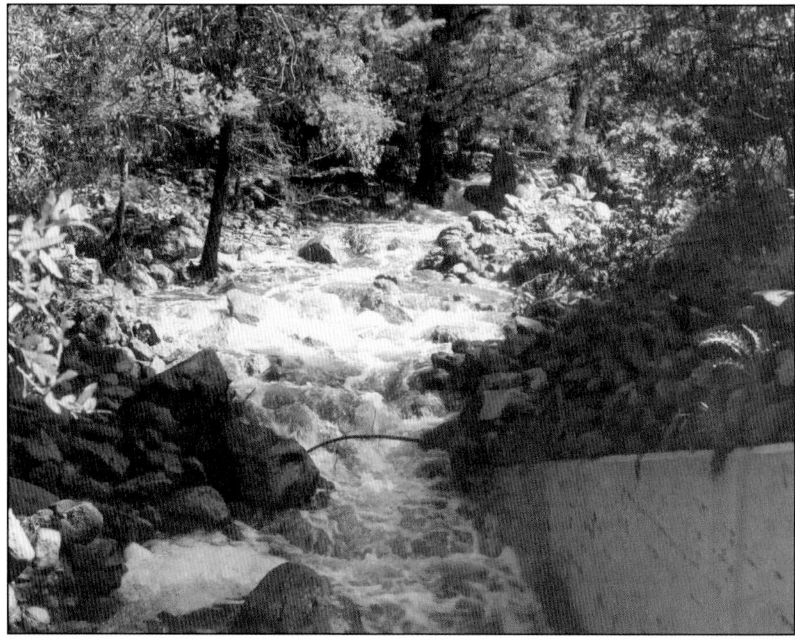

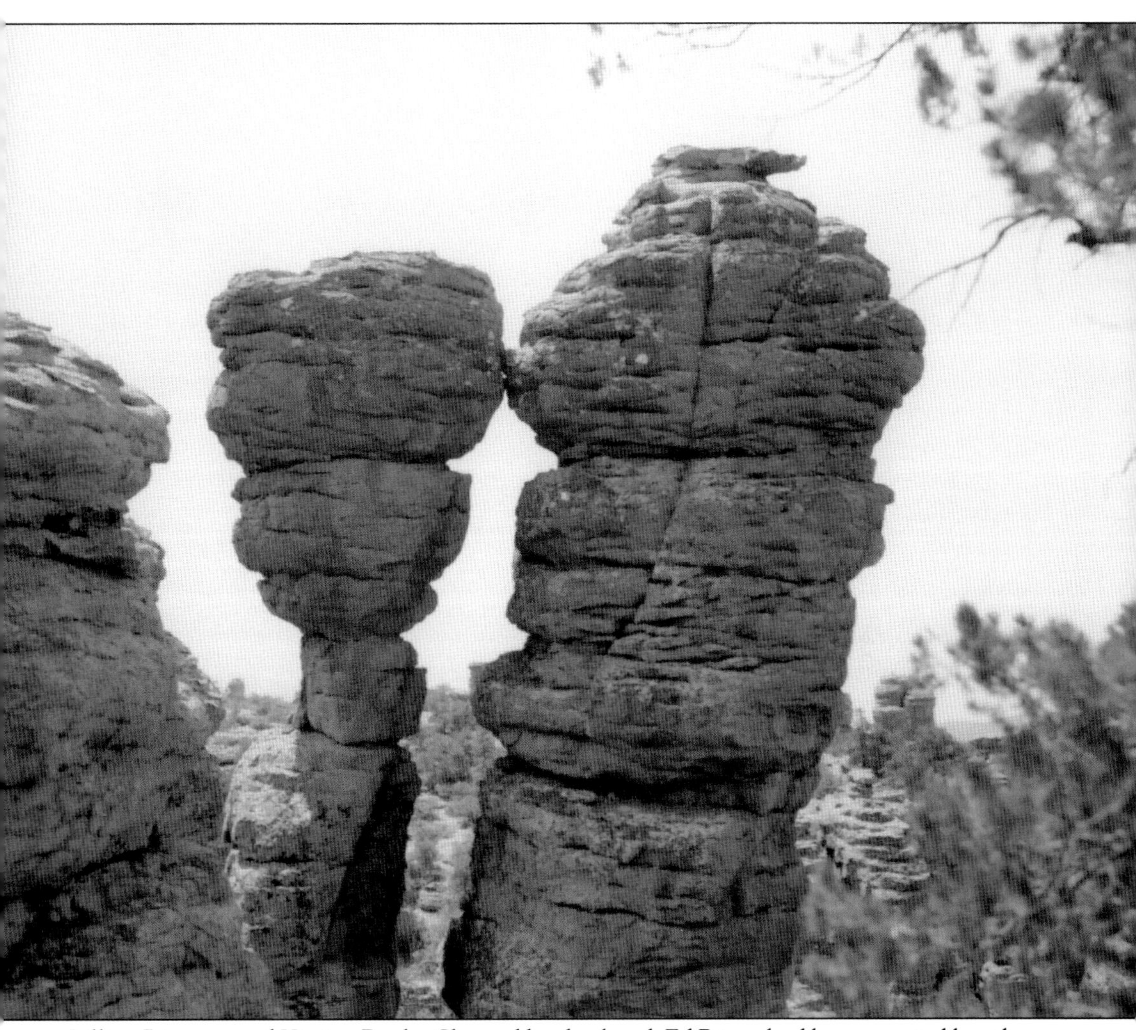

Lillian Riggs named Kissing Rocks. She and her husband, Ed Riggs, had been married less than a year when they began promoting the Wonderland of Rocks and their Faraway Ranch as a tourist destination. Beginning with connections Ed created while he lived in Douglas, the couple put together a chain of people that convinced Pres. Calvin Coolidge to declare the Wonderland a national monument on April 18, 1924. That happened slightly more than 18 months after Ed and Lillian's wedding.

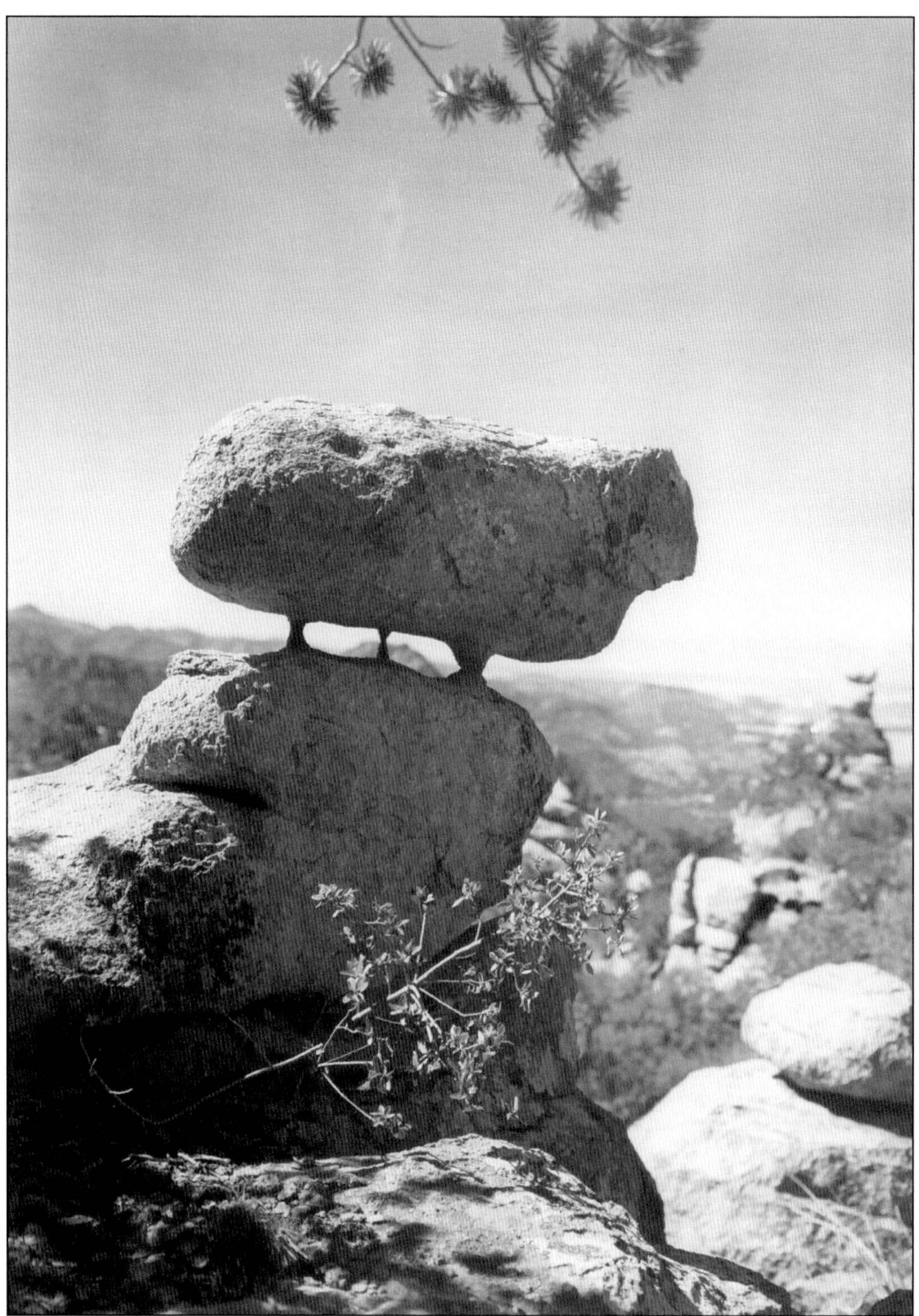

Sheep Rock became one of the Wonderland of Rocks' iconic formations after Marvin Irwin photographed it in the early 1920s. Chiricahua National Monument visitors today, however, will not see Sheep Rock, because it collapsed in the 1950s. Since then, other formations have seemingly disappeared because tree growth now obscures the line of sight to some formations, locations of other formations are not known to today's monument staff, or names have become politically incorrect. Instead, visitors are encouraged to let their imaginations soar as they hike monument trails and come up with their own names for the variety of shapes they see.

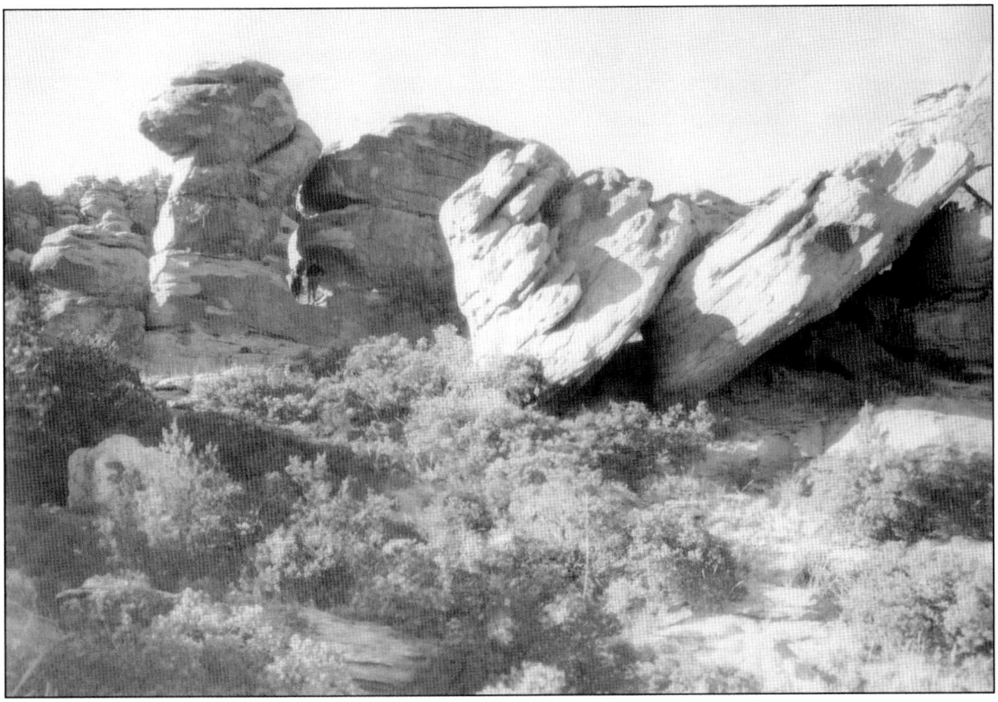

Occasionally, formations like the one above cease defying gravity and collapse. This formation slid apart long ago; a horse and rider are on the left. Other well-known formations, such as the rock below leaning onto Big Balanced Pinnacle, changed—in this case, because the tree died and disintegrated.

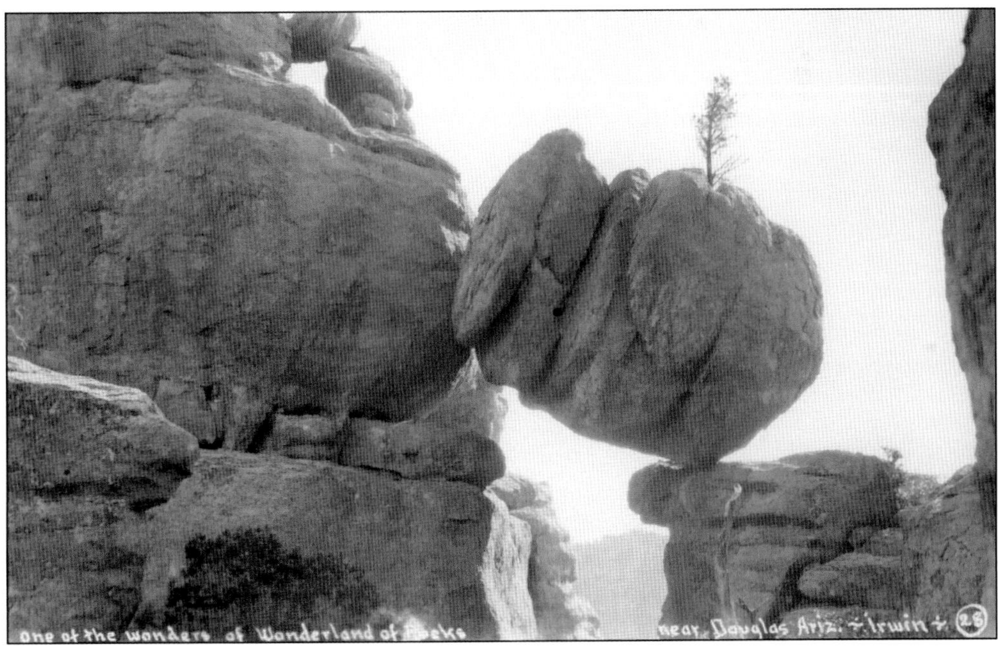

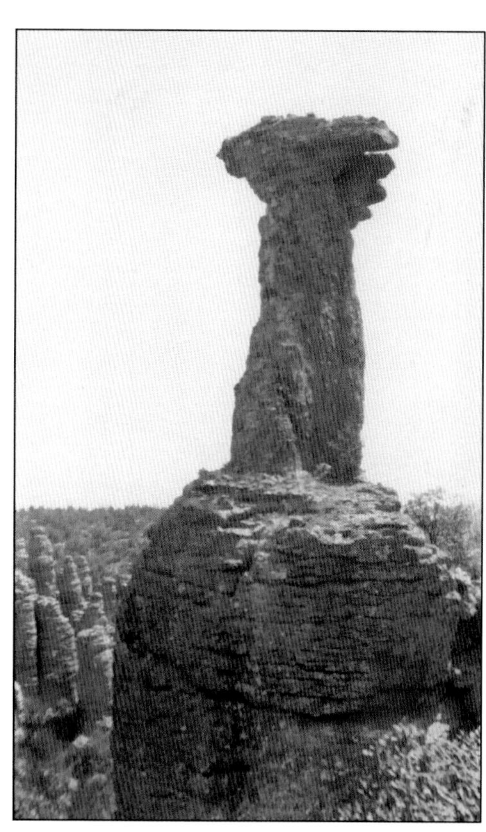

Formations named by Lillian Riggs include the Hammer, also known as Thor's Hammer (left). Its name undoubtedly came from Lillian giving a nod to her Swedish heritage. The 150-foot-tall Totem Pole (below) is where Lillian and Ed stopped to eat lunch during their first mutual exploration of the Wonderland of Rocks in 1921.

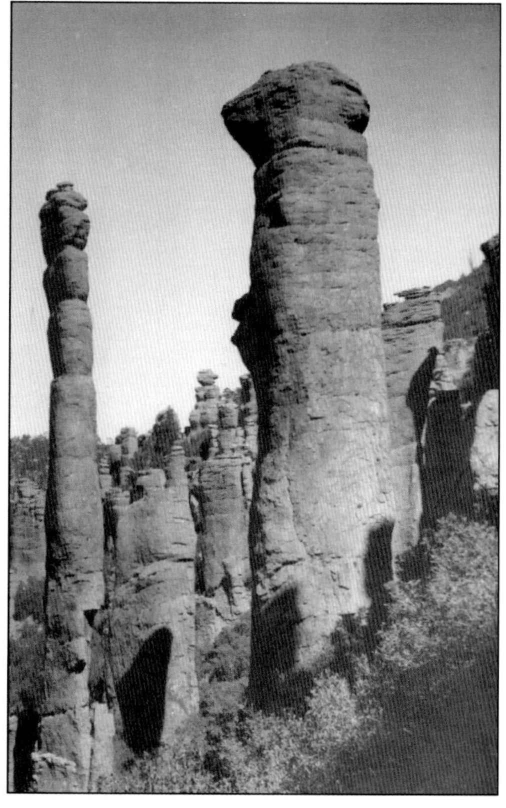

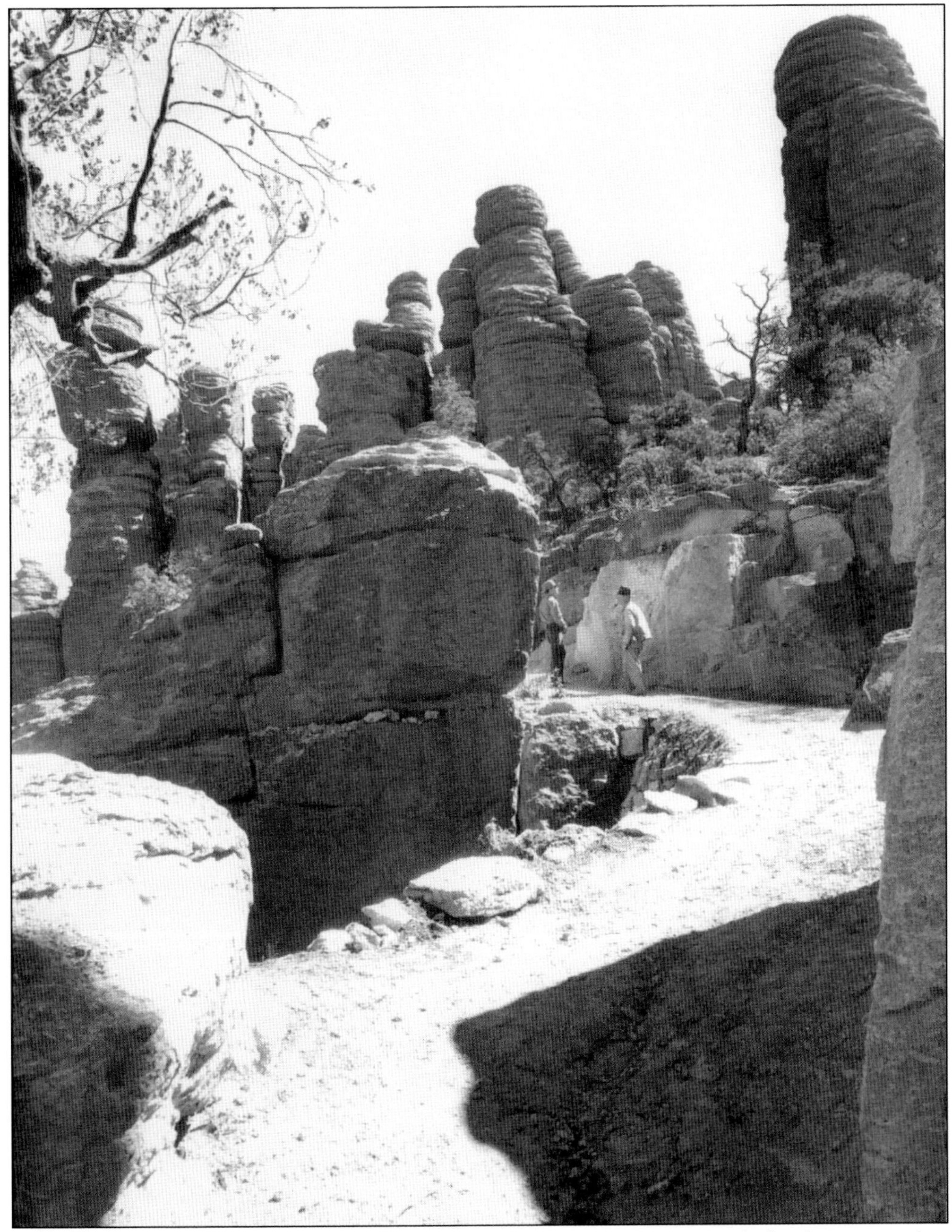

This National Park Service ranger and Chiricahua Monument visitor might be discussing what is around the next bend on the Echo Canyon Trail. The National Park Service's mission is to preserve and protect the variety of natural and cultural resources found on Chiricahua National Monument and more than 400 other sites across the United States.

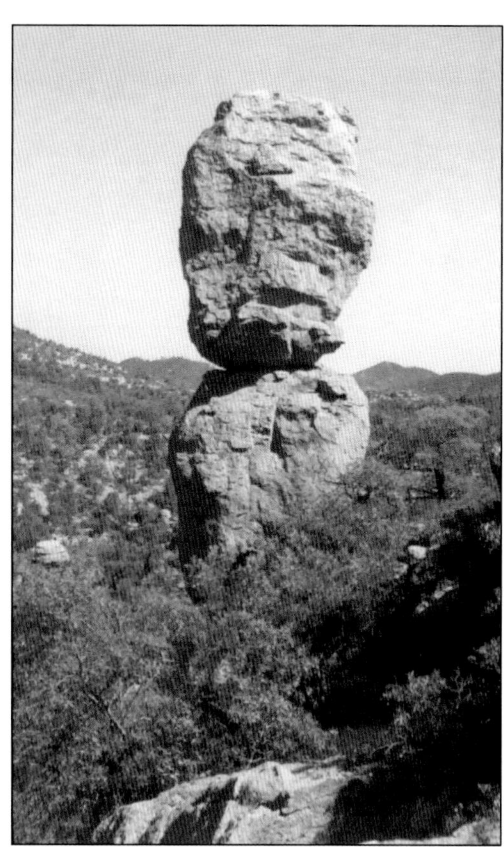

Pinnacles are sometimes called hoodoos, a geological term describing bizarre pillars whether massive or human-sized, like the two shown here. Chato, the Apache leader on page 62, supposedly told American settlers in Bonita Canyon that the rocky area to the east was sacred because spirits of the dead lingered there.

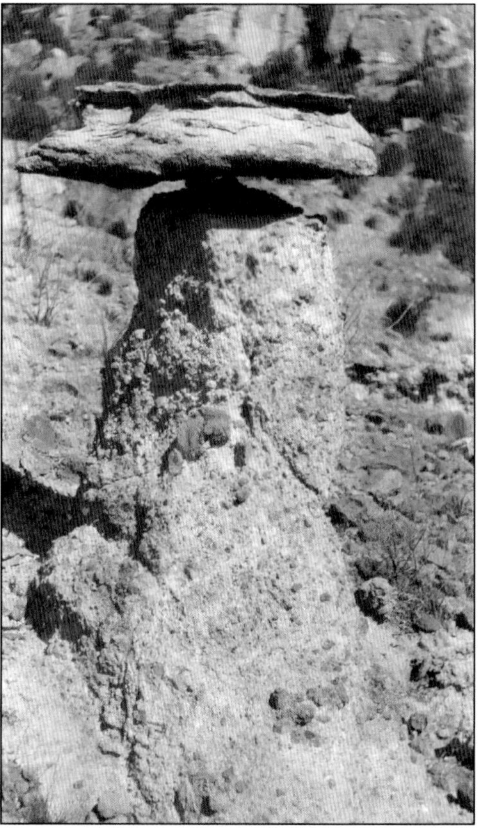

National Park Service ranger Suzanne Moody encourages monument visitors taking photographs to go for grand scenic vistas. But she also advises people to focus on details such as the rough texture and curving cracks seen in these photographs of two different sets of hoodoos.

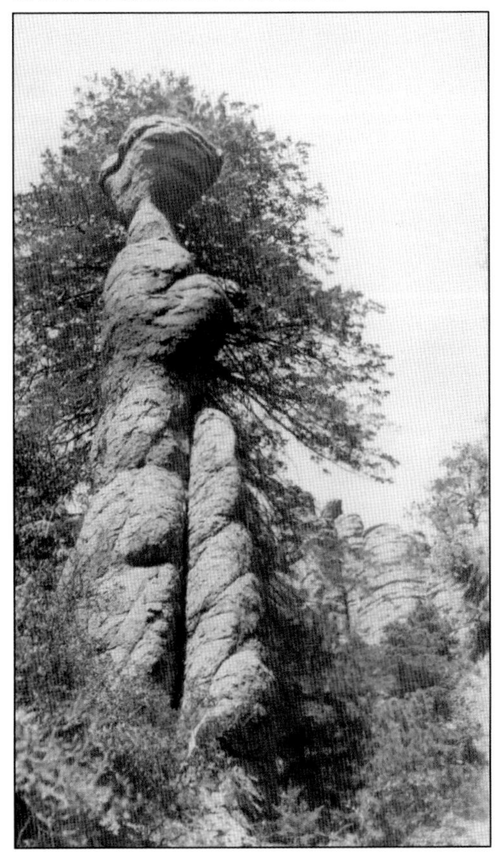

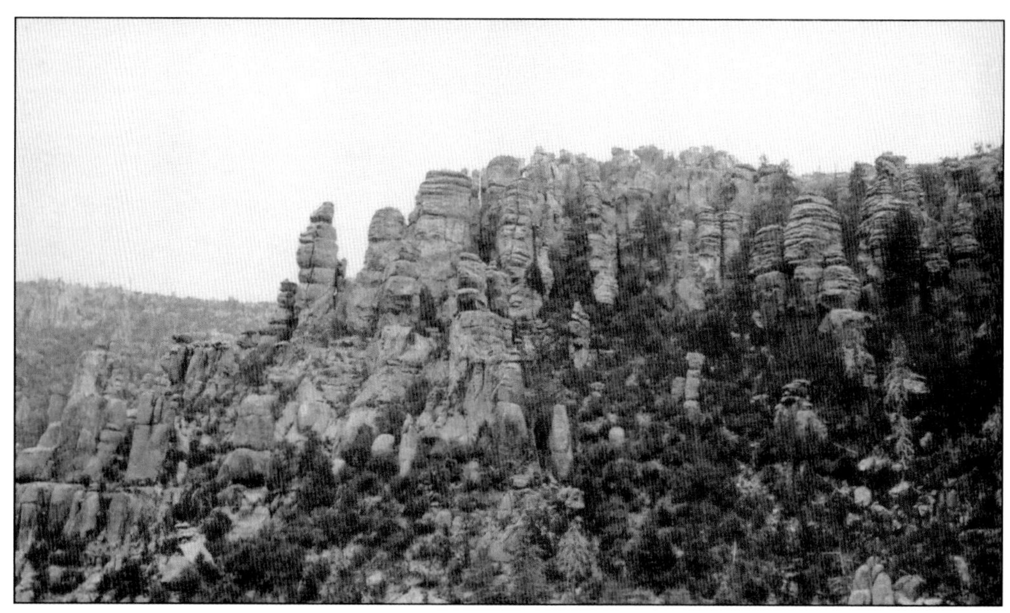

Visitors to Chiricahua National Monument will always see something interesting, whether it is just around the next curve of Bonita Canyon Drive (above) or the view looking west from Inspiration Point (below). The Hailstone Trail clings to the canyon side, and the large hill on the right is Sugarloaf, whose 7,310-foot summit is the monument's highest accessible point. There is an easy trail to the CCC-constructed fire lookout on Sugarloaf's summit.

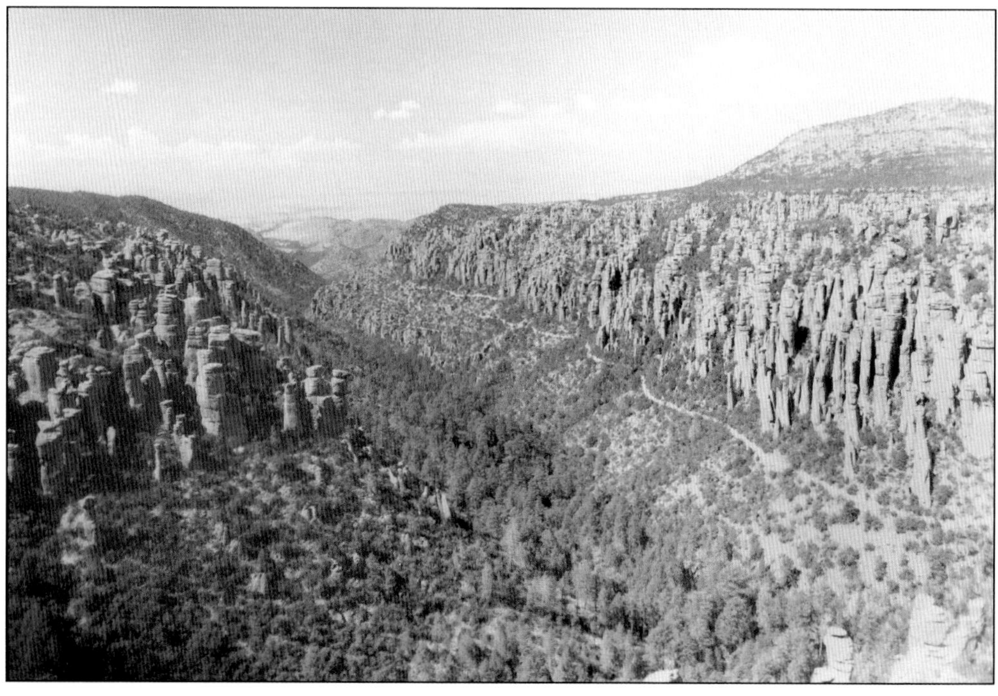

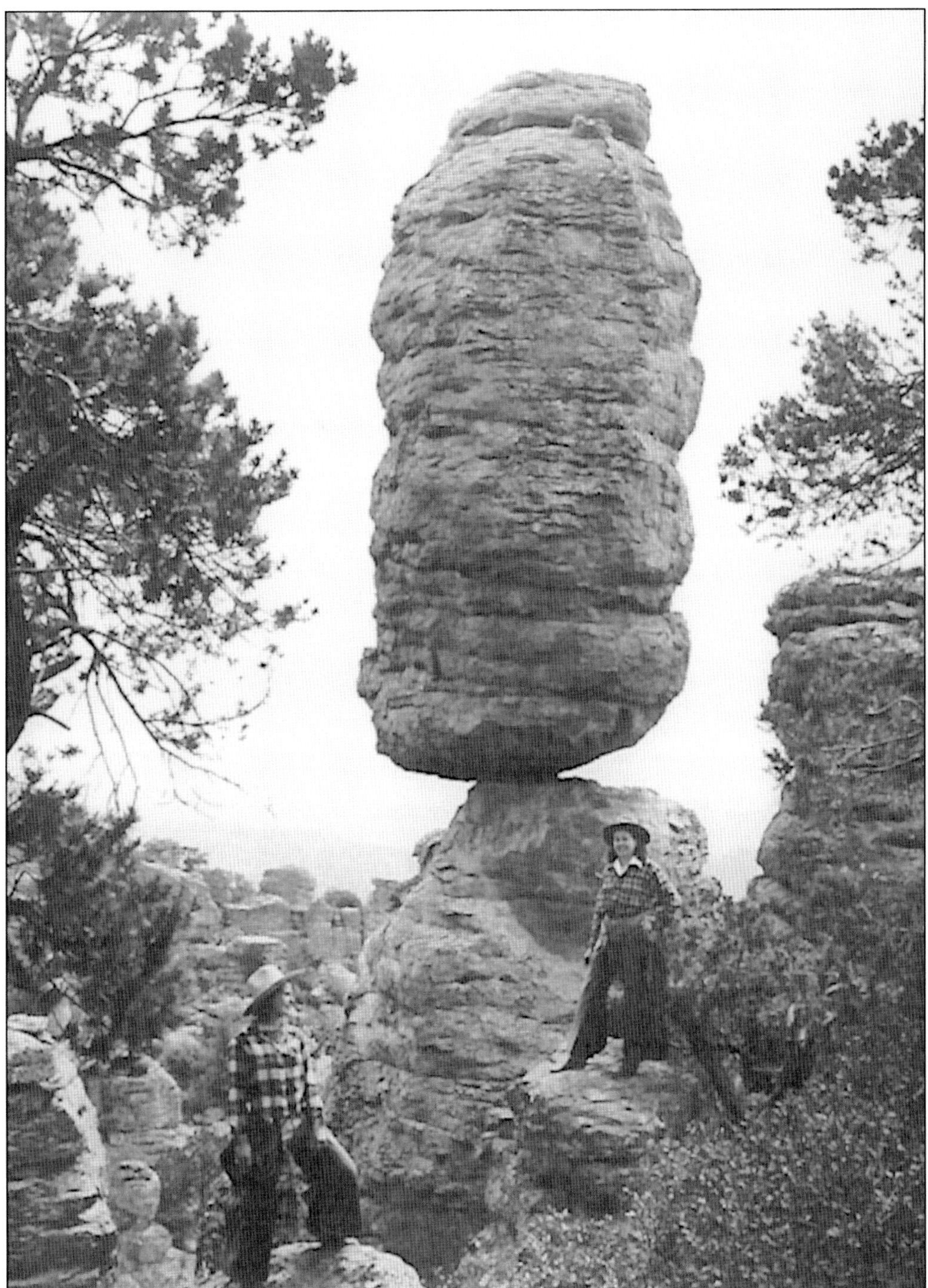

Clover L. Kline, modeling classic Western wear for an admirer at Big Balanced Pinnacle, worked in the late 1940s at Faraway Ranch. There, she met Lillian's nephew, Stan Hutchison, son of Hildegard Erickson and Jess Hutchison. Clover and Stan married and raised three daughters in California, thus becoming one of a half-dozen couples who found romance at Faraway while living or working there.

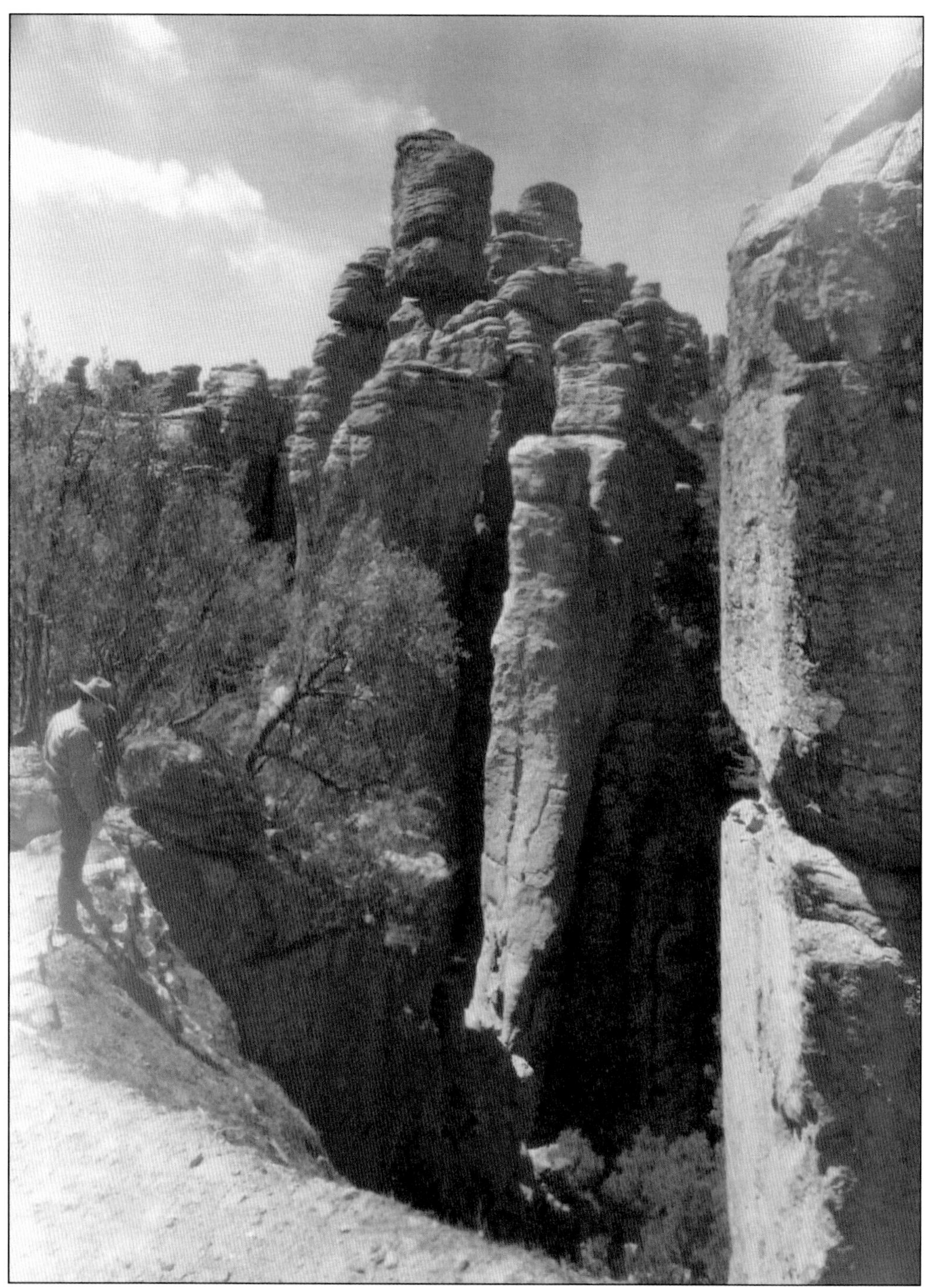

Perhaps this unidentified park ranger is contemplating the superb work done by Civilian Conservation Corps members in the 1930s as they constructed Echo Canyon Trail. Designed by Ed Riggs, the trail connects with the Hailstone Trail to form one of two major loops that hikers and horseback riders can cover within Chiricahua National Monument.

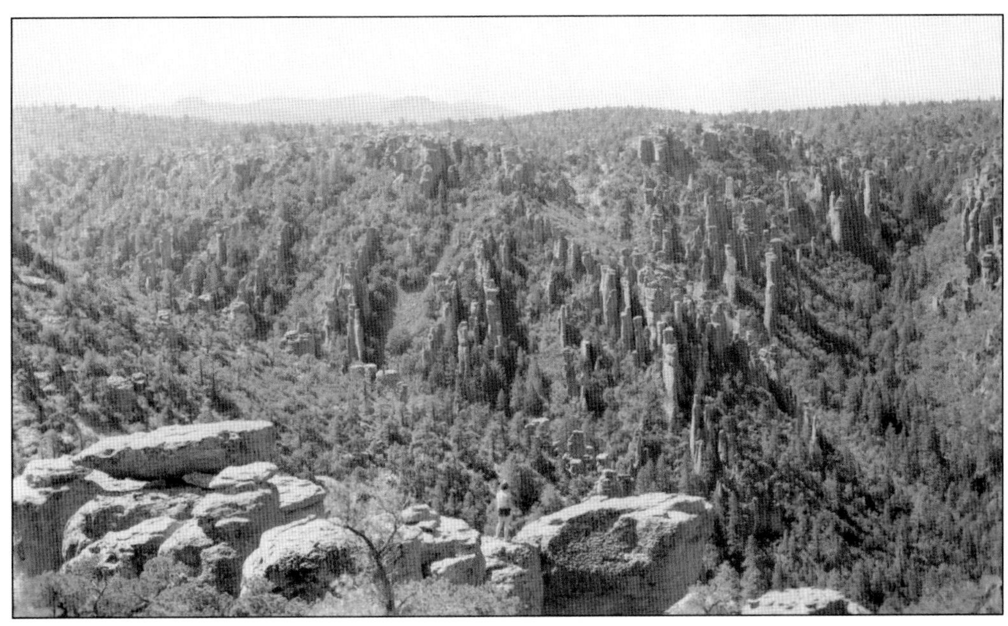

Prolific Western author Zane Grey mentions columns of "marching rocks," such as these, in two of his novels, *Wild Horse Mesa* and *Vanishing American*. The rock formations of Chiricahua National Monument are unlikely to vanish, because 86 percent of the monument was declared a wilderness area in 1976. This provides additional federal protection and preservation measures.

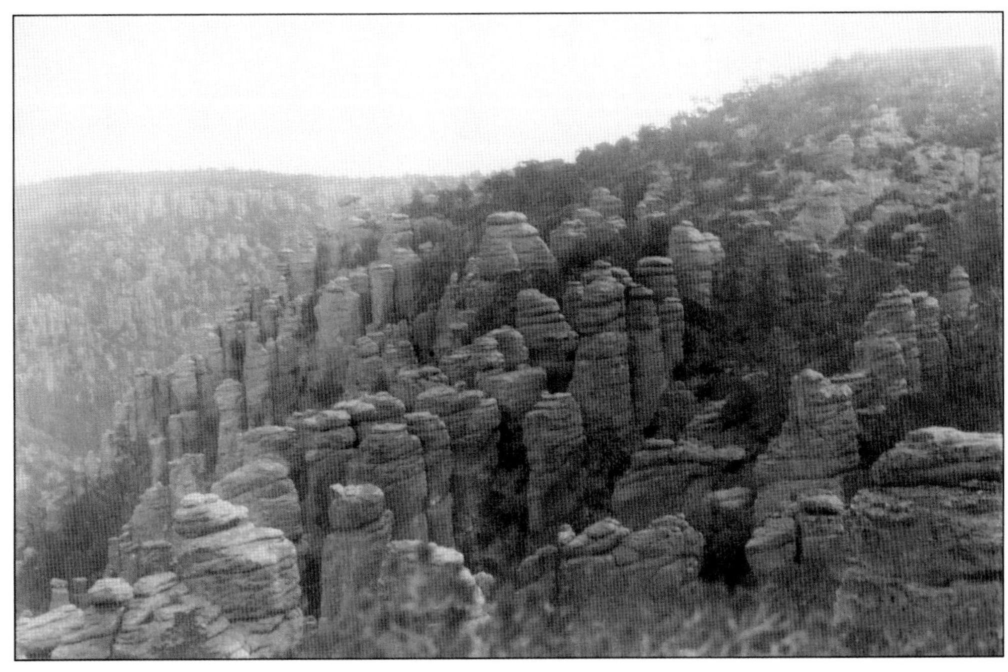

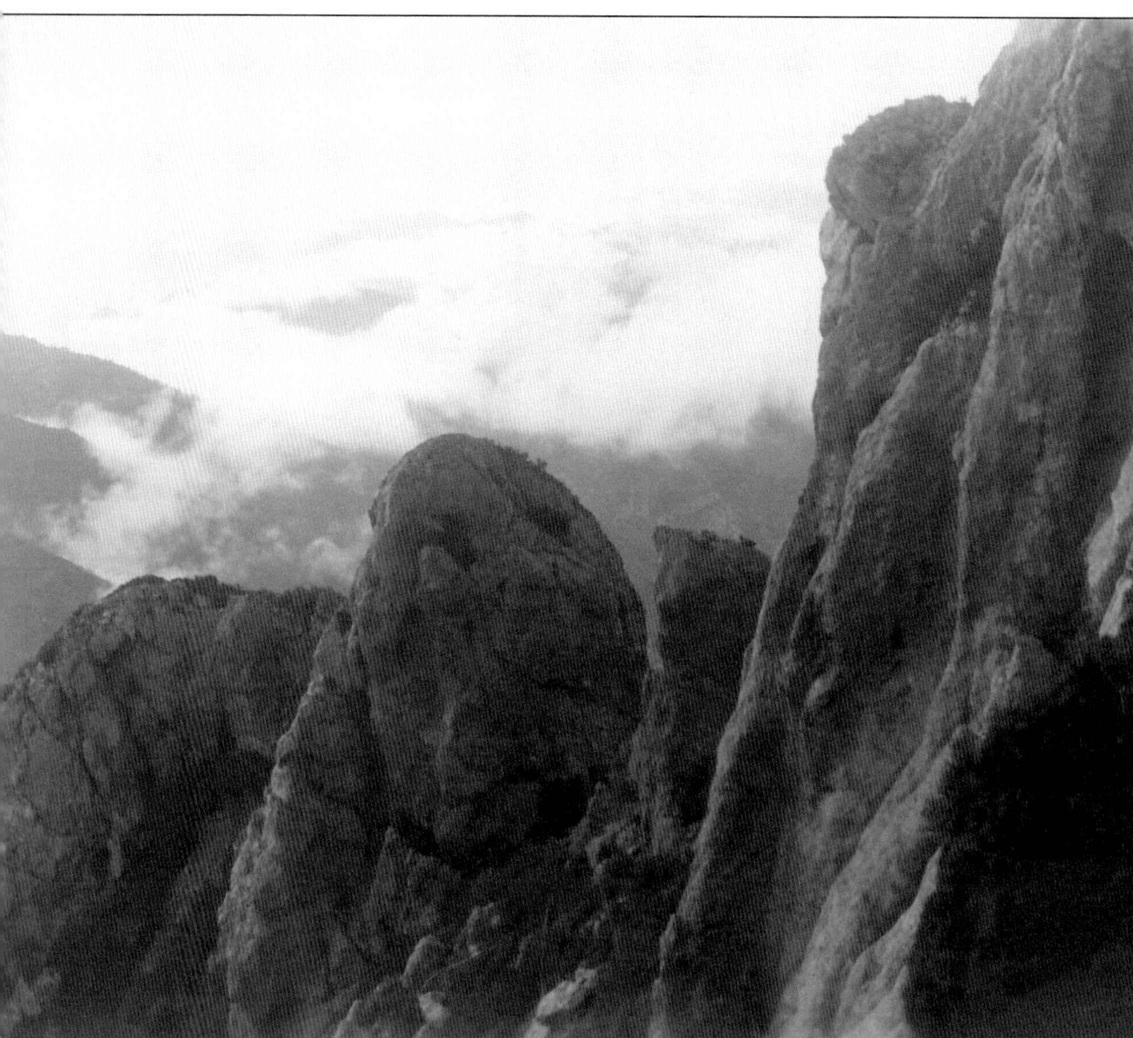

Anyone visiting Chiricahua National Monument soon realizes the formation known as Cochise's Head, seen on pages 104 and 116, dominates the area. The formation casts a spell over the northern portion of the Chiricahua Mountains, as an unidentified photographer acknowledged when he wrote the caption for this photograph he took of fog swirling around Cochise's Head following the rain of a summer thunderstorm: "It sure was a lonesome feeling to stand alone on the Old Boy's Nose with the world completely shut off by fog, and hear the rumble of thunder reverberating in the distant clouds."

Four

APACHES AND FORT BOWIE

National Park Service archaeological surveyors found traces of prehistoric Native Americans within Chiricahua National Monument, but its usage by people known as Chiricahua Apaches is legendary. They called the place Land of Standing Up Rocks.

Their Athabaskan language suggests Apaches reached the Southwest not long before Spanish conquistadors traveled through southern Arizona in the 1540s. The Spanish encountered the nomadic Apaches, who became even more mobile after acquiring Spanish horses.

Apache men hunted deer and antelope in the valleys surrounding the Chiricahuas, while the women foraged for edible plants. Their survival depended upon locating every water source, such as a spring and creek in Bonita Canyon.

Horses enabled an Apache raiding economy in which first Spanish, then Mexican, and finally American settlers were victims. Apaches killed or ran off livestock, stole or devastated crops, and made mining a perilous business. Traveling in southern Arizona or northern Mexico was a death-defying experience in the 1860s and 1870s.

In that period, there were six Apache tribes, of which the Chiricahuas (Chokonen) were one. They lived in three bands. The Southern band, whose most famous leader was Geronimo, ranged in northern Sonora and Chihuahua, Mexico. The Central band, led by Cochise, occupied southeast Arizona and southwest New Mexico. The Eastern band, with Victorio as its most well-known leader, lived in western New Mexico.

Moreover, band members lived in small community groups that could and did act independently. This fractionalized structure hindered American efforts to place Chiricahuas on a centralized reservation.

It also led to confusions such as Lt. George Bascom incorrectly blaming Cochise's band for the abduction of a Mexican boy that spiraled into a vortex of hostage taking and killing followed by a war that ended only with the intercession of Tom Jeffords. The story is romanticized in the novel *Blood Brother* and the film *Broken Arrow*.

After Cochise's 1874 death, Geronimo's band became the focus of pacification efforts. Much of this endeavor originated from Fort Bowie, an Army camp eight miles north of Bonita Canyon. Gen. George Crook led the first effort, but ultimately Gen. Nelson Miles brought about Geronimo's surrender in 1886.

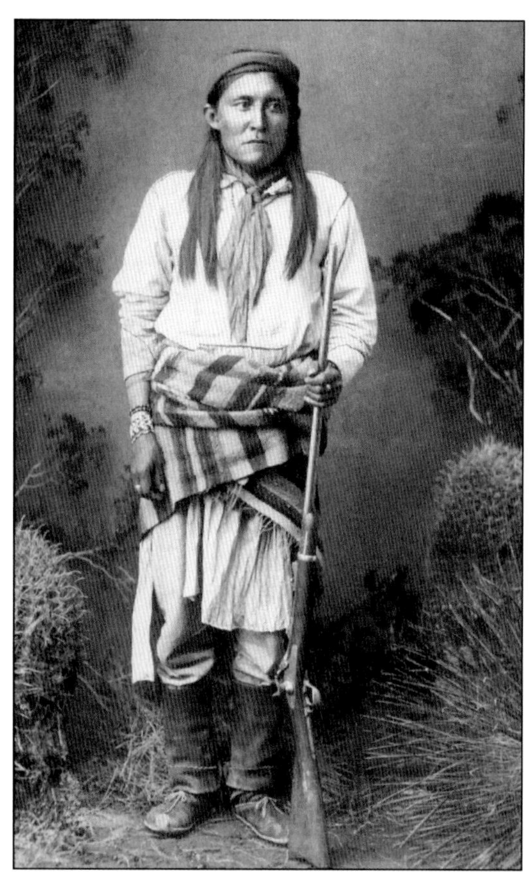

Leaders of the southernmost band of Chiricahua Apaches included Chato, left, and Geronimo, below. The Southern band lived mostly in northern Sonora and Chihuahua, Mexico, but regularly raided in the United States. Following the 1872 death of Cochise, leader of the Central band, and the 1874 closure of the Chiricahua Reservation in the Sulphur Springs Valley, elements of the Central and Southern bands combined. They became the focus of the US Army, which did not overcome these Apaches until Geronimo's surrender in 1886. Geronimo and his followers were shipped as prisoners of war, first to Florida and then Oklahoma, where Geronimo died in 1909.

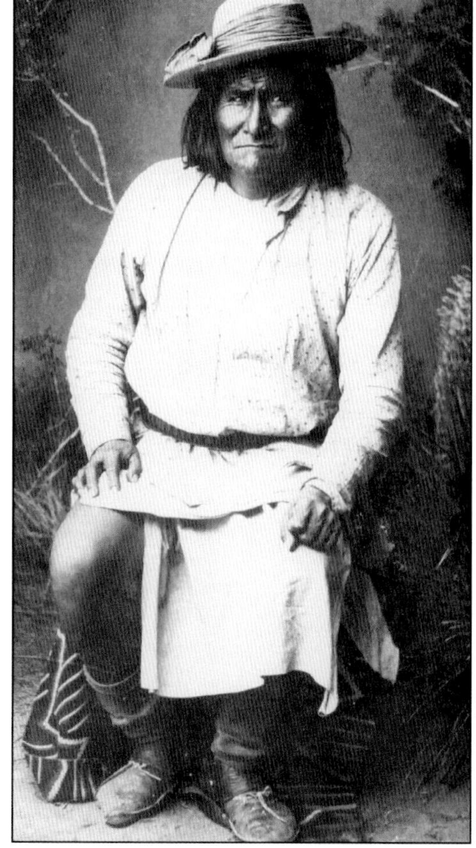

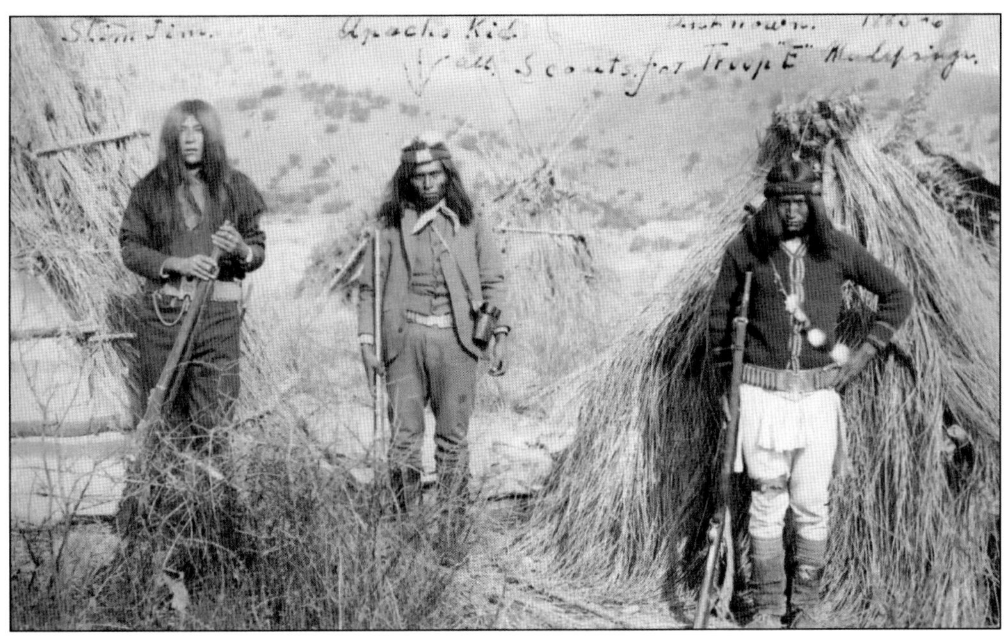

Because Chiricahua Apaches lived in small independent groups with no overall structure, one group could be at peace with its neighbors while fighting another group. Apache enemies, such as Mexican militias, often allied with "peaceful Apaches" and used them to kill other Apaches. The US Army also utilized this tactic by recruiting Apache scouts who trailed other Apaches. In the photograph above, three of these scouts are, from left to right, Slim Jim, Apache Kid, and an unidentified man in a bivouac at Mud Springs, a few miles north of today's Douglas, Arizona. The heliograph shown below was also at Mud Springs. The arrow points at a mirror used to flash Morse code.

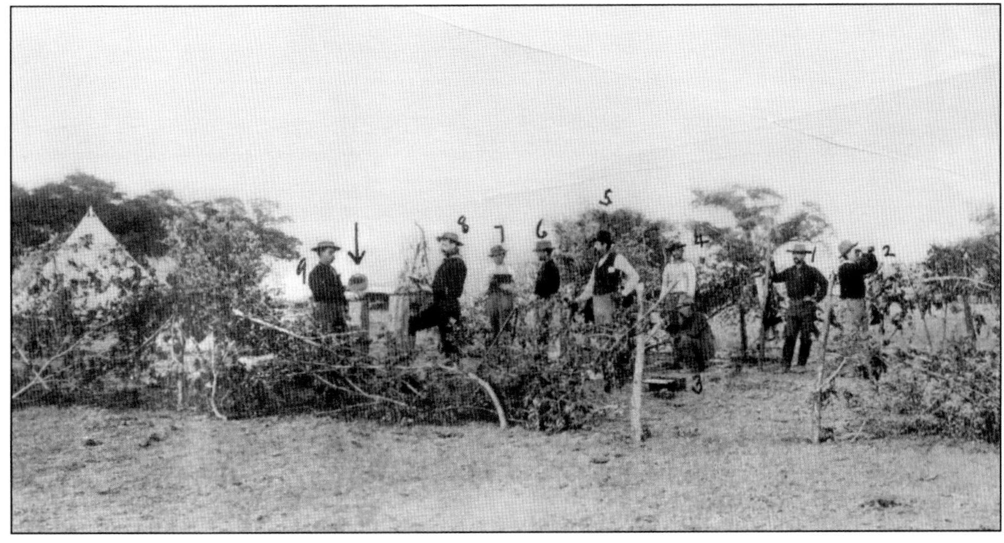

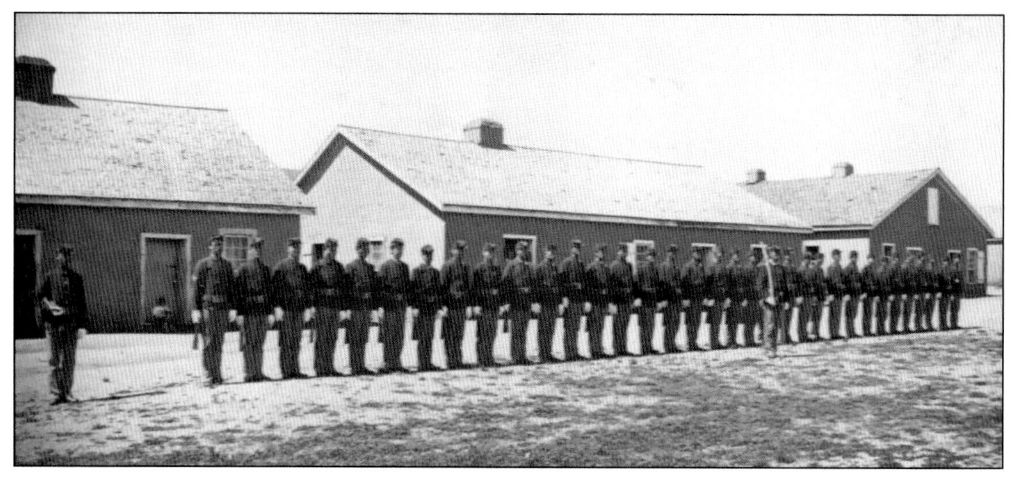

The 4th Cavalry was a US Army regiment chasing Apaches in southern Arizona and New Mexico in the late 1800s. At one point, the 4th operated out of the middle Rio Grande valley at Fort Craig, New Mexico. This is where the photograph above was taken of the regiment's Troop E standing in review. The photograph below shows what must have been Troop E's "foreign legion." The men are, from left to right, S.R. Goenhnour, Geyza Kanovics, and Neil Erickson. Swedish-born Erickson had stowed away on a ship to the United States and enlisted in the Army to avenge his father's 1871 death at the hands of Indians.

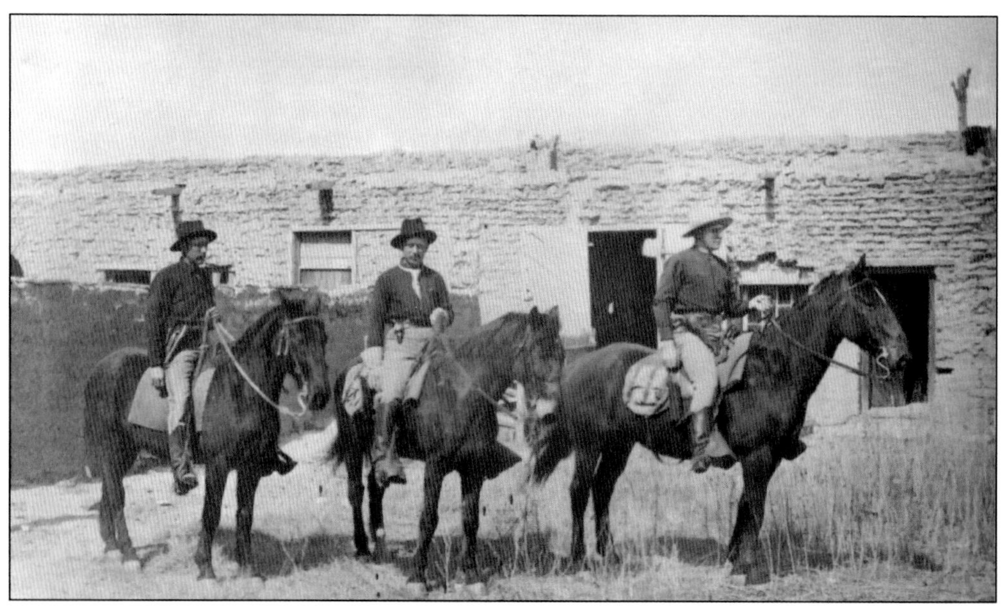

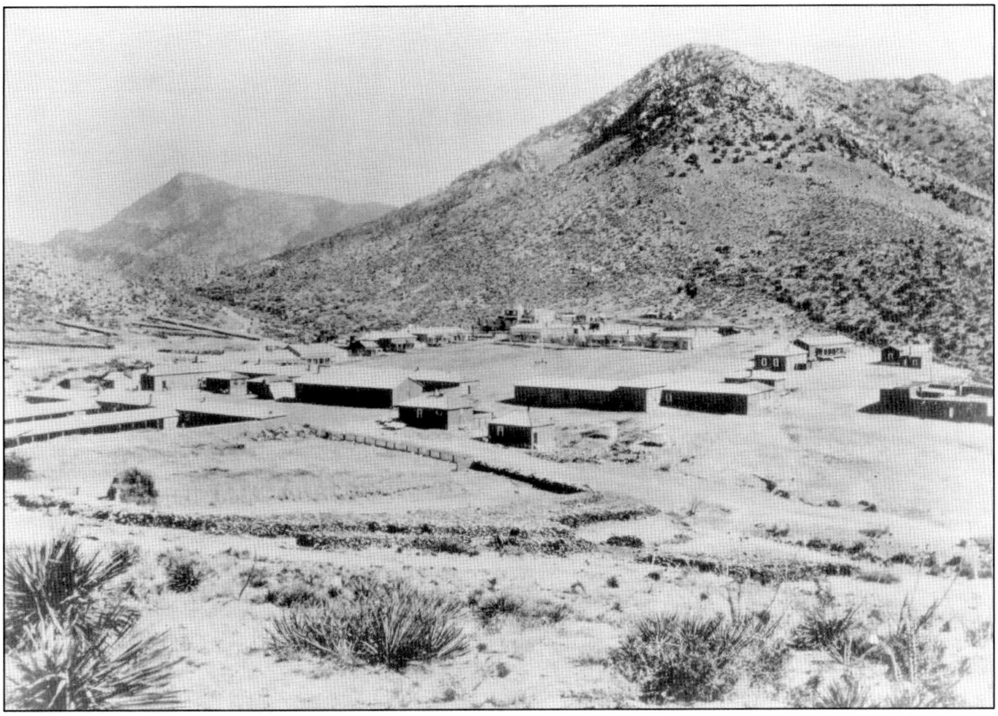

In 1884, the 4th Cavalry moved to Arizona, and Erickson ended up at Fort McDowell, east of Phoenix. It was a hardship for Erickson, because he had met Emma Peterson while at Fort Craig and fallen in love. A fellow Swede, Peterson kept house for a 4th Cavalry officer, and when he was assigned to Fort Huachuca, she moved there. Later, she went to Fort Bowie and ran a boardinghouse. Fort Bowie (above) was a staging and supply center straddling an important pass through the Chiricahuas. Another reason for its importance was nearby Apache Spring, the area's only reliable water. Living on Fort Bowie were about 100 civilians and 200 soldiers, including members of a band (below).

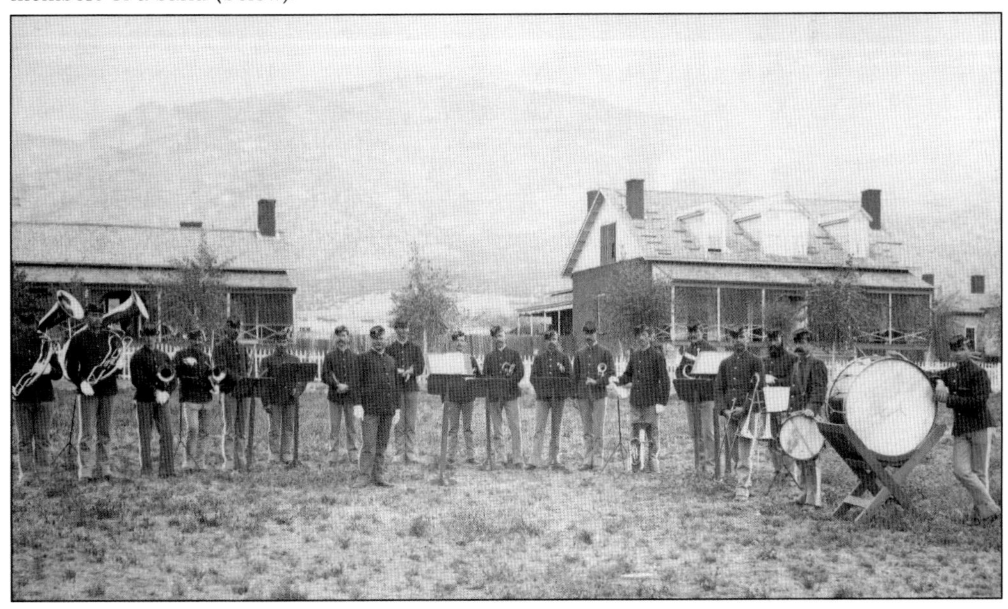

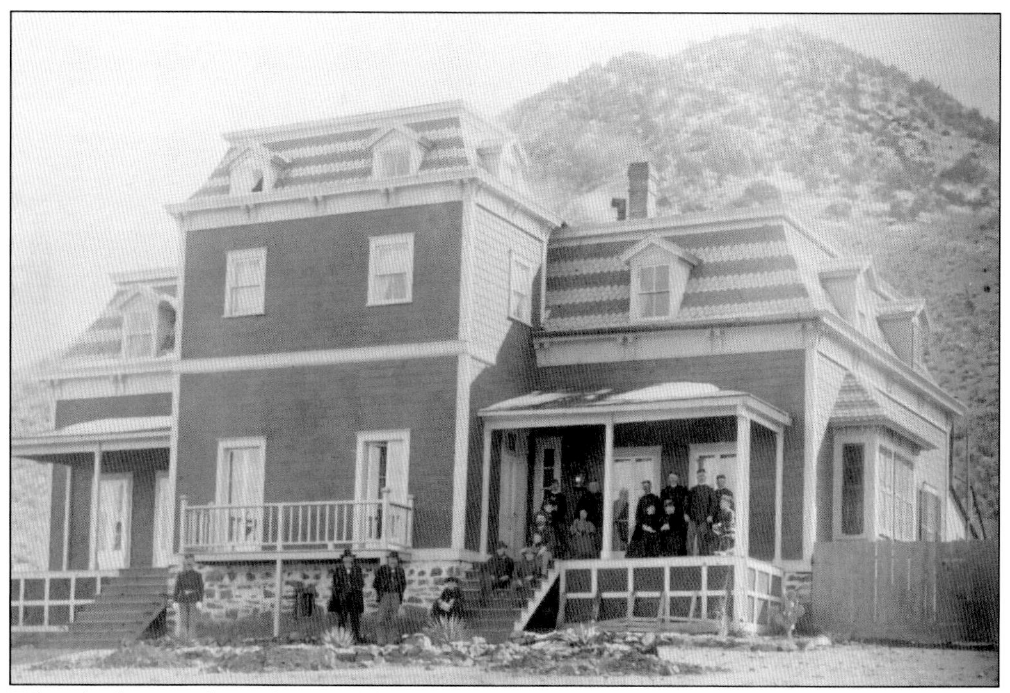

When looking at the multistoried house that was Fort Bowie's commanding officer's quarters (above), it is hard to believe the house and post disappeared so quickly and so completely (below). The fort's life began on July 27, 1862, when the 5th Regiment of California Volunteers established the post and named it after unit commander Col. G.W. Bowie. While it was initially adjacent to Apache Spring, soldiers moved Fort Bowie slightly eastward in 1868. The installation came to include adobe barracks, houses, corrals, a trading post, and a hospital. Despite this seeming permanency, orders closed Fort Bowie on October 17, 1894, and little remains today. The ruins are open to the public as Fort Bowie National Historic Site.

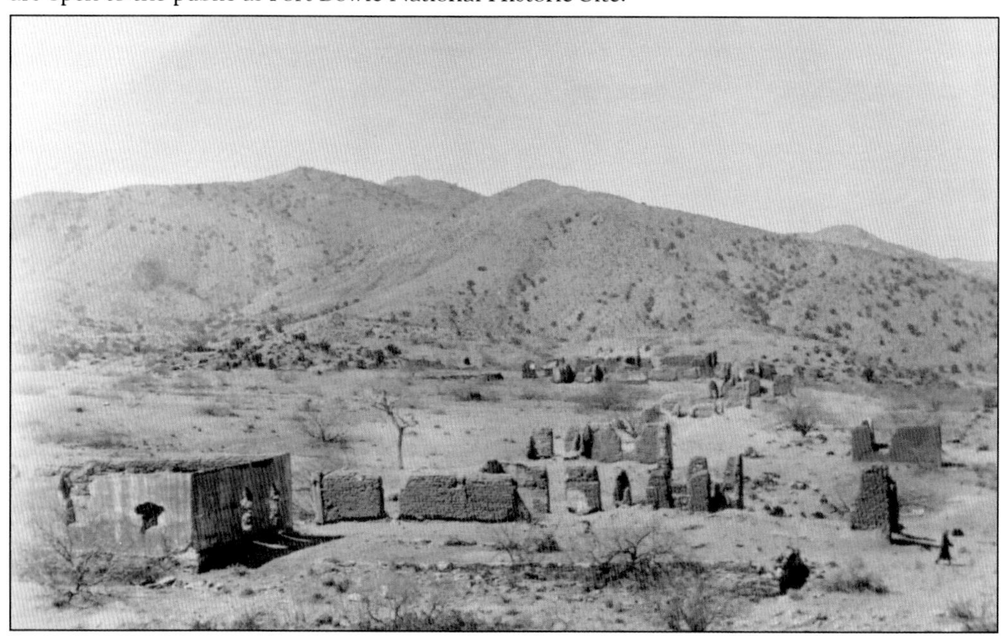

Five

Buffalo Soldiers and the Garfield Monument

One tactic American Army generals George Crook and Nelson Miles used as they attempted to subdue Chiricahua Apaches in 1885–1886 was control of southern Arizona's water resources. To this end, they posted soldiers at every water source, including 10th Cavalry troopers at Bonita Canyon.

Formed in 1866, the 10th was one of two US cavalry regiments composed of black enlisted men and white officers. The 10th became a mainstay while fighting Plains Indians in the 1870s and earned the nickname buffalo soldiers.

In 1885, the 10th marched to Fort Bowie and then dispersed to locations scattered around southern Arizona. Three troops—E, H, and I—were consecutively stationed in Bonita Canyon between September 1885 and September 1886, when Geronimo and other bands finally surrendered.

From Bonita Canyon, the 10th patrolled the surrounding country, was part of a courier system, acted as a secondary defensive line, and prevented Apaches from using Bonita Spring. The soldiers lived in tents, while their commander occupied a two-room cabin already on-site.

Duty was not particularly onerous. Wagons from Fort Bowie brought hay for horses and supplies for men, which they augmented with vegetables, fruits, and eggs purchased from farmer Ja Hu Stafford, who lived east of camp, and beef bought from Louis Prue, who lived southwest of camp.

To alleviate boredom, the buffalo soldiers created a monument. They shaped local rocks into blocks and carved their names or initials, dates, and other information into the blocks. The soldiers inscribed "In Memory Of Jas. A. Garfield" on a large centerpiece.

A Civil War general elected to Congress in 1862, Garfield strongly supported black suffrage and education. He became the 20th US president in 1881 but was shot within months of his inauguration and died before completing a year in office.

The buffalo soldiers put their blocks into a three-tiered monument and then marched away to other assignments. It remains the only engraved monument constructed by soldiers in the United States.

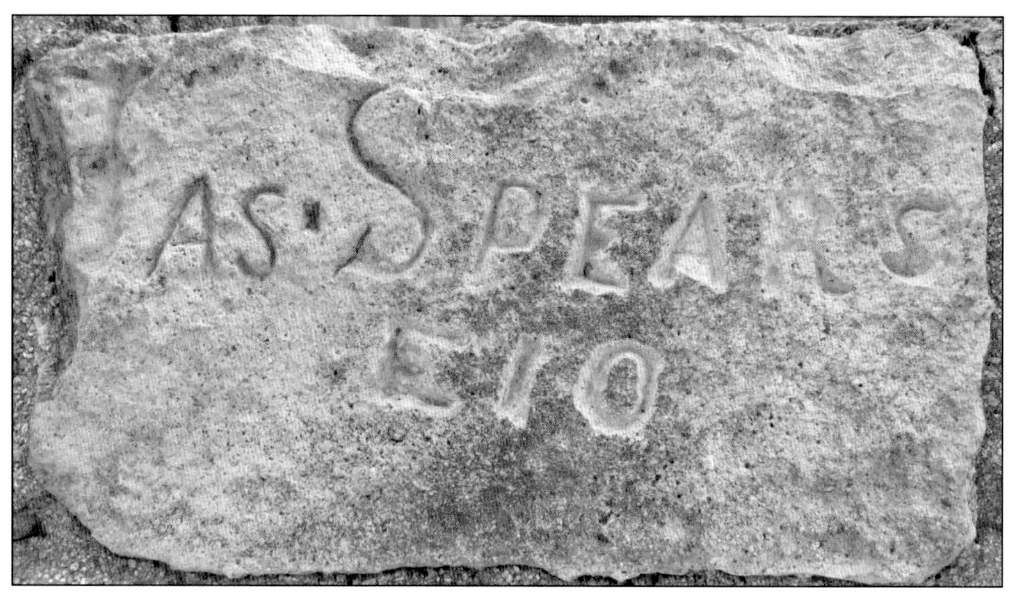

During 1885–1886, three troops of 10th US Cavalry took turns living in Bonita Canyon. They were black men commanded by white officers and tasked with preventing Chiricahua Apaches from using Bonita Canyon's water. This left the buffalo soldiers with spare time, which they filled by shaping local rocks into blocks and carving their names or initials, dates, and other info. Research by National Park Service experts revealed that the top block bears the name of James A. Spears, a Troop E sergeant. The block below includes a hammer and horseshoe and the initials J.W.R. for John Robinson, Troop E's blacksmith. His name appears on two additional blocks. (Photographs by Suzanne Moody.)

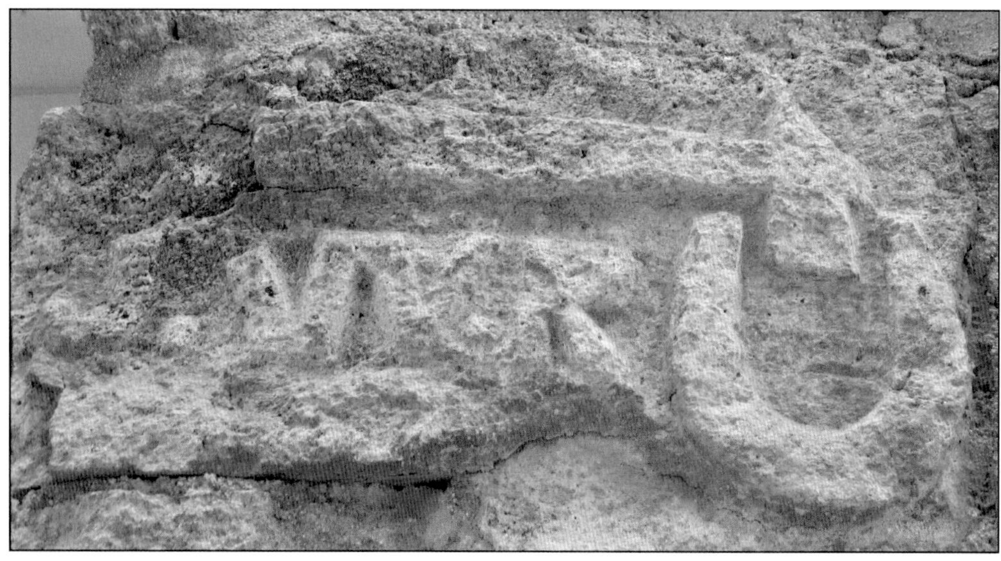

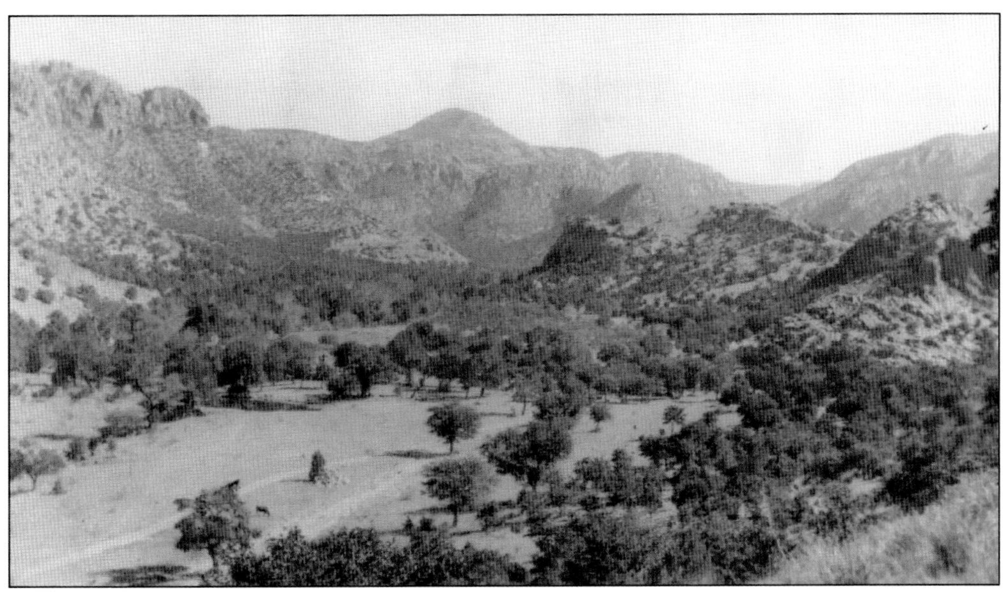

The buffalo soldiers assembled their inscribed blocks into a three-tiered monument with a centerpiece honoring James A. Garfield. The 20th president of the United States, Garfield consistently advocated black education and suffrage before his assassination in 1881. The one-of-a-kind monument stood in Faraway Ranch's west pasture for three decades (above), but it was falling apart by 1924 (below). Ed Riggs then took the blocks and used them to create a fireplace on the north side of the Faraway house, thus preserving a unique piece of American history.

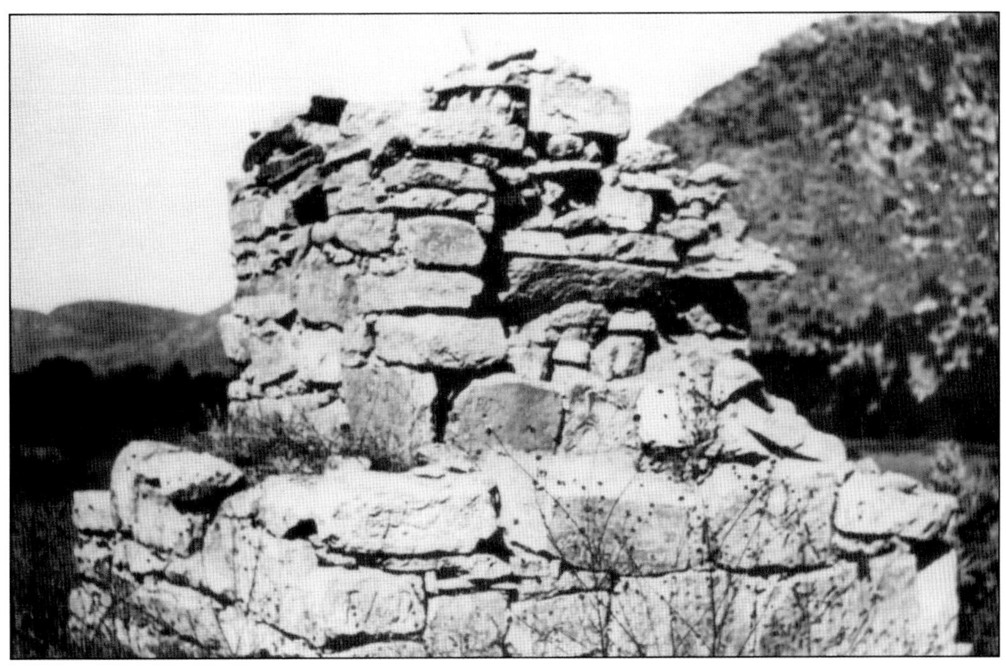

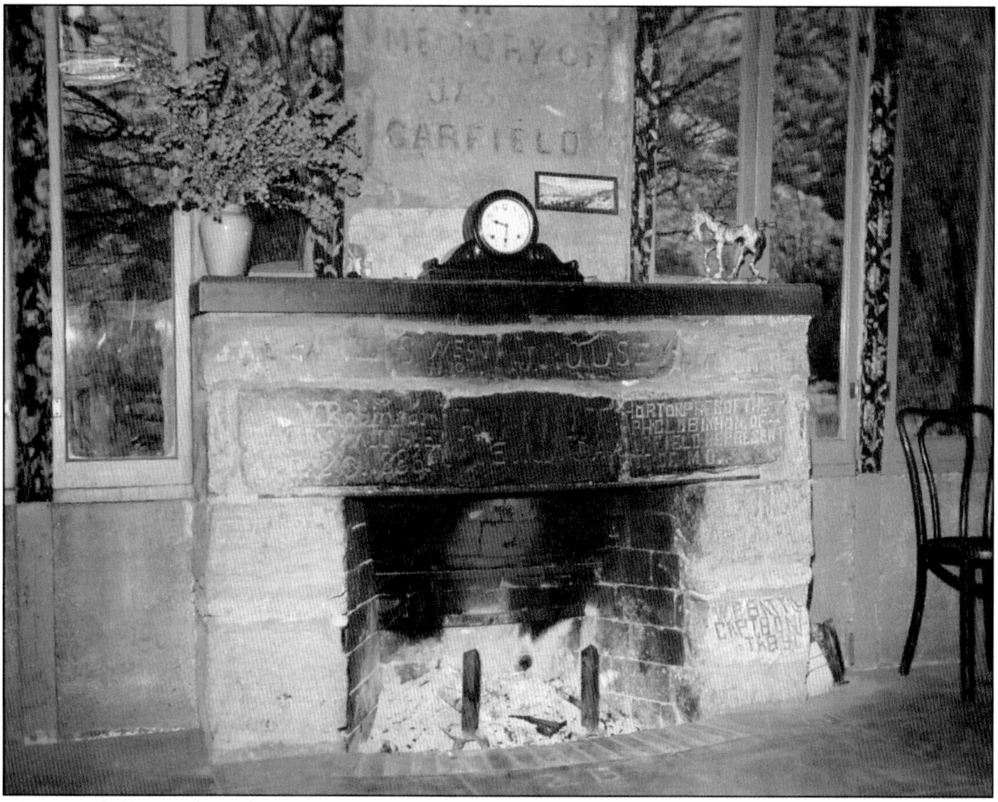

The Garfield fireplace dominates a large dining room on the north side of the Faraway Ranch house. These two views clearly show the Garfield centerpiece. A smaller block worth noting is the one directly under the bony horse statuette. It reads "H.O. Flipper" and obviously is a 10th Cavalry tribute to the first black graduate of the US Military Academy at West Point. Below the Flipper block is one apparently made by George Horton. It is believed that Horton, a Troop H member who was promoted while at Camp Bonita, played a leading role the monument's creation.

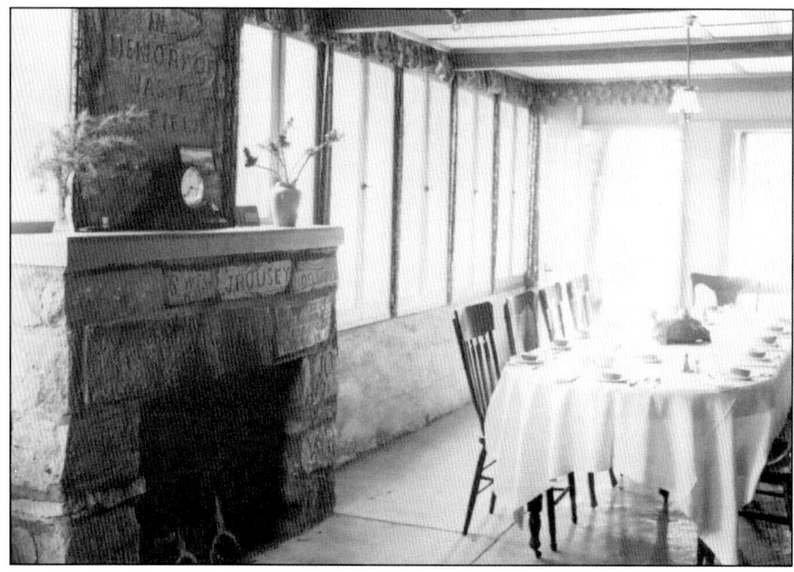

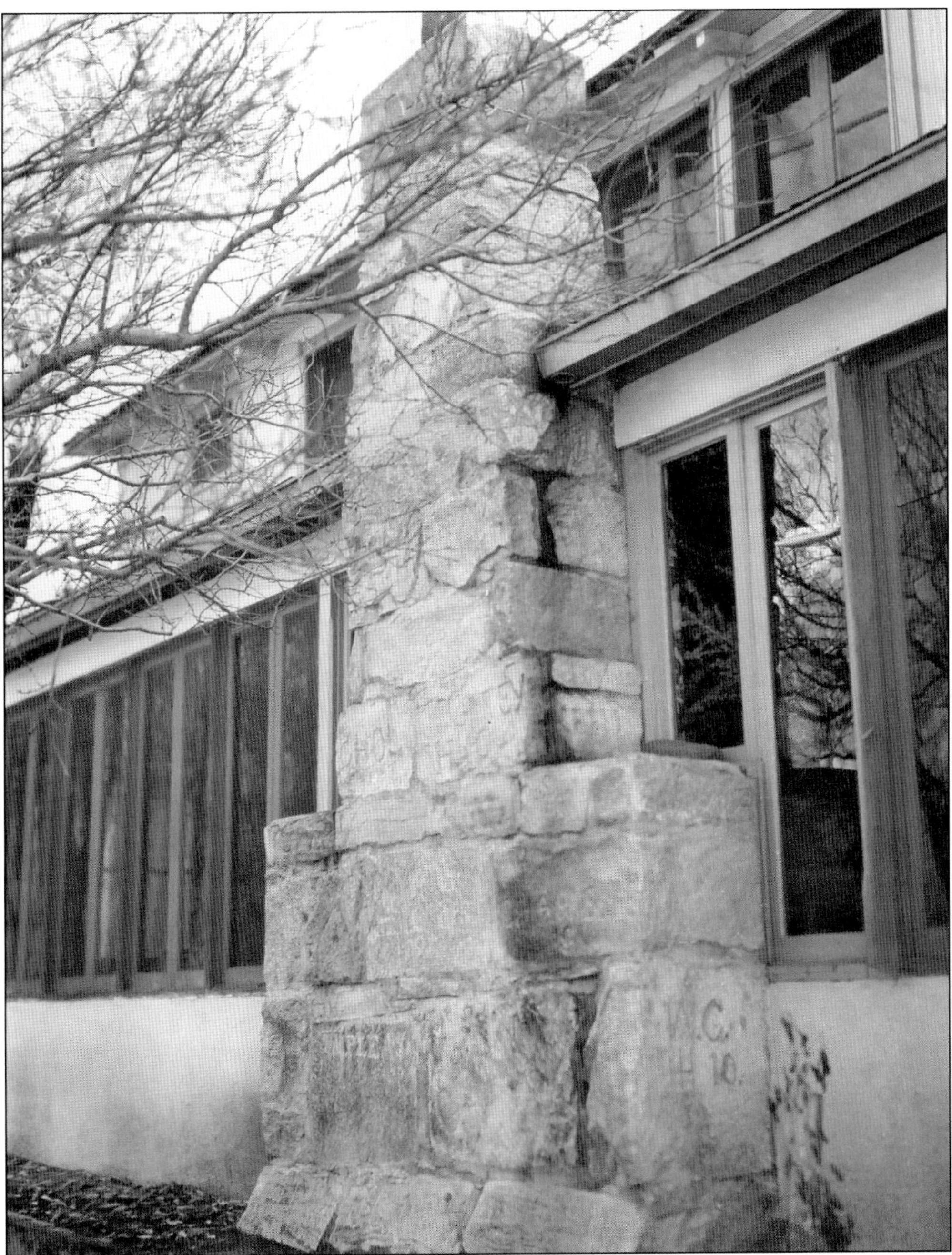

The Garfield fireplace's exterior shows many blocks with decipherable information. "W.C." visible on the large lower-right block are the initials of Webb Chatmoran, a private in Troop H. A small block above Chatmoran's is that of S.R. Miller. His records show that he enlisted on November 23, 1881, in Washington, DC, and also was in Troop H. So was Pvt. Michael Finnegan, whose block bears the three interlocked ovals that are the insignia of the Odd Fellows, a fraternal order.

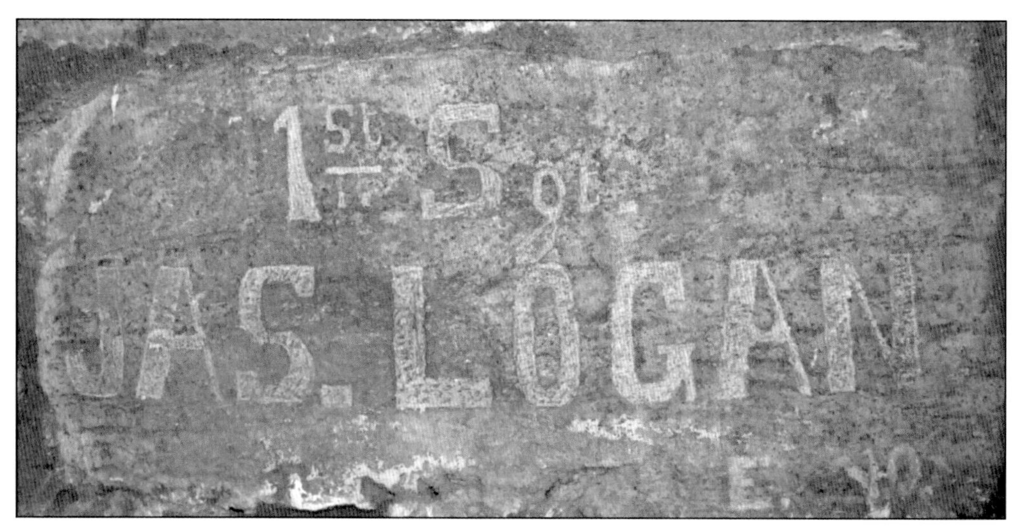

One Garfield Monument block with particularly crisp lettering is that of 1st Sgt. James Logan, a Troop E leader (above). Like Troop E blacksmith John Robinson, Logan has three blocks in the monument. The photograph below shows the block of Sampson West, a private in Troop H. All the fireplace blocks are from Troops E or H, with one exception. The one created by Troop I bears the initials of eight members of that troop. (Photographs by Suzanne Moody.)

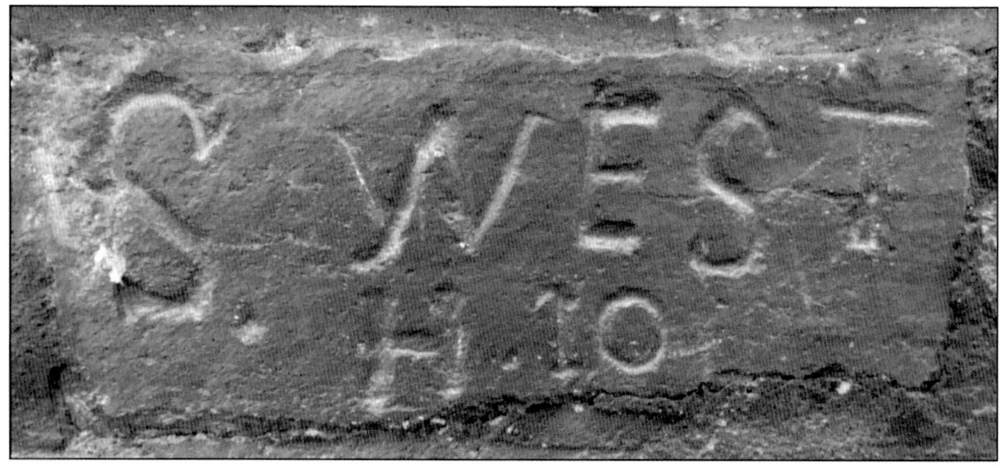

Six

Homesteaders and Ranchers

The first North Americans living in the Bonita Canyon vicinity were the Louis Prue and Brannick Riggs families. Canadian-born Prue, a US Army veteran and rancher, arrived late in 1878. The Riggs family showed up early in 1879, and they too ran cattle in the Sulphur Springs Valley.

In 1880, Riggs recommended Bonita Canyon as a homestead location to Ja Hu Stafford. Born in North Carolina, Stafford had lived a transitory life until he met Pauline Madsen, daughter of a Danish convert to the Mormon Church. Ja Hu was baptized in that faith in 1880, the same year the couple moved to Bonita Canyon.

They built a two-room log cabin, which they expanded as their children were born. They planted fruit trees and put in a garden watered by an irrigation ditch drawing upon Bonita Creek.

Sometime before 1885, a man named Newton built a cabin a half-mile west of the Staffords. It housed 10th Cavalry officers and then became the nucleus of a home constructed by Neil Erickson.

His was a poor Swedish family. His father had immigrated to United States but was killed by Indians. This so affected Neil that in 1879 he stowed away on a ship going to America. He joined the Army, rising to sergeant's rank in the 4th Cavalry.

While Neil was stationed at Fort Craig, New Mexico, a friend introduced him to Emma Peterson, who also was Swedish. Neil courted Emma as they both moved to Arizona, but it took four years for Neil to convince her to marry him.

In that period, Emma visited Bonita Canyon and fell in love with it. She acquired the Newton property, and not long after she and Neil married in 1887, Neil went to Bonita Canyon and began turning the cabin into a secure home. A few months after the 1888 birth of daughter Lillian, the Ericksons moved to Bonita Canyon, where Ben and Hildegard were born.

In 1890, a renegade Apache couple, believed to be Massai and his wife, fled through Bonita Canyon. Neil and Prue trailed the pair eastward and thus were the first American settlers to enter what became Chiricahua National Monument.

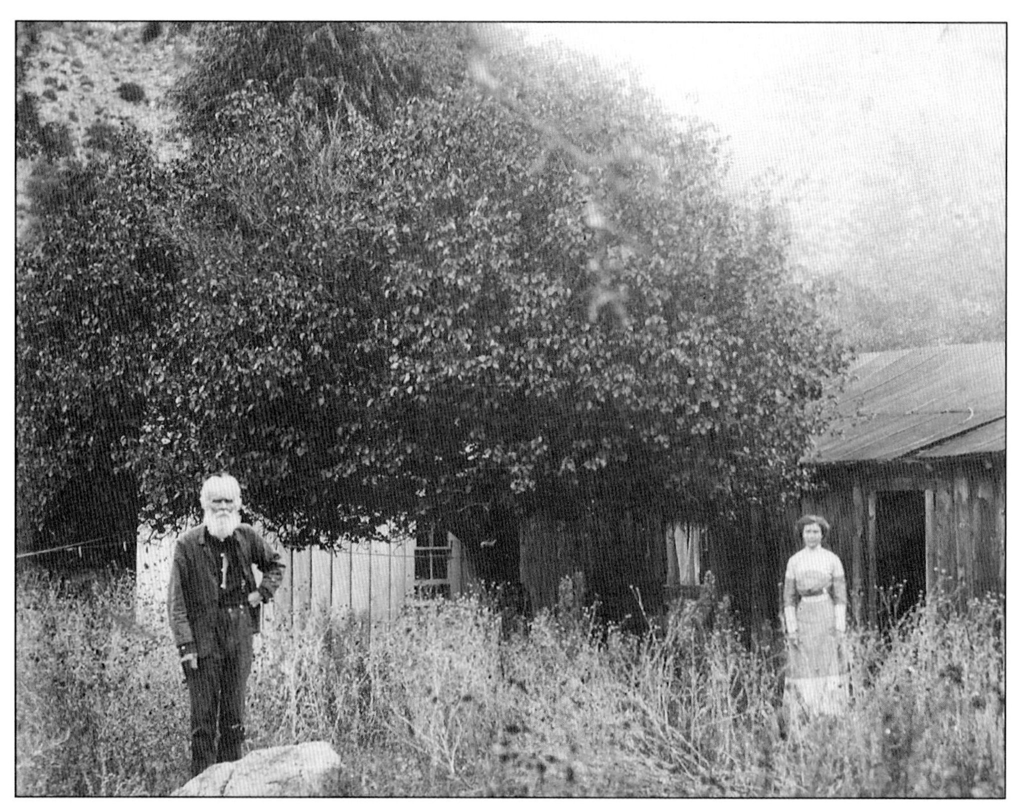

The first North American settlers in the Bonita Canyon area arrived in 1878 and 1879. They were ranchers Louis Prue and Brannick Riggs. The latter encouraged Ja Hu Stafford to homestead in Bonita Canyon. Given a name apparently derived from Old Testament prophet Jehu, Stafford was born in 1834 in North Carolina. He roamed the West until he met Pauline Madsen, daughter of a Danish convert to the Mormon Church. Ja Hu was baptized in that faith in 1880, the same year the couple moved to Bonita Canyon. They built a log cabin, farmed, and reared five children. Two are shown here with their father, Pansy at the cabin door above and Clara in a more formal pose at left.

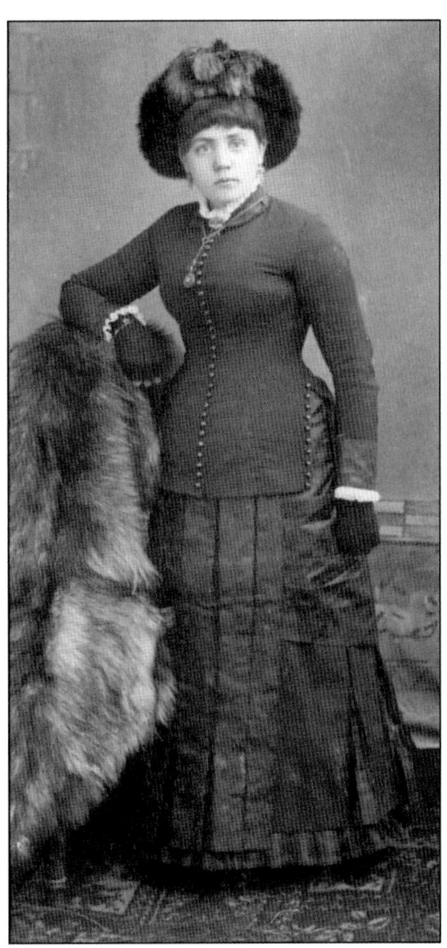

Joining the Staffords in 1888 in Bonita Canyon were Swedish immigrants Neil and Emma Erickson. They had met and courted while living on Army posts in New Mexico and Arizona, Neil as a sergeant in the 4th Cavalry and Emma as a housekeeper and boardinghouse manager. While living at Fort Bowie, Emma visited Bonita Canyon and acquired land there before her January 25, 1887, marriage to Neil. The couple moved to Bonita Canyon shortly after the February 9, 1888, birth of their first child, Lillian Sophia, at Fort Bowie.

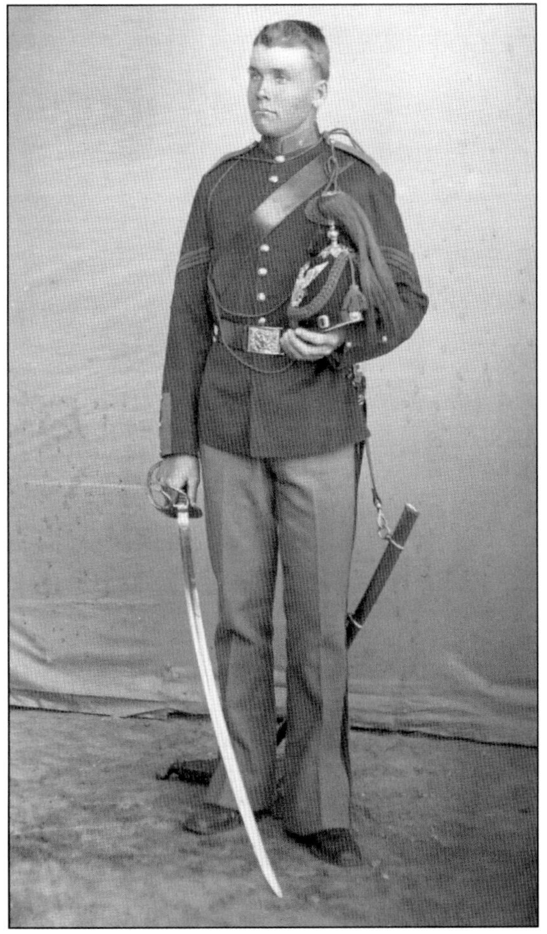

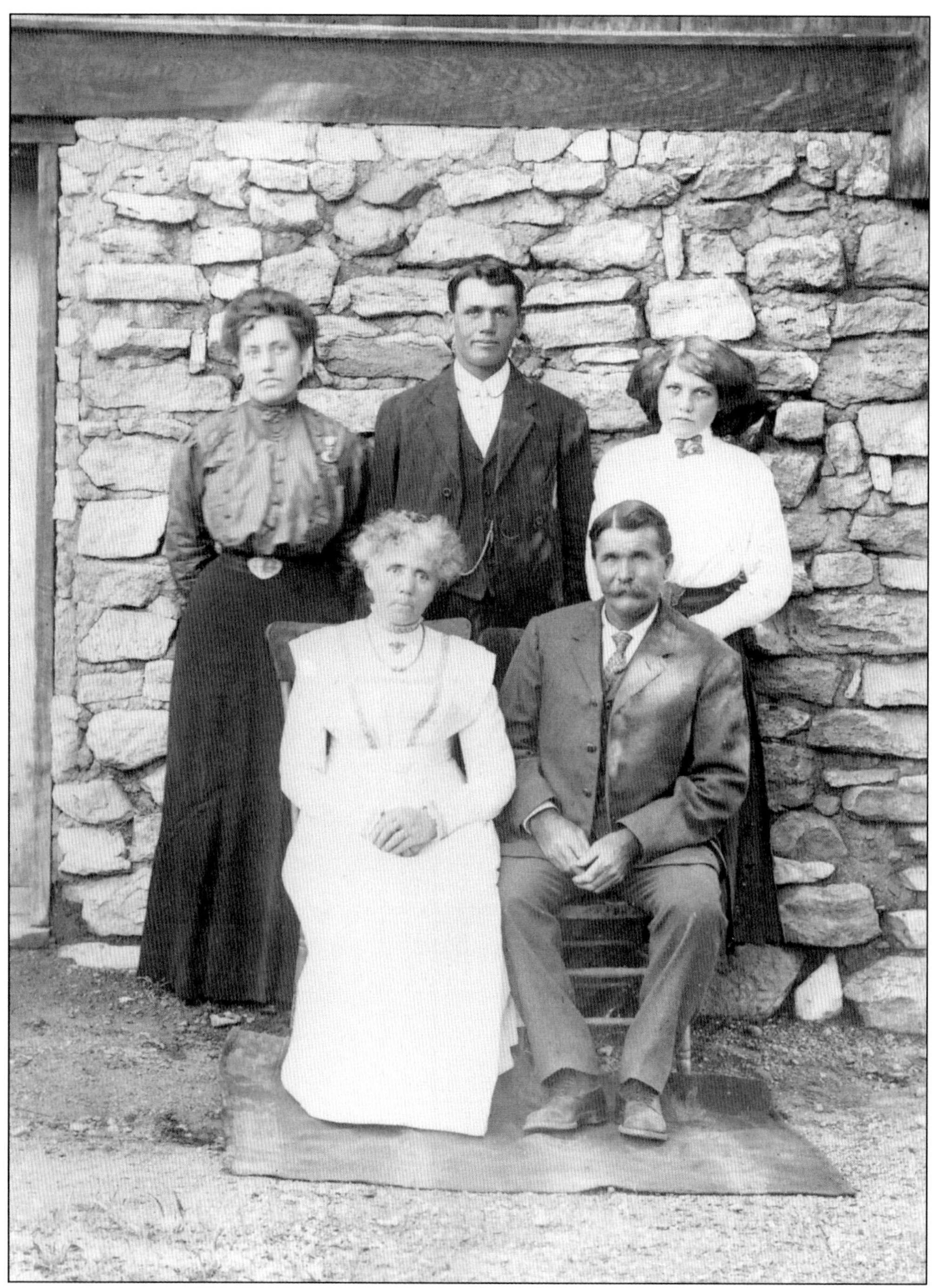

Upon their arrival in Bonita Canyon, Emma and Neil Erickson moved into a two-room cabin built by a man named Newton. The cabin was where commanding officers of the 10th Cavalry had lived. Neil added rooms to the cabin's side and eventually put up a second story. This home welcomed Louis Benton Erickson, born in 1891, and Helen Hildegard Erickson, born in 1895. This photograph was taken about 1914 in front of the Erickson house with Emma and Neil seated in front of their children—from left to right, Lillian, Ben, and Hildegard.

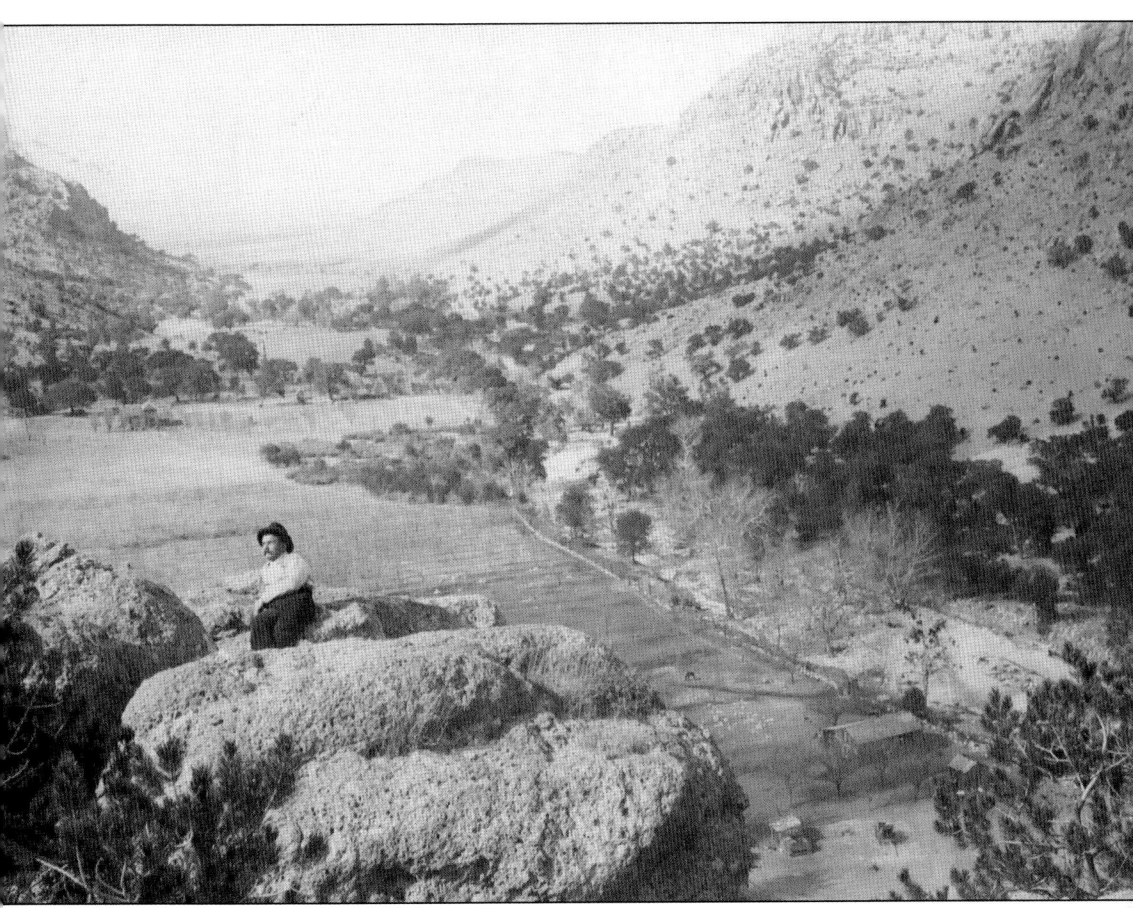

Neil and Emma Erickson followed the Staffords' lead and planted a vegetable garden and fruit trees and ran some livestock in Bonita Canyon. But with much the same circumstances then as today for many small farmers, the Ericksons needed another income source to thrive. For much of 1890–1894, Neil worked in Bisbee as a freelance carpenter and for a copper mining company. He returned home often enough that he posed for this photograph, which shows him reclining on a rocky hilltop east of his home and the Staffords'. Their cabin and some outbuildings are at the lower left. Bonita Creek runs past the cabin. The dark line between the cabin and a grazing horse is apparently an irrigation ditch off the creek. It would have watered the orchard whose rows stretch toward Neil's house, just visible above his head. Neil was also on hand in 1890 when two Apache renegades fled through Bonita Canyon. They perhaps were Massai and a woman. Erickson family lore declares that ex-soldiers Neil and Prue trailed the couple eastward into the rhyolite columns and other features of eastern Bonita Canyon. They were thus the first North American settlers known to see what 25 years later became Chiricahua National Monument.

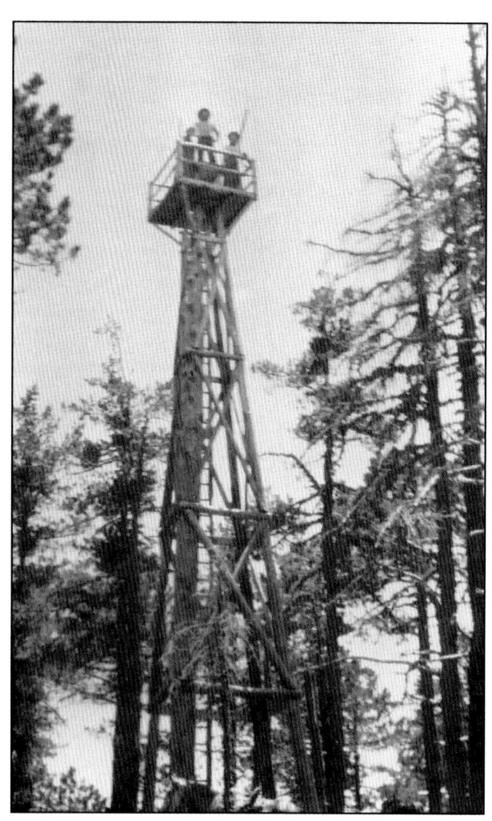

In 1903, Neil received a federal appointment as ranger of the Chiricahua Forest Reserve, part of the newly formed Coronado National Forest. The job let him work out of his home, and its salary sent his three children to school in Illinois, where Emma's brother lived. Rangers were expected to erect fire lookouts (left) and patrol their area (below). Neil is on the left riding in Rustlers Park atop the Chiricahuas. The place was so named because rustlers would supposedly keep stolen cattle there until their changed brands healed.

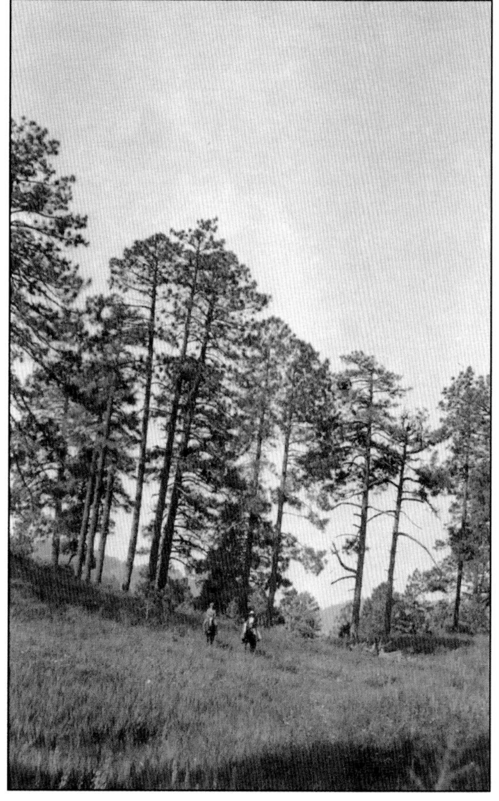

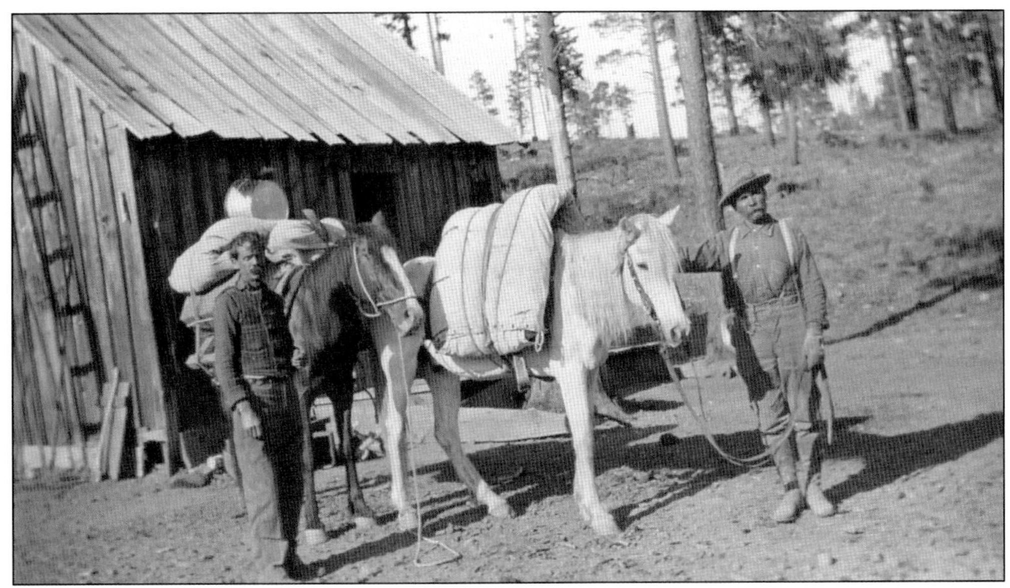

Among the duties of early-day forest rangers like Neil Erickson was construction of Forest Service cabins and other facilities. Above, Neil is standing with Tom, his favorite horse, who has a tent roped to his saddle. Neil's companion, Dr. Wethered, leads Dandy, who bears a packsaddle with the two men's additional gear. The Forest Service cabin behind them was in Barfoot Park. Below, Neil is talking into a field telephone at Old Headquarters Camp on the side of Chiricahua Peak. The phone line, attached mostly to trees, was a semi-reliable way for Forest Service personnel in the Chiricahua high country to communicate with fellow rangers at headquarters, first in Paradise and later in Portal, villages on the east side of the mountains.

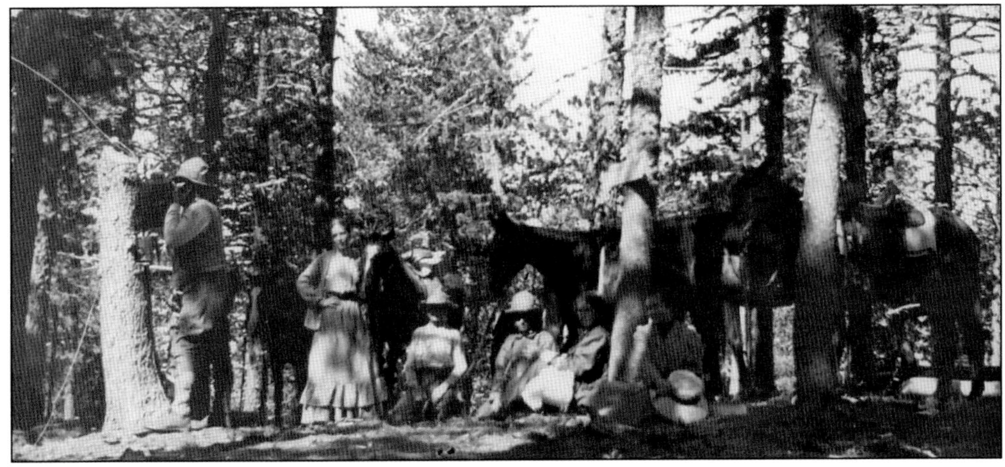

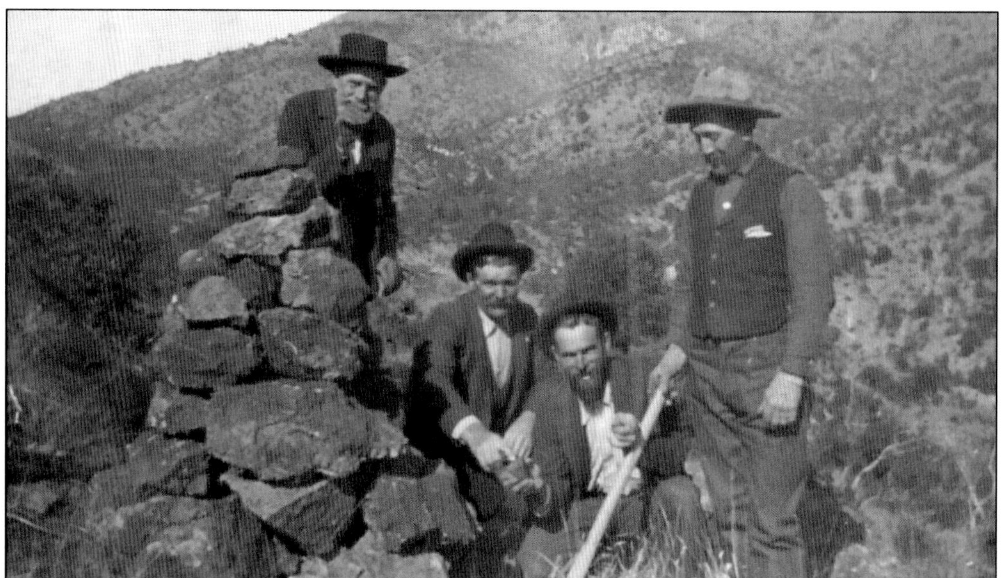

The 13 members of the Riggs family were neighbors of the five-member Erickson family. The Erickson youngsters attended the primary grades at El Dorado School, located in Riggs Settlement, a few miles from the Erickson homestead. Between 1887 and 1891, the Ericksons got their mail at Riggs Settlement from the Brannock Post Office, which was the misspelled first name of the Riggs patriarch. Another link between the families is shown above. From left to right, Brannick Riggs, Neil Erickson, Brannick's son Brannick Benjamin, and Brannick's son-in-law Thomas B. Stark have piled rocks to make a mine location cairn in Bonita Canyon. Pictured below, Stark's wife, Martha, rode sidesaddle and kept her apron on even as an older woman, something a Faraway Guest Ranch visitor would come to appreciate (see page 106).

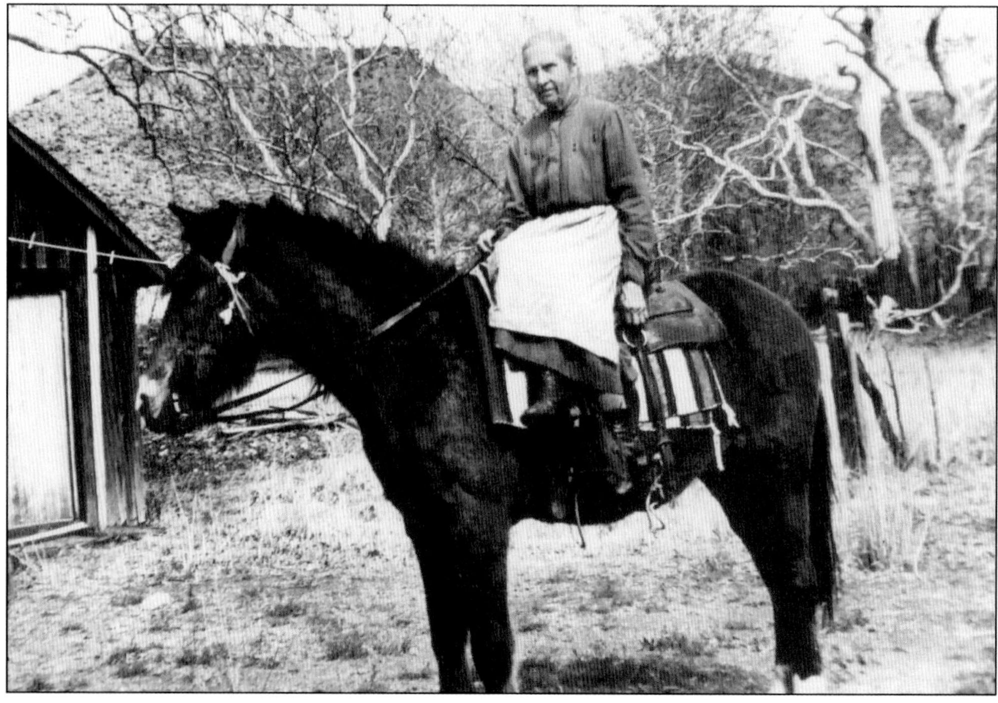

Another connection between the Riggs and Erickson families is that both sent sons to serve in the US Army during World War I. Ben, who had worked for the Forest Service before joining up, poses in his Army uniform in front of the Erickson house before leaving (right). Edward Murray Riggs's path to the military was more complicated. The son of Thomas Jefferson Riggs and grandson of Brannick, Ed grew up punching cows but had some college education as well as a mechanical flair. In 1908, he married Gaye Moore, and they lived in Douglas, where Ed was a partner with Gus Hines (below) in the Douglas Motor Company. After Gaye died from smallpox in 1917, Ed left his children, Murray and Eula Lee, with Gaye's family and joined the Army, which sent him to MIT to take engineering courses. After World War I was over, Ed and Ben returned to Arizona, Ed to a Douglas automotive businesses while Ben established his own homestead.

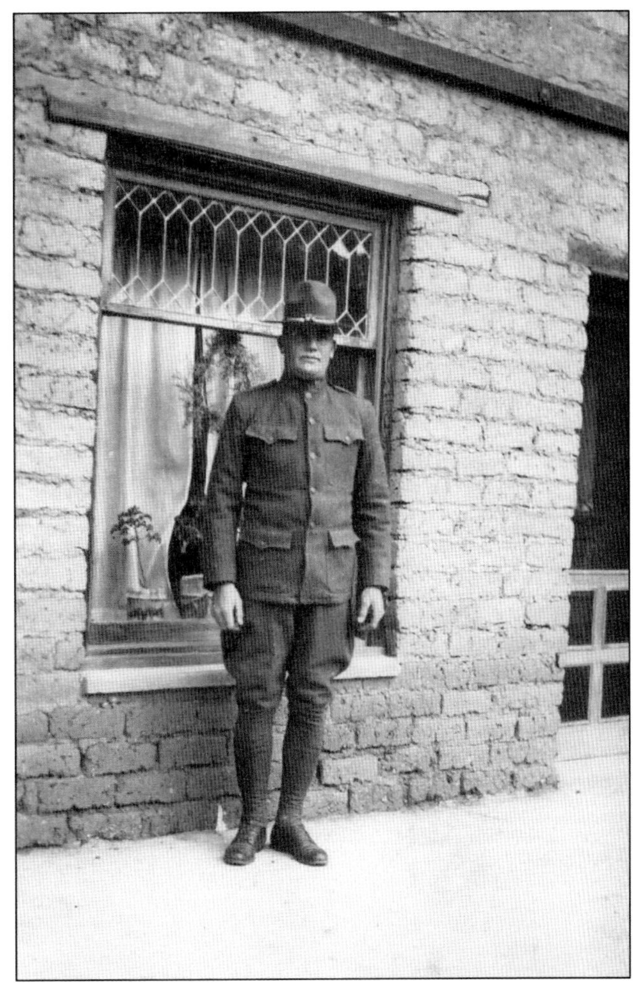

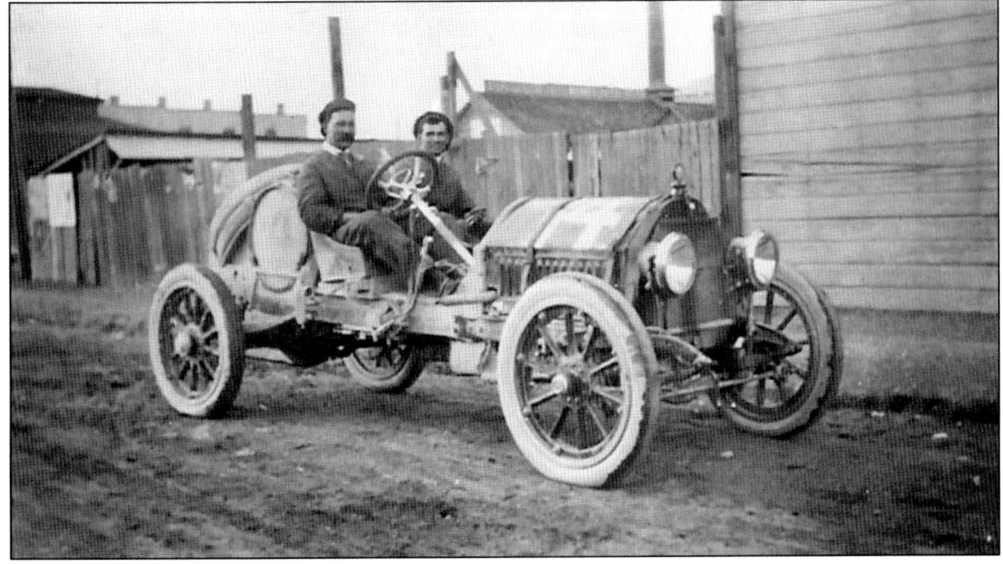

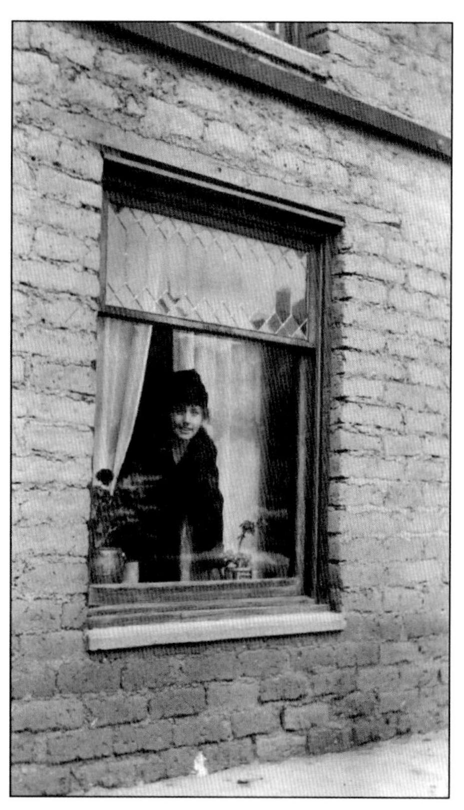

The World War I years were also eventful for the Erickson sisters and their ranch home. Lillian, looking out the front window at left, taught in nearby schools and so went home to Bonita Canyon on weekends. Hildegard helped her parents around the farmstead, which included a garden, orchard, chicken coop, and pen for the wiggling, squealing piglets she is holding below. The Ericksons also pastured dairy cows and a few head of beef cattle. This bucolic lifestyle began changing after Hildegard got the idea to share her home with guests.

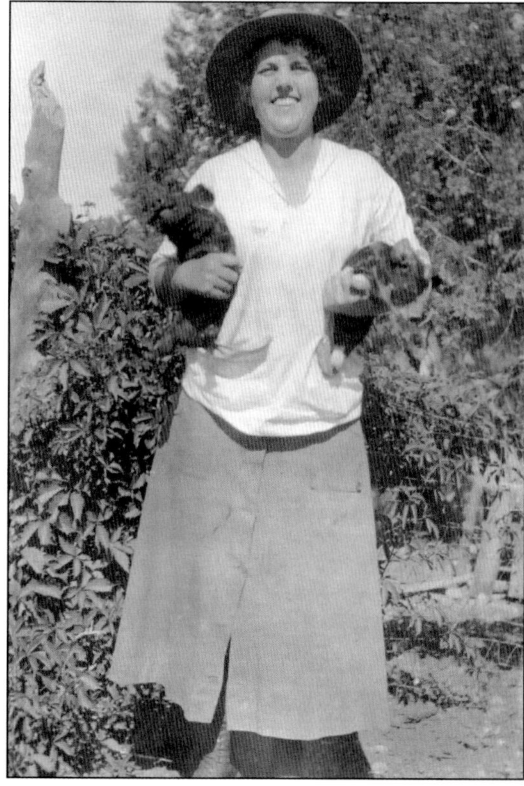

Seven

Faraway's First Years

During the 1890s, Neil Erickson endured working in the mining town of Bisbee to support his family in Bonita Canyon. In 1903, he was appointed a Coronado National Forest Reserve ranger with a home office. Neil's activities included surveying and mapping, fire prevention and control, timber and grazing permit issuance, and trail construction.

This position enabled the Ericksons to send their children to school in Illinois. Lillian became a teacher, but Ben and Hildegard returned home without college diplomas. Ben joined the Army during World War I. Afterwards, he resumed Arizona life, married, ranched, and worked for the Forest Service. In 1917, Hildegard set an entirely new course after her parents moved away for Neil's latest Forest Service posting.

Hildegard wrote friends in Douglas and Bisbee and invited them to the ranch for weekend stays, complete with meals and horseback excursions. At first, Lillian did not like the idea of a guest ranch business, but its success soon won her over. She even gave the ranch a new name, Faraway, because it was so far away from everything.

In 1920, Hildegard married and moved to California. Lillian continued operating one of Arizona's first guest ranches by herself. In 1923, she married Ed Riggs, an old friend who was by then a widower with two children. Ed was a grandson of Brannick Riggs and thus reared as a rancher. He had also attended college, served in the Army, and run a Douglas business.

Newlyweds Ed and Lillian looked for ways to expand the guest ranch business and soon came up with one. In 1900 as boys, Ed and Ben climbed to the top of what is now called Sugarloaf Mountain. Ed thus saw the rock formations Neil Erickson glimpsed in 1890. But like Neil, Ed could not exploit the area's potential immediately.

That waited until 1921, when Ed took photographs and showed them to Douglas residents. They took more photographs and displayed them at the Cochise County Fair, which started a chain of events resulting in creation of Chiricahua National Monument.

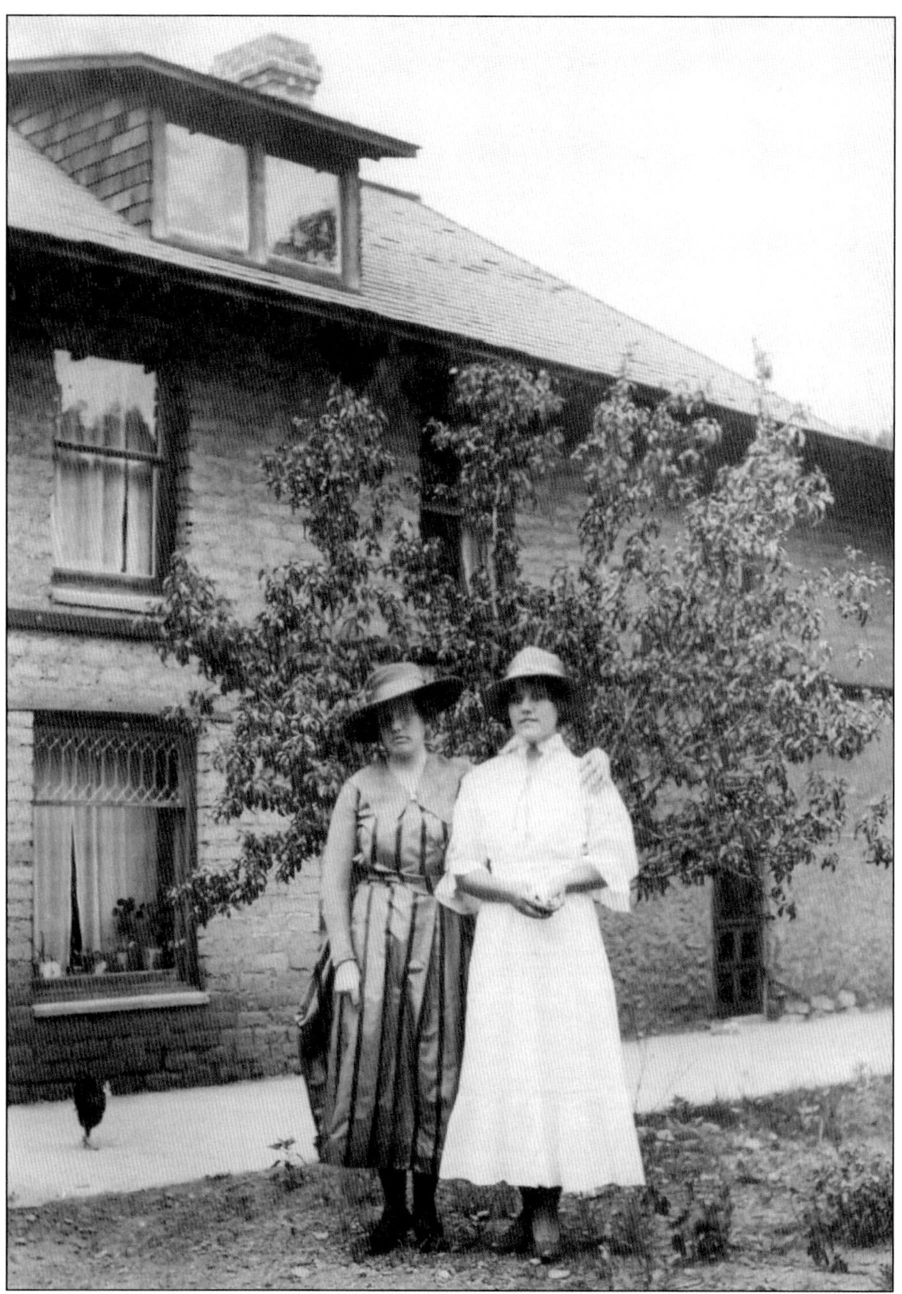

In June 1917, federal authorities consolidated southern Arizona's various forest reserves into the Coronado National Forest and transferred Neil from the Chiricahua to the Dragoon Mountains. He and Emma lived almost directly west across the Sulphur Springs Valley, 40 miles from Bonita Canyon. Neil had just finished enlarging the Bonita Canyon house, and so that summer Lillian and Hildegard had plenty of room to host parties for friends. It did not take Hildegard long to come up with the idea of offering meals and horseback trips to paying customers. One Sunday, Douglas osteopath Dr. Paul Collins showed up in his car with his sister, Ruth, and three of her teacher friends. Hildegard (right) quickly prepared a meal, and the Erickson sisters, shown here about 1918 in front of their home, were in business.

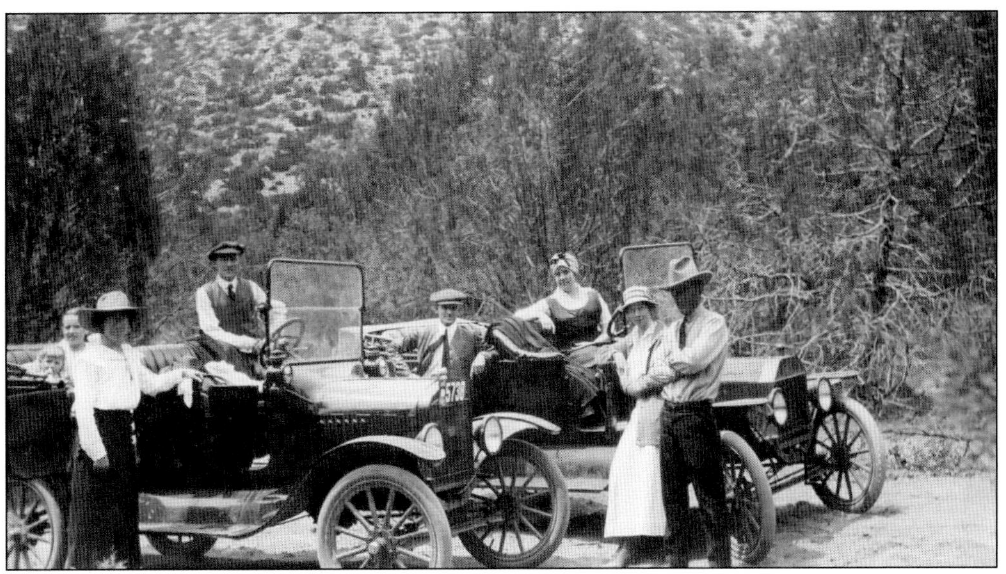

Hildegard picked exactly the right time to attempt a guest ranch startup. Following World War I, more and more Americans took to the roads for vacations or day trips, such as these people at Faraway (above). In 1917, Cochise County began constructing local motorways, including ones connecting Douglas with Bonita Canyon. In 1920, the county built a 23-mile cement road between Douglas and Bisbee. It was Arizona's longest hard-surfaced highway and attracted many out-of-state travelers. Entrepreneurs such as Douglas businessman Ed Riggs, with his for-hire car (below), capitalized on the post–World War I automobile craze.

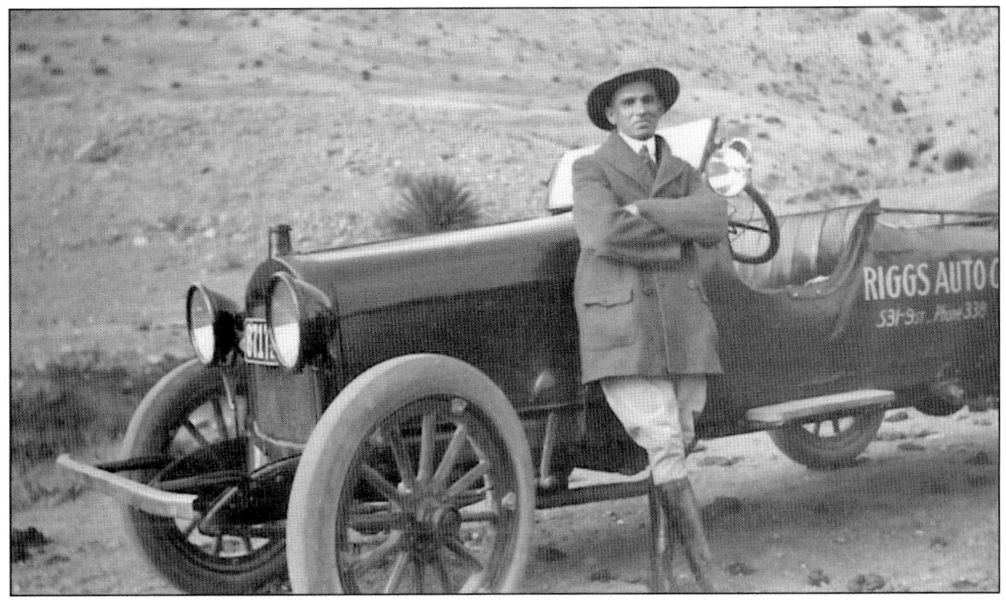

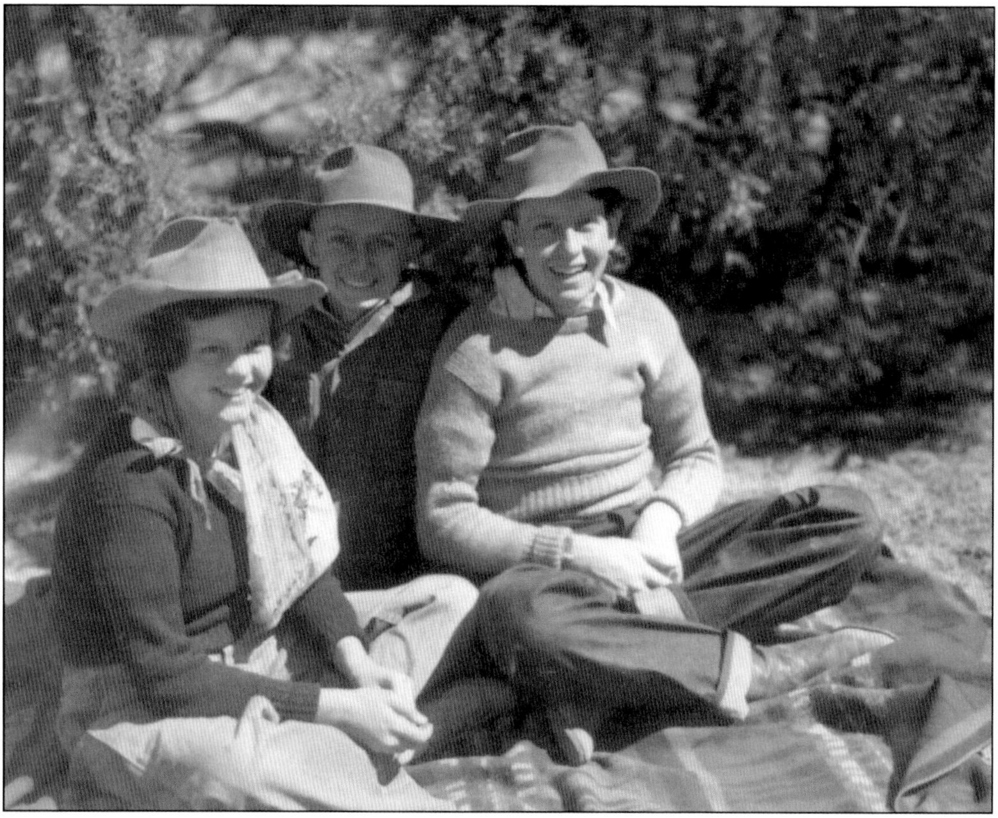

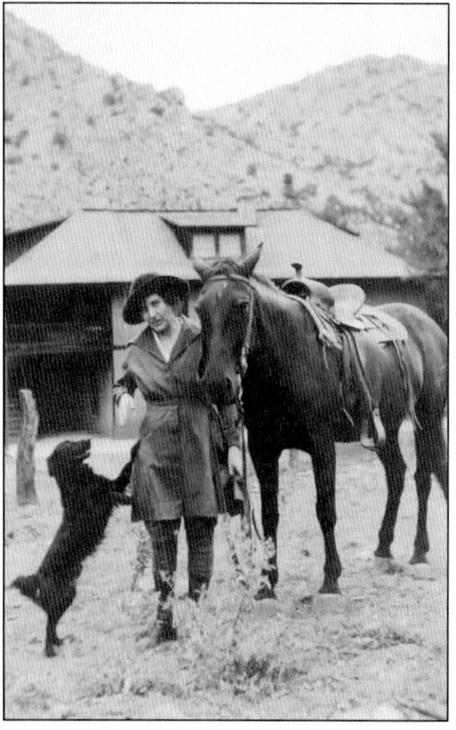

At first, Lillian did not like Hildegard's guest ranch idea, because she feared people would look down upon the Ericksons. But as Lillian helped Hildegard and was around guests such as the "happy campers" above, she changed her mind. Lillian took guests on rides, as at left, and came up with the name Faraway Ranch because "it was so far away from everything." Lillian always insisted Faraway was a guest ranch, not a dude ranch, because a "guest ranch invites a different and better class of people than does a dude ranch."

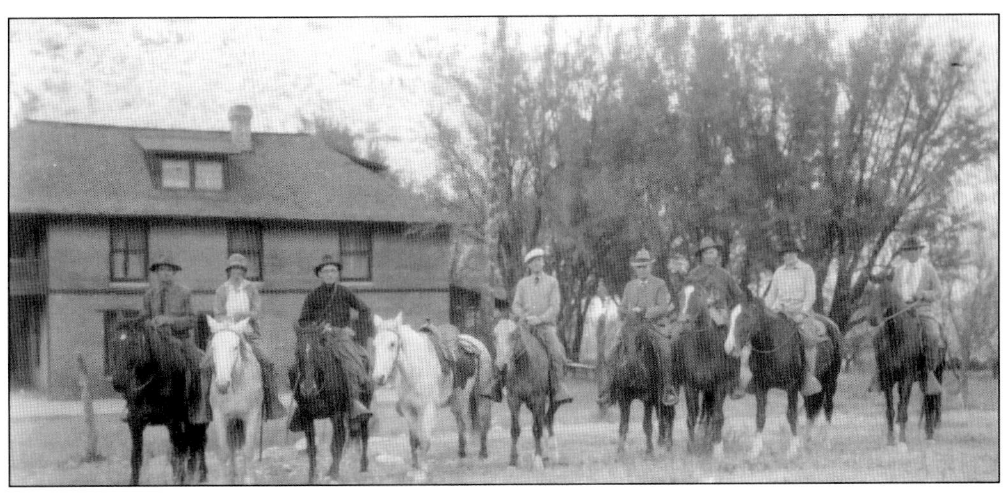

From the beginning, Faraway Ranch's strongest attraction to visitors, such as those above, was horseback trips. During Faraway's first years, guests wanted to ride in the Chiricahua Mountains' forest greenness. So Hildegard, seen below, and Lillian would guide riders out of Bonita Canyon and south to Pinery Canyon, where trails climbed up into the mountains.

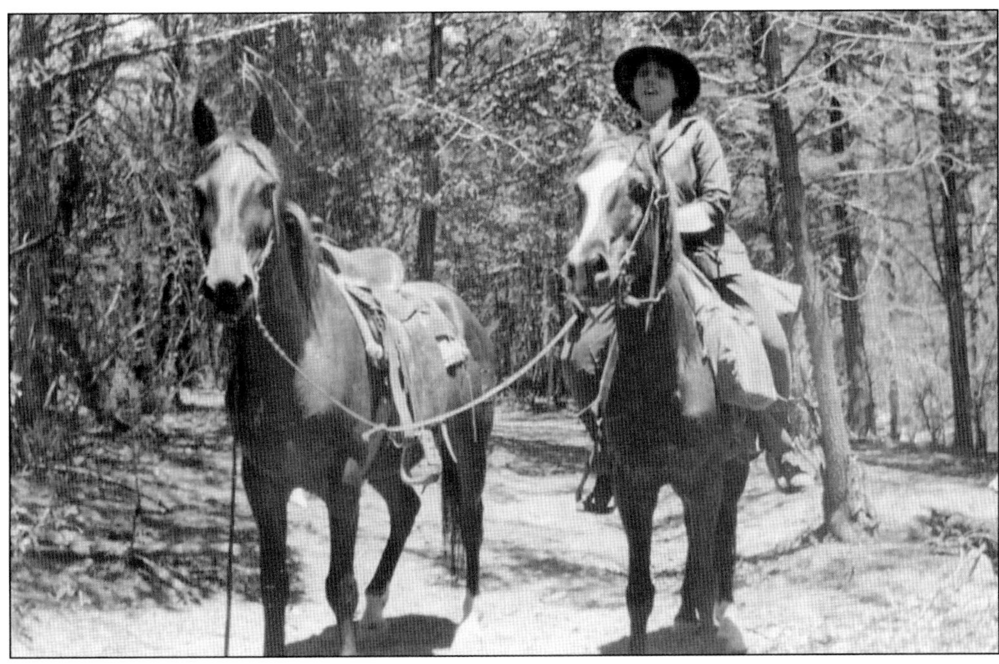

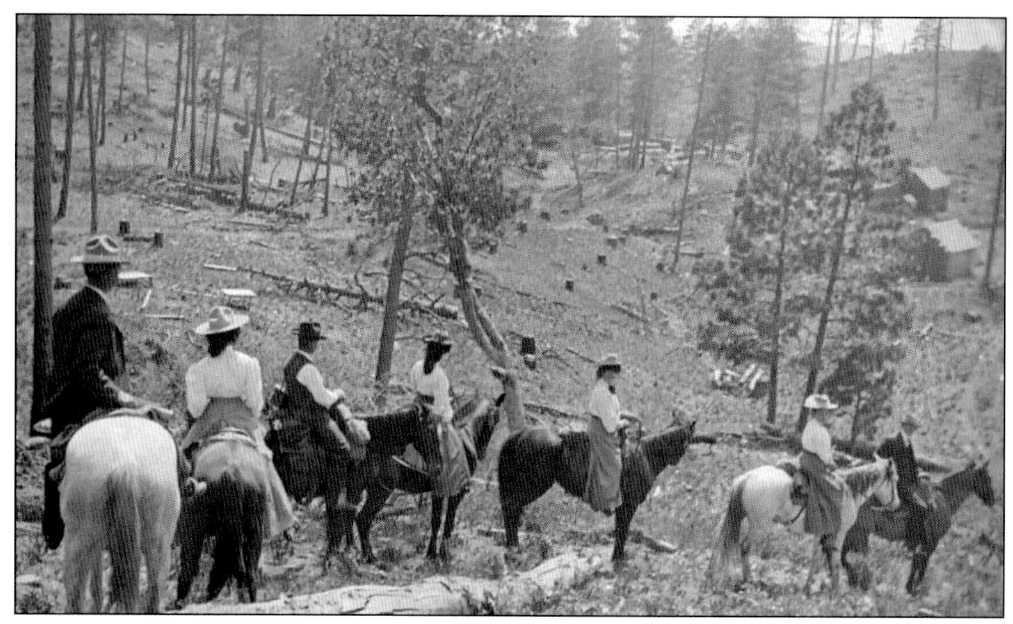

After climbing up Pinery Canyon, riders from Faraway worked their way toward Barfoot Park (above). Note that the cabins in this photograph are the same type as the one on page 79. Once in Barfoot Park, it was an easy ride for Faraway guests south to Rustlers Park and then to Round Park (below).

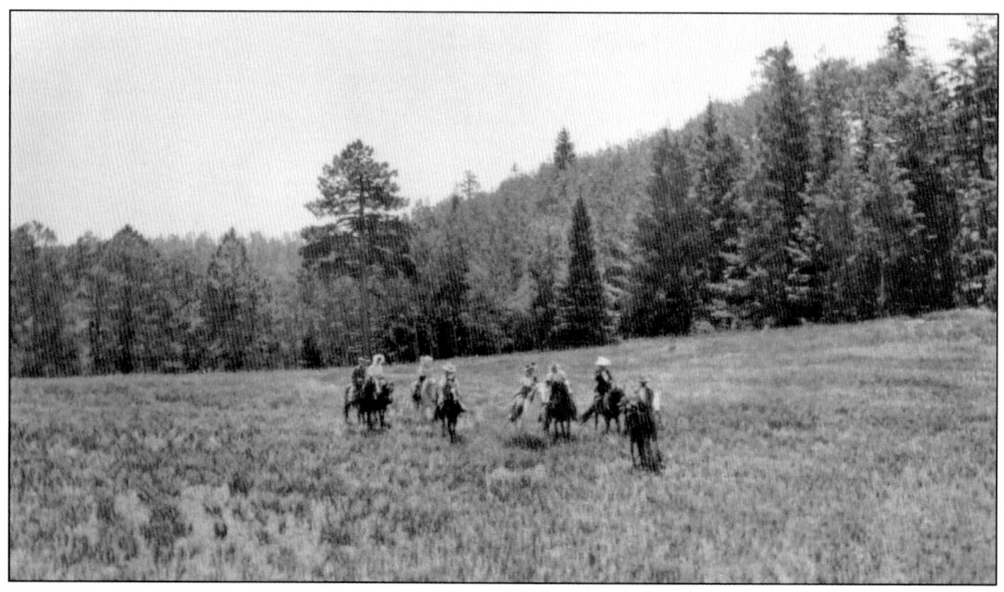

Ben occasionally took time away from his own homestead to help his sisters at Faraway. At right, he is handing reins to a female guest. Such attention must have pleased Faraway's visitors, including the one below, who is dressed to the hilt in 1920s-style cowboy garb and perched on the gate of Faraway's horse corral.

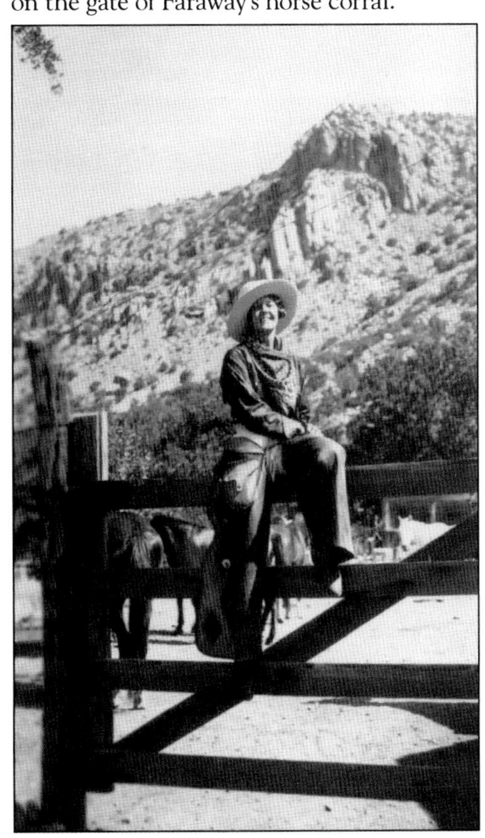

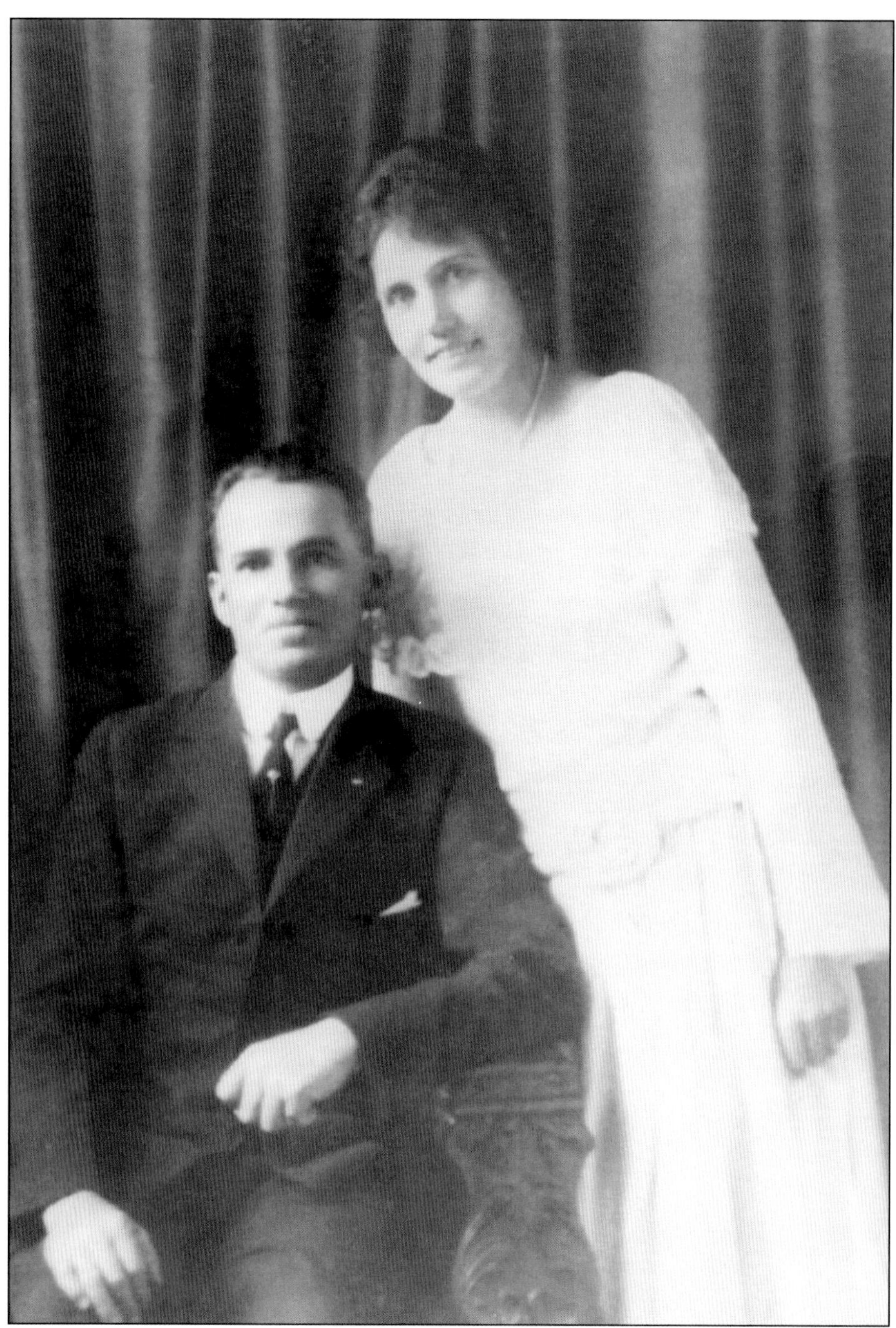

In the 1920s, all three Erickson children married. The first was Hildegard, who wedded Jess Hutchison in 1920, moved to California, and had three children. Lillian ran Faraway by herself for three years and then married the perfect helpmate, Ed Riggs, on February 26, 1923. The couple's obvious happiness in this wedding photograph boded well for Faraway. In 1927, Ben married Belle Underwood, a widow with two sons. Like Lillian had with Ed's two children from his first marriage, Ben acquired an instant family. He supported his with a Forest Service job that eventually took him to central Arizona.

Faraway in its 1920s–1930s heyday (right) was a substantial house in a picturesque setting. Guests could stay in one of several upstairs rooms and eat home-cooked meals in one of two downstairs dining rooms. The Stafford cabin also accommodated visitors. Ja Hu died on November 14, 1913; the Erickson sisters bought the property in 1918. Faraway guests who participated in ranching activities, such as cattle roundups, ate out of an authentic chuck wagon (below).

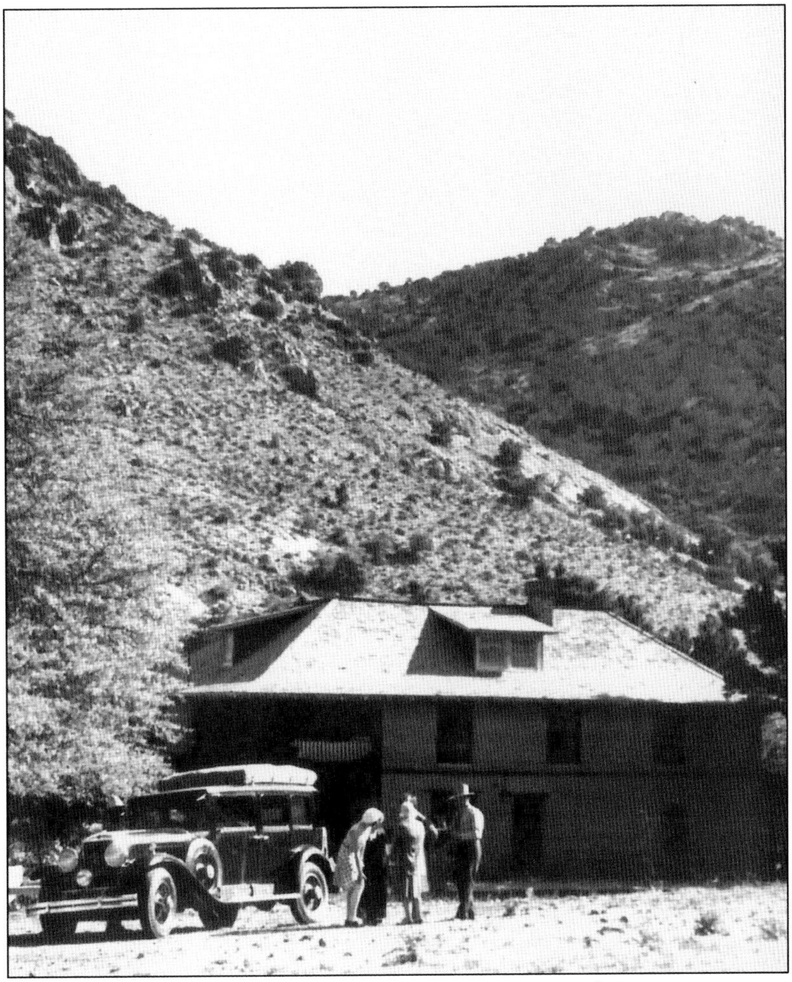

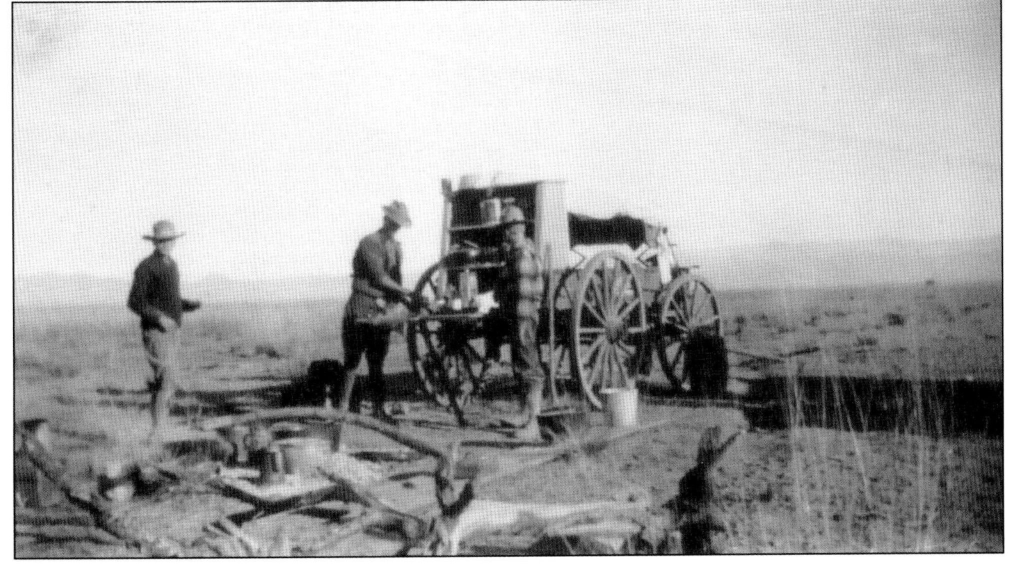

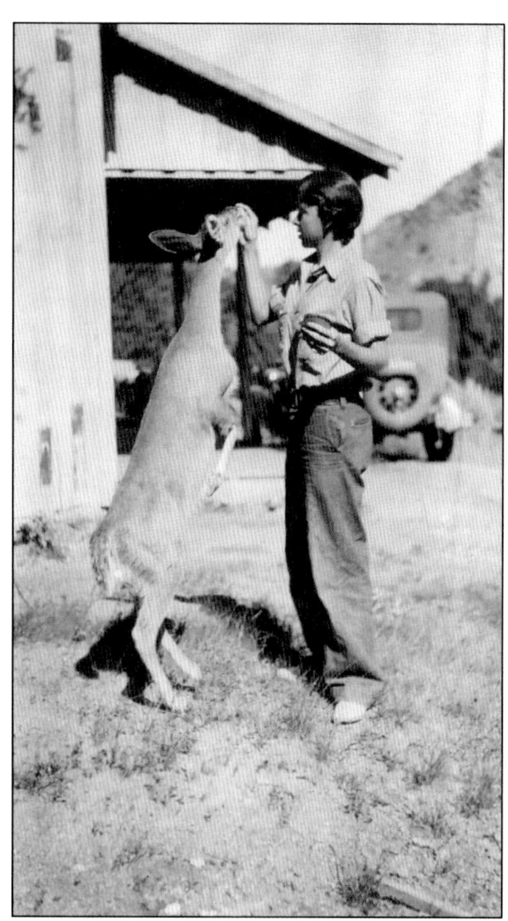

Ed and Lillian upgraded Faraway's house to make it comfortable for guests. They also provided a "Western experience" combined with special attractions. The latter included this rescued mule deer (left). Named Shiva, the deer was a great favorite at Faraway in the 1920s. So was a swimming pool (below) built during the same decade. Behind the swimmers, notice the garden rows watered by pool overflow. Another Faraway amenity was a "cypress bower" for couples wishing to marry in a pastoral setting.

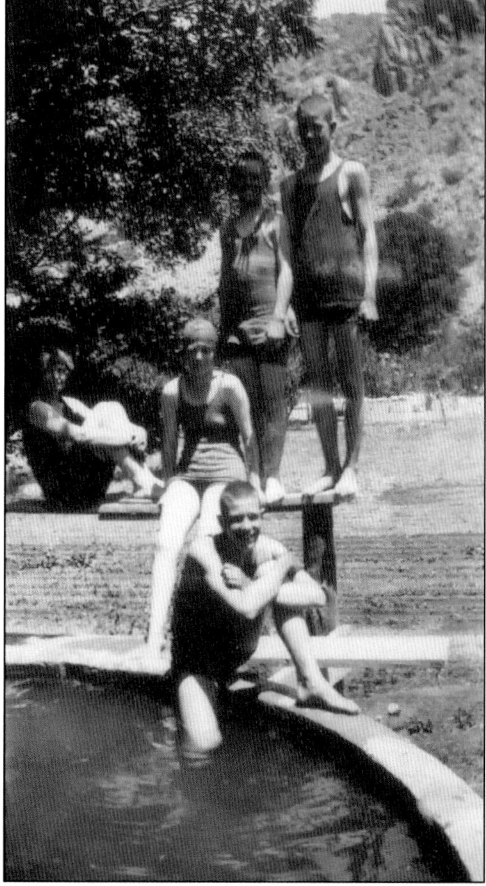

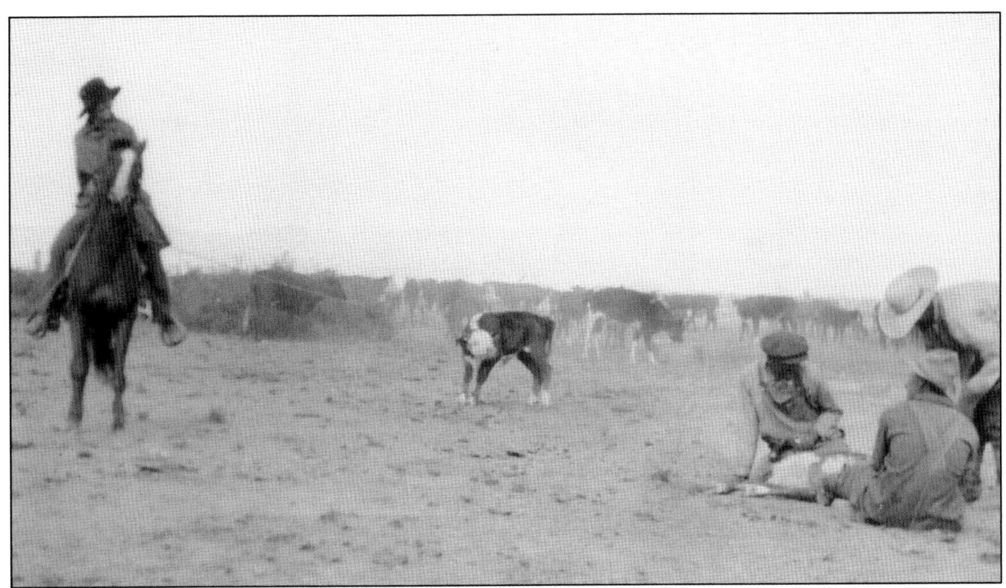

People who knew Lillian well said she enjoyed the cattle ranching portion of Faraway more than the guest ranch side of the business. In the photograph above, she is pulling a roped calf to be branded at Frank Geers's ranch, 18 miles southwest of Faraway. Lillian and Ed owned land west of Bonita Canyon in the Pat Hills and called it the Holderman place. That is where they are in the photograph below, along with Ralph Souers (center), who briefly had a private boys' school at Faraway before he moved it to Turkey Creek, south of Faraway. Souers had been the schools superintendent in Douglas and held that job in Bisbee after the Great Depression closed his Turkey Creek school.

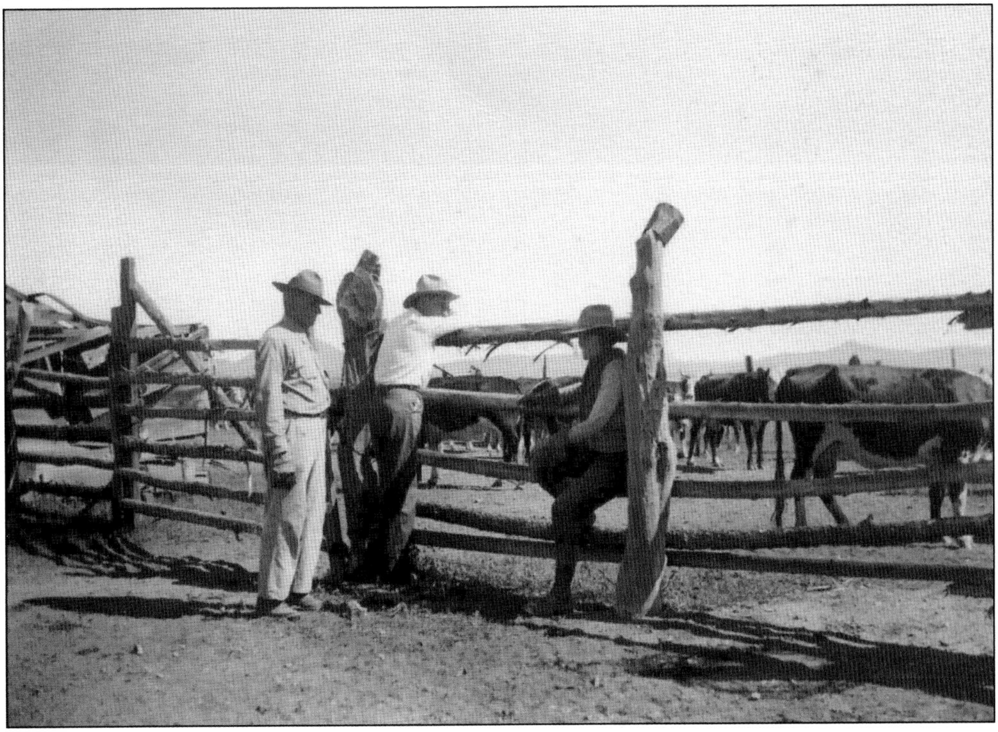

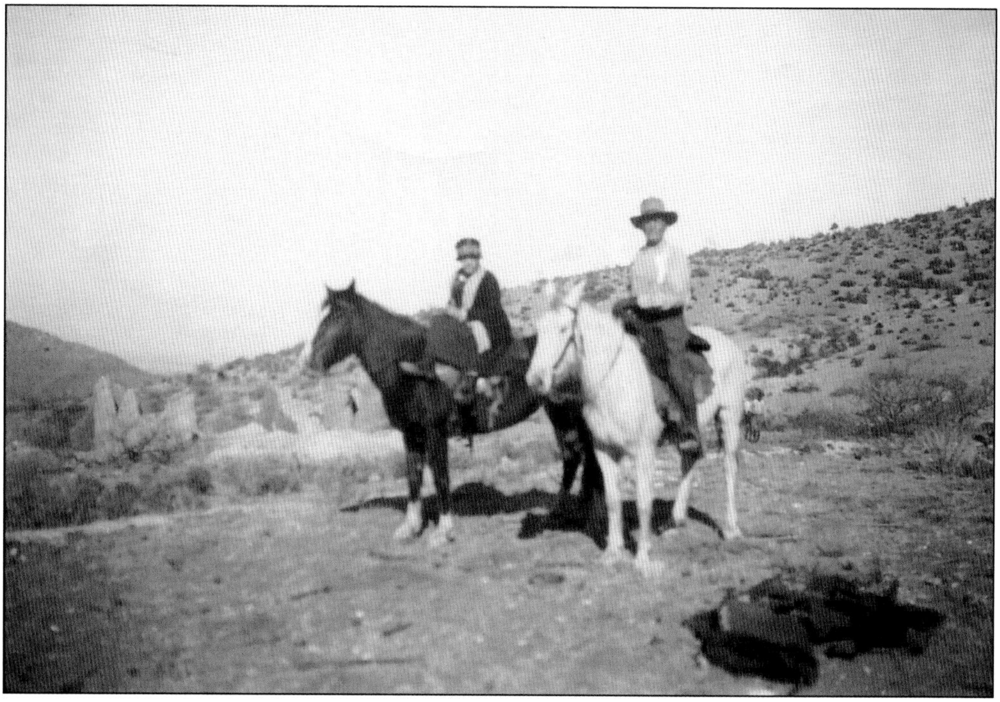

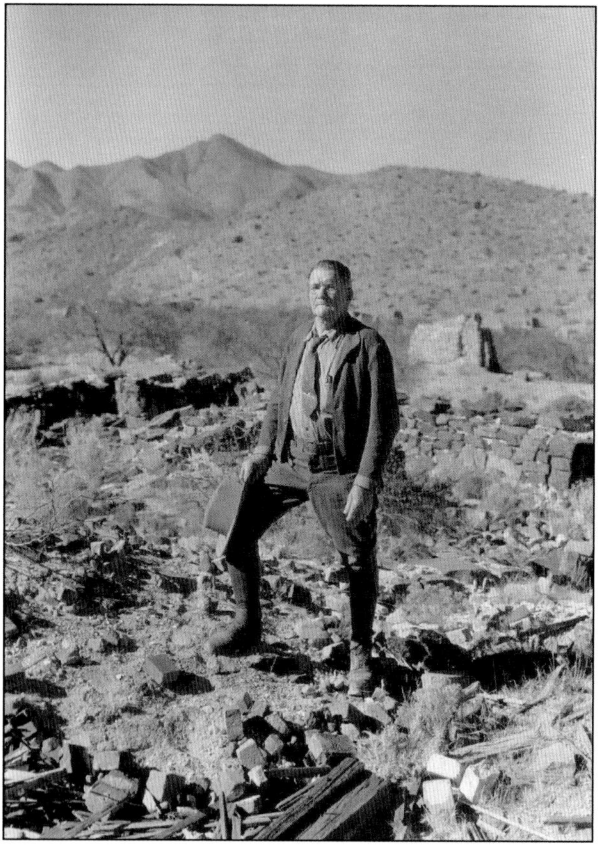

A horseback day trip for Faraway guests in the 1920s–1930s could be to the ruins of Fort Bowie. In 1932, Neil and Emma rode to the place where they had courted 45 years earlier (above). When Neil (left) retired from the Forest Service in 1927, he was the district's second-longest-tenured employee. In 1932, the Forest Service named a Chiricahua peak for Neil, honoring his service as a soldier and ranger. In retirement, Neil and Emma spent time at Faraway with Lillian and Ed and in California with Hildegard and Jess. In 1937, Lillian celebrated Neil and Emma's 50th anniversary with 200 party guests at Faraway. Neil died eight months later.

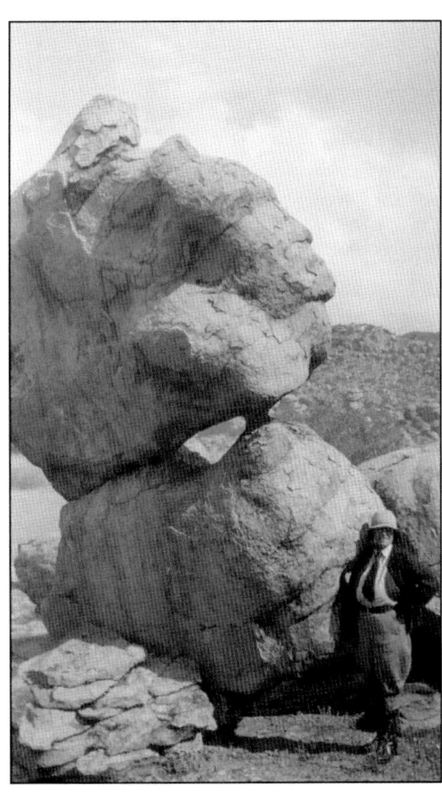

In 1921, before Lillian and Ed married, some hunters from Douglas stayed at Faraway. When one wounded a deer, Ed and Lillian trailed the creature eastward from the ranch up Rhyolite Canyon. After spotting unusual rock formations, they decided the area "should be opened up so that our guests could ride into it, and we could enjoy it," Lillian recalled. She and Ed began hacking out a trail. Ed took photographs of some formations and displayed them at the Cochise County Fair in Douglas. This helped bring visitors to Faraway, such as this unidentified female (right) and Douglas physician James J.P. Armstrong (below). (Below, courtesy of Douglas Historical Society.)

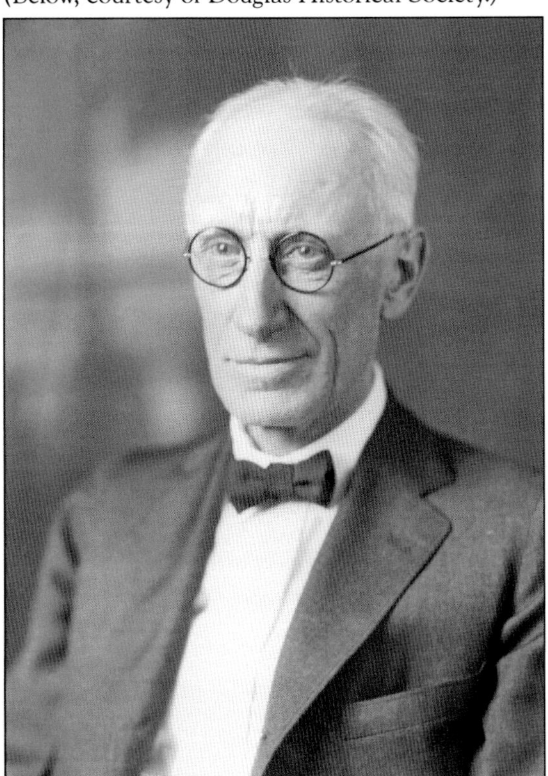

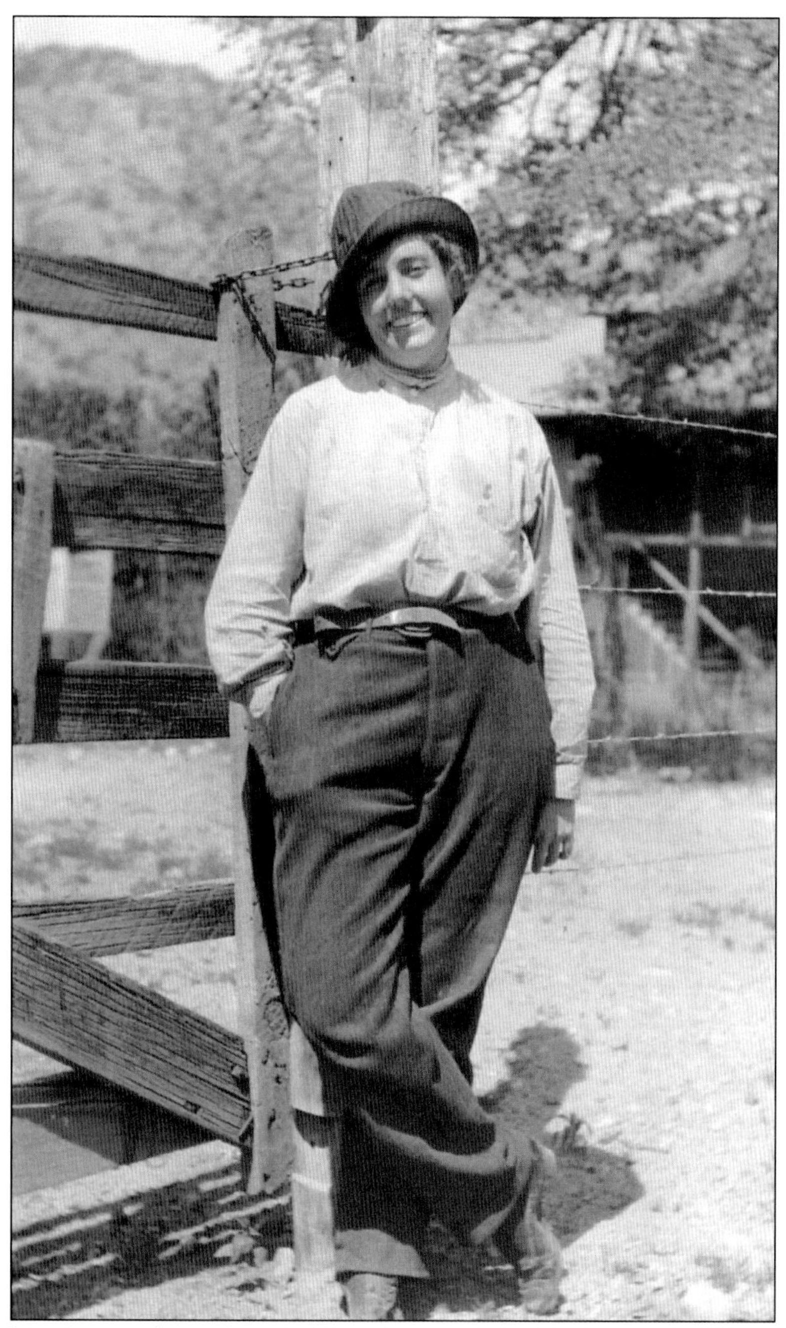

Lillian Erickson Riggs, radiating feminine appeal while dressed in masculine clothing, undoubtedly appreciated the paradox she presents in this early 1920s photograph. She was a female who had capably run a complex business by herself during a time when few women did so. On the one hand, the business required that she charm guests with an idyllic version of country life. On the other hand, it demanded her participation in gritty cattle handling tasks. Lillian's manner and way with words made her an effective promoter of Faraway and the Wonderland of Rocks, but she realized that the price of such promotion was having thousands of people descend upon the area and change it simply by being there.

Eight

Creating and Developing Chiricahua National Monument

On August 5, 1923, Arizona governor George W.P. Hunt got out of a vehicle parked in Faraway's front yard. Wearing his trademark white linen suit, Hunt posed for photographs and then mounted a burro for a trip into the Wonderland of Rocks.

Hunt returned in agreement that the name was a good one. He convinced Calvin Coolidge that the area deserved federal recognition, and on April 18, 1924, the president signed a proclamation creating Chiricahua National Monument.

This increased Faraway business, enabling Ed and Lillian to improve the ranch house and add other structures for guest accommodations, such as a swimming pool. One main house improvement was the creation of a large dining room with a fireplace incorporating blocks from the Garfield Monument, which had fallen into disrepair.

The couple offered guests participation in ranching activities, but riding monument trails was the main draw. Ed played a large role in the creation of those trails. At first, just he and Lillian cleared brush. Then, encouraged by Douglas friends, Ed got Forest Service permission to build permanent trails.

This occurred shortly before the Forest Service and Cochise County began constructing roads to provide better access to Bonita Canyon. In 1933, the National Park Service took over monument management, and the agency oversaw completion of a paved road to Massai Point. Its dedication in 1934 attracted 10,000 people.

Members of the Civilian Conservation Corps provided the labor to build monument roads. They also constructed a campground, visitor center, Massai orientation station, Sugarloaf fire lookout, and 12 miles of monument trails, included Ed's masterpiece, Echo Canyon Trail.

CCC Camp NM-2-A was east of Faraway on land leased from Ed and Lillian. The CCC enrollees were mostly teens from impoverished families. Each CCC worker earned $30 a month; of this, $25 was sent to his family. The CCCers also gained valuable experience many used when they entered the military during World War II.

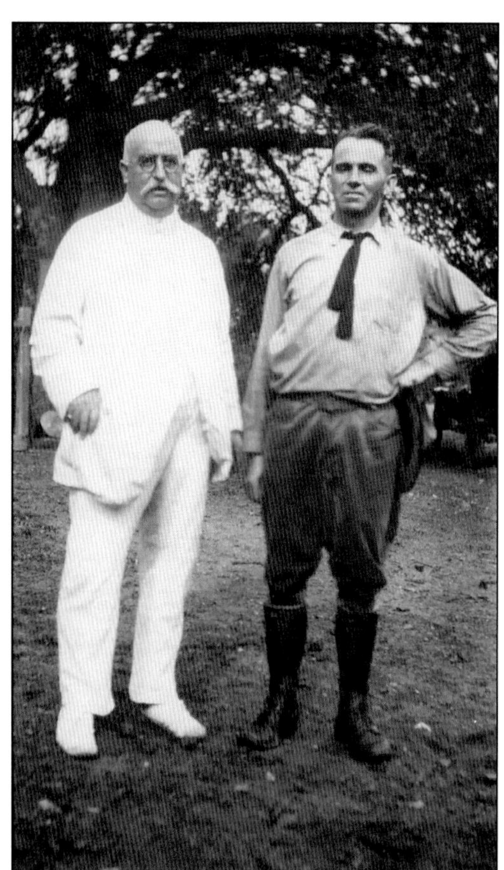

George W.P. Hunt was serving the fourth of his seven terms as Arizona governor when he arrived at Faraway Ranch on August 5, 1923. He brought with him an entourage of 60 people, including an official photographer who snapped the photograph at left of Hunt with Ed Riggs. Hunt held a camera when he posed with Dr. James J.P. Armstrong, one of several Douglas residents who had exhorted Hunt to visit Faraway. Armstrong took some of the first photographs of the Wonderland of Rocks. He also urged a professional Douglas photographer, Marvin E. Irwin, to take photographs.

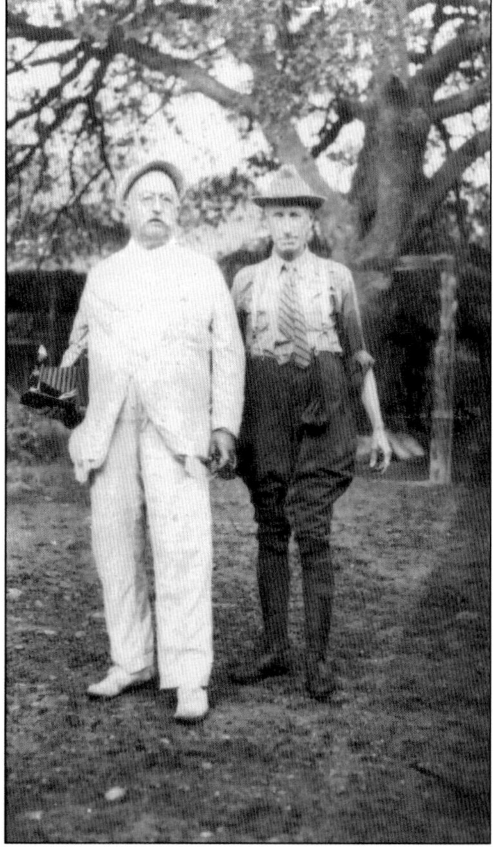

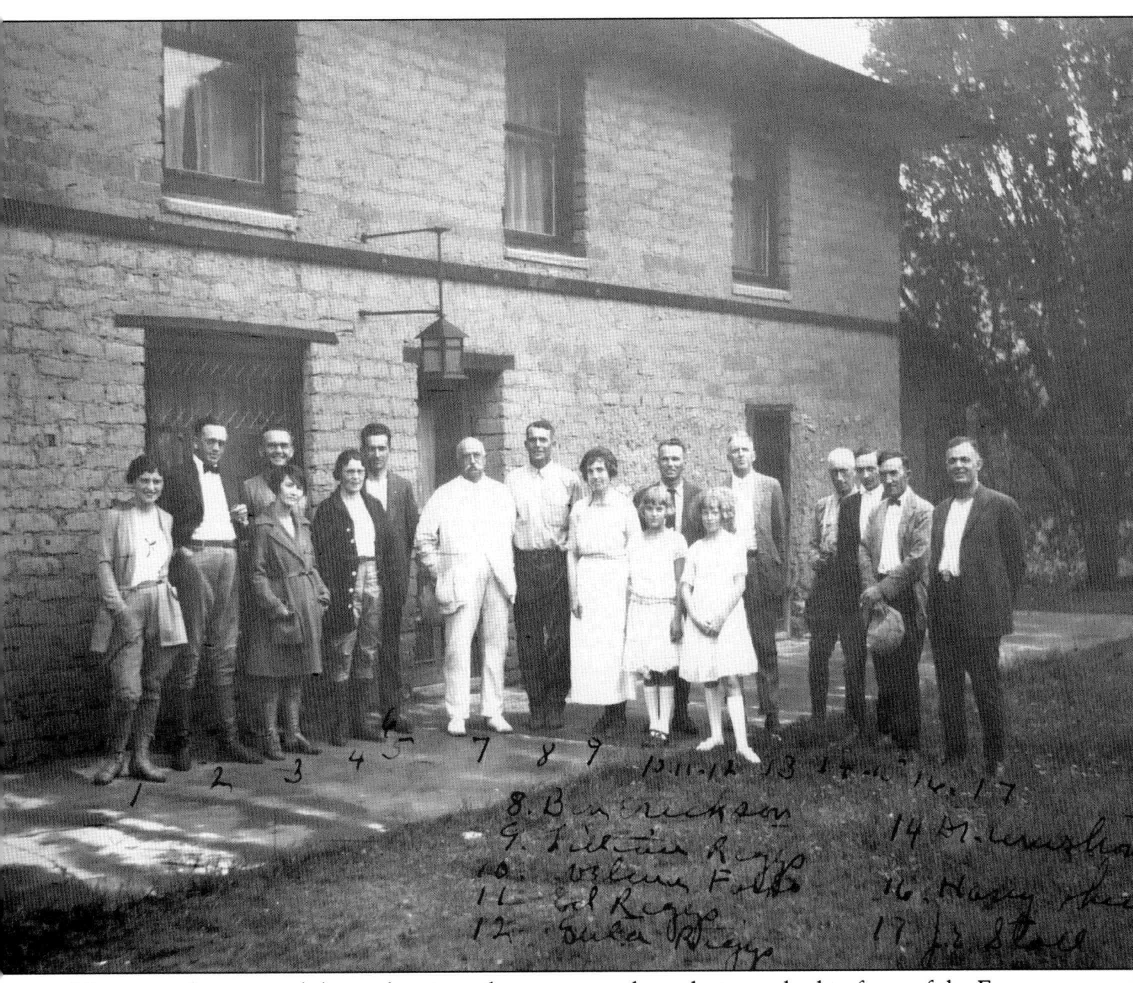

These people arranged themselves into three groups when photographed in front of the Faraway Ranch house with Arizona governor George W.P. Hunt in his all white suit. No identifications are available for the group on the left. The tall man in a white shirt with dark pants next to Hunt is Ben Erickson. Next to Erickson is his sister, Lillian Riggs. Next to her is her husband, Ed Riggs. Next to him is his former brother-in-law, Charles Fokes. The girls in front are Velma Fokes (left) and her cousin Eula Lee Riggs. Velma's mother, May, took care of Eula Lee and her brother, Murray, when Ed Riggs joined the Army during World War I following the 1917 death of his wife, Gaye, from smallpox. The person wearing glasses in the right-hand group is Dr. James J.P. Armstrong. The other three men have not been positively identified, but they are possibly members of Douglas's American Legion post, which took a leading role in the early promotion of the Wonderland of Rocks.

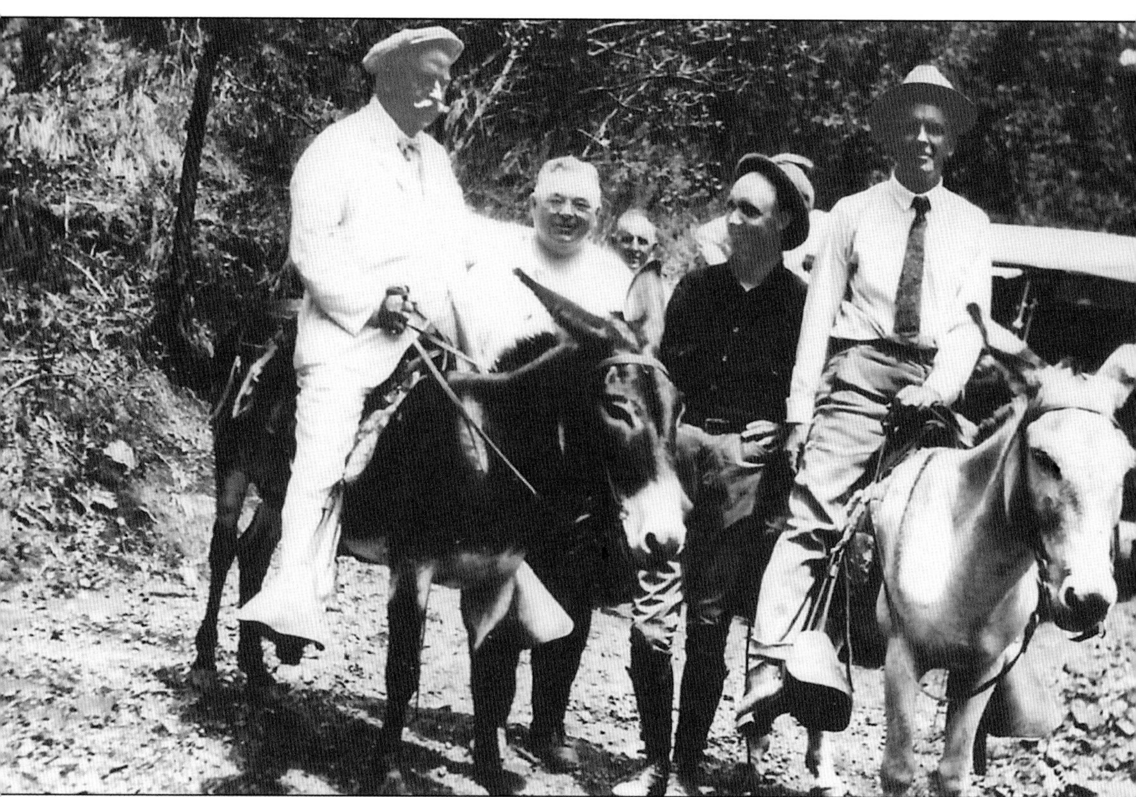

The three men with mustachioed Arizona governor George W.P. Hunt were Douglas residents. On the left is Harry Clark, superintendent of the Calumet & Arizona Mining Company copper smelter. Clark became the owner of a place on the eastern side of the Chiricahuas that now is the Southwest Research Station. David O'Neil (center) was manager of Douglas's streetcar system at the time. He went on to manage Douglas's famous Gadsden Hotel and become an Arizona state tax commissioner. Shelton Dowell (right) was manager of an important early Douglas business, the Arizona Gypsum Plaster Company. He later served on the Arizona Highway Commission. They were just three Douglas community leaders who urged Hunt to approach federal authorities about proclaiming the Wonderland of Rocks a national monument. Their effort paid off on April 18, 1924, when President Calvin Coolidge did just that.

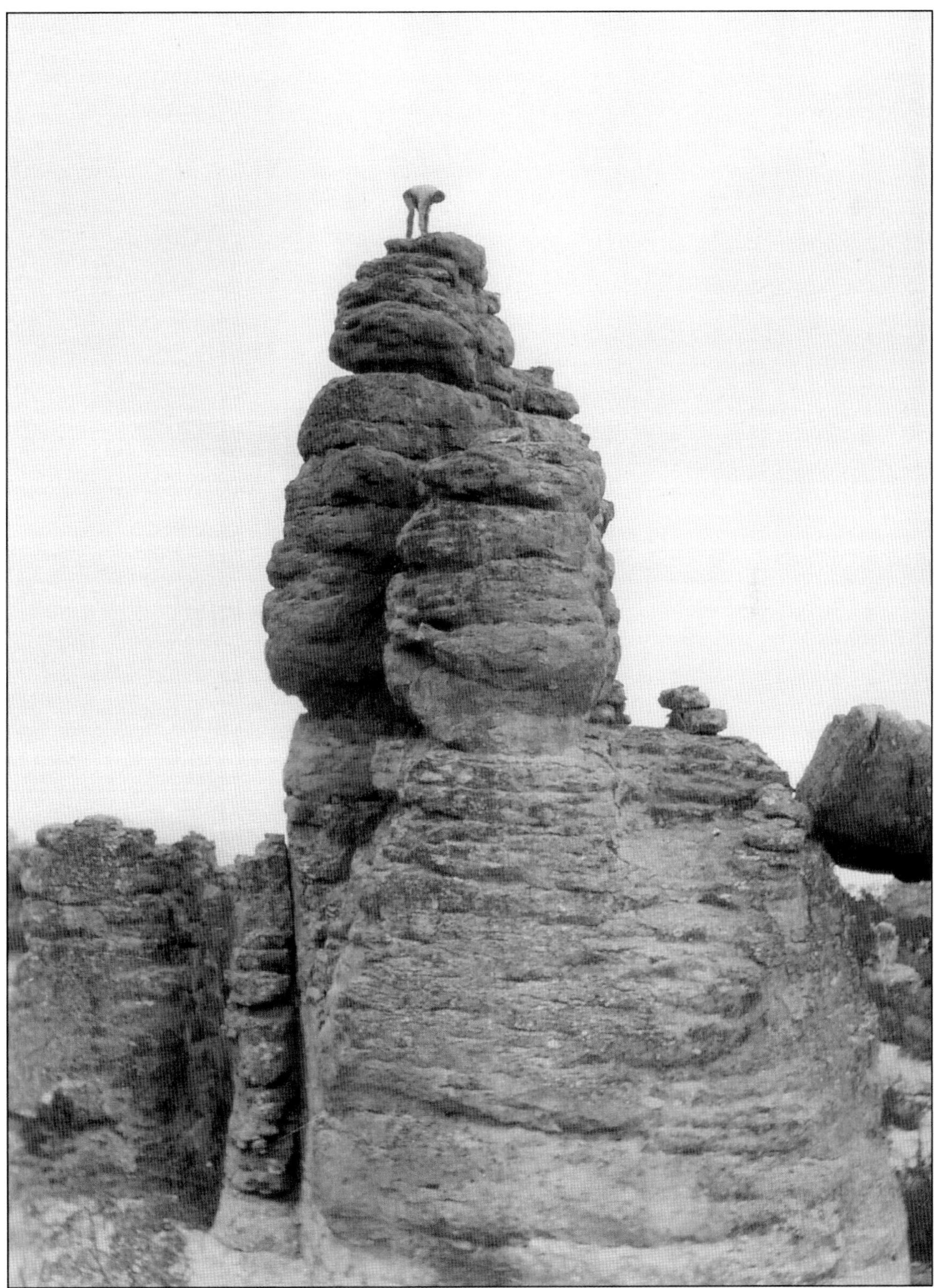

Douglas resident David C. O'Neil is credited as the first person to climb a pinnacle in the Wonderland of Rocks. This photograph of him topping out was probably taken by Douglas photographer Marvin Irwin in 1923. "Today, climbing rocks and pinnacles isn't permitted in the interest of visitor safety and preservation of the formations," said Chiricahua National Monument ranger Suzanne Moody. "Technical climbing isn't allowed either, partially because rhyolite is brittle enough that it doesn't reliably hold gear."

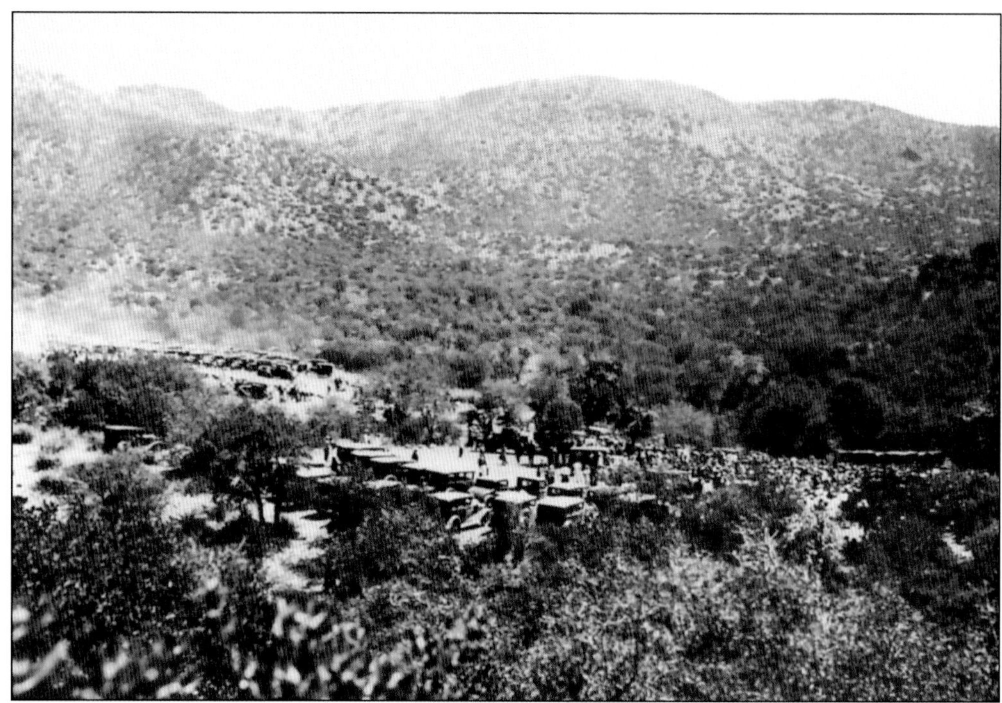

Although the Wonderland of Rocks became Chiricahua National Monument in 1924, it did not draw many visitors in its first 10 years of existence. Roads to the monument were rudimentary and signage almost nonexistent, and there was no road at all east of Faraway Ranch, just a trail axed out by Ed and Lillian Riggs. That began to change in 1932, as the Forest Service and Cochise County government built new roads and improved existing ones to the monument. The process slowed as the Great Depression deepened but accelerated when the National Park Service took over monument management in 1933. The next year, hundreds of cars and thousands of people attended a ceremony dedicating a road up Bonita Canyon to Massai Point. (Both, courtesy of Douglas Historical Society.)

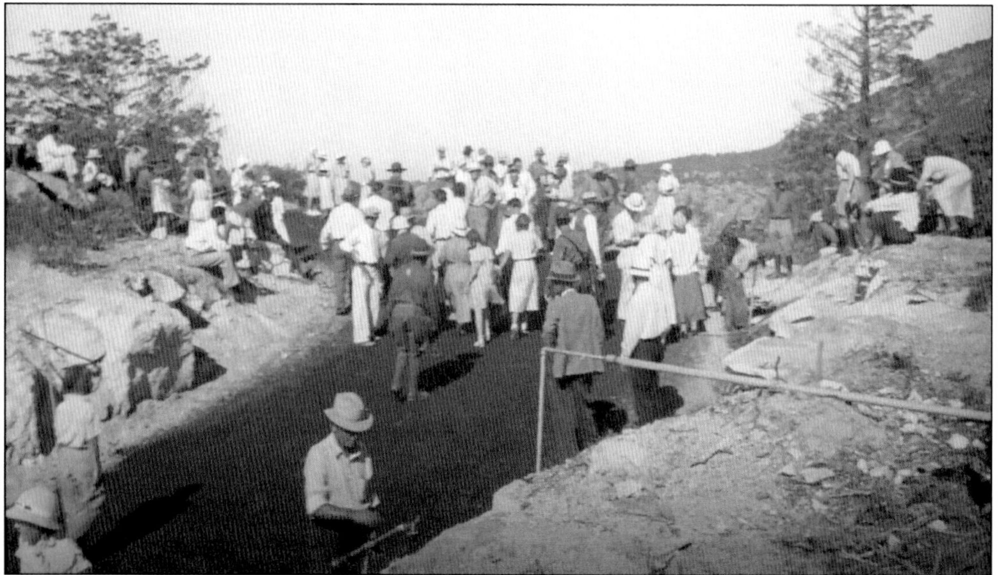

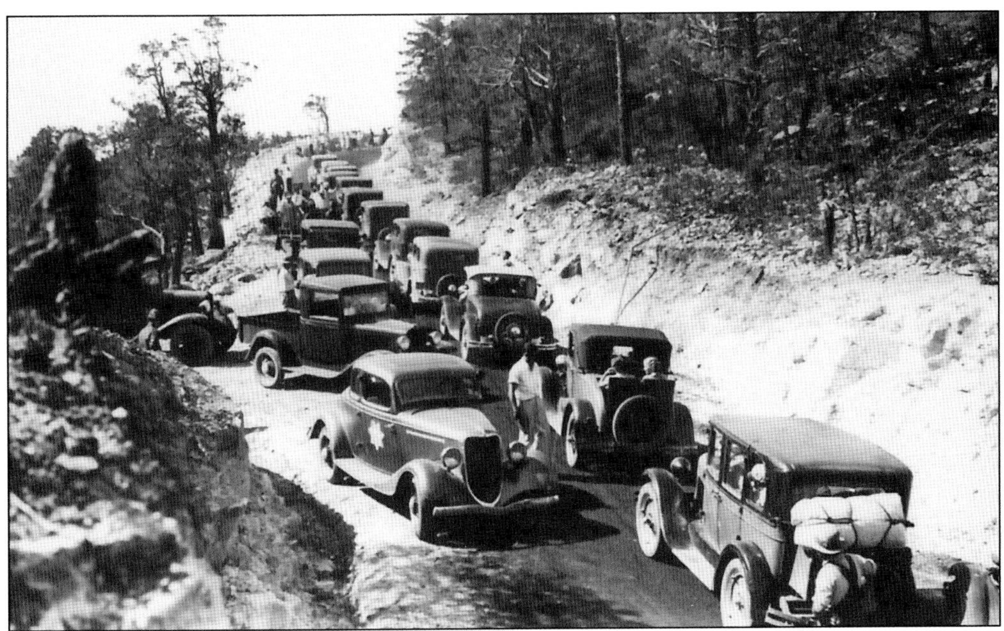

The dedication of Bonita Canyon Road on September 3, 1934, drew an estimated 10,000 people. There were so many vehicles that at first authorities retained a couple of hundred at the ranger station, but their drivers would not be denied and drove up the canyon anyway. People who reached Massai Point saw a dedication ceremony at which Arizona's first female congressional representative, Isabella Greenway; Sen. Henry Ashurst; and Gov. B.B. Mouer all spoke. Entertainment included performances by Douglas's and Bisbee's high school bands and a tug-of-war between Bisbee miners and Douglas smeltermen (Bisbee won). The crowd good-naturedly stood in line to receive free plates of barbecued beef and beans. (Both, courtesy of Douglas Historical Society.)

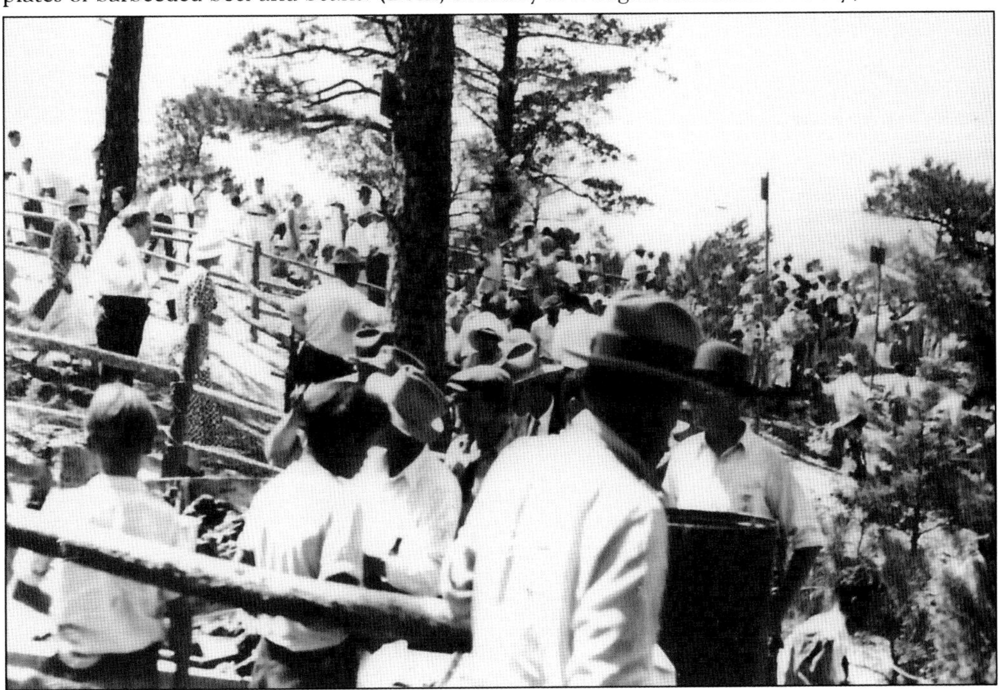

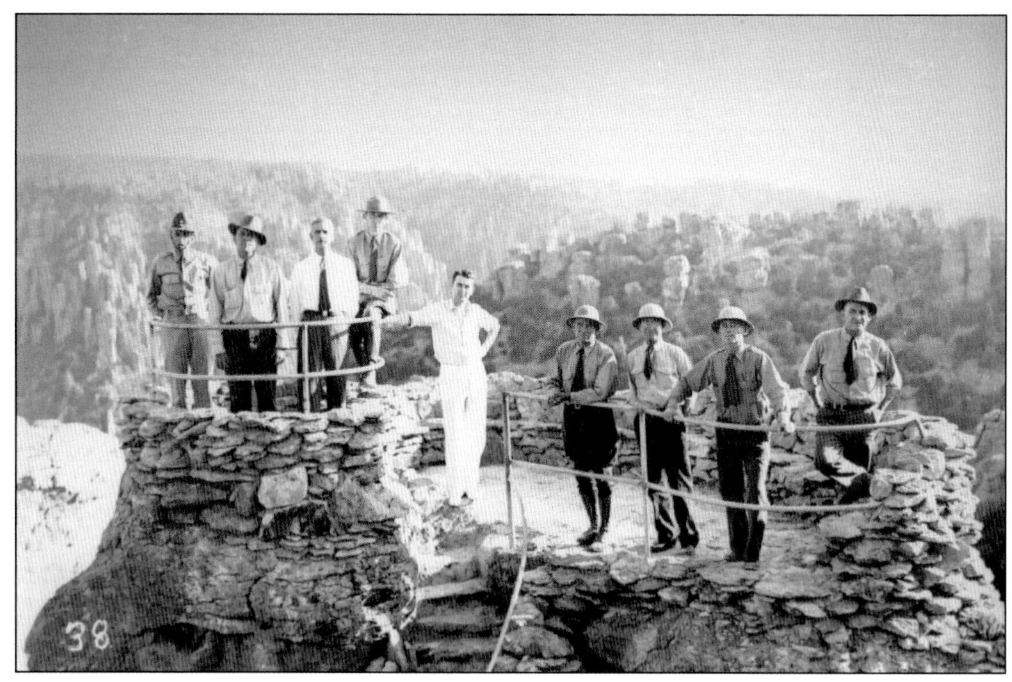

A platform at Massai Point (above) held National Park Service and other officials who had their photograph taken during the dedication of the Bonita Canyon Road. The officials include Ed Riggs (fourth from right), a foreman helping build trails and other NPS facilities. At Massai Point, those facilities include a short loop trail and orientation center. It was constructed by CCCers after the ceremony. They hauled in supplies packed on burros to the location (below). Note the up close and personal view of Cochise's Head behind the crew.

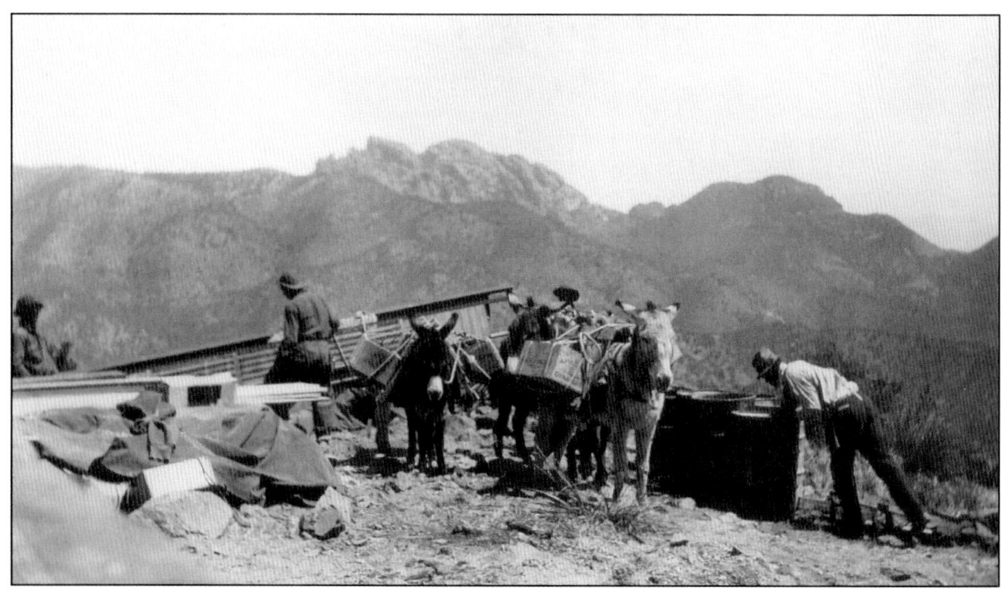

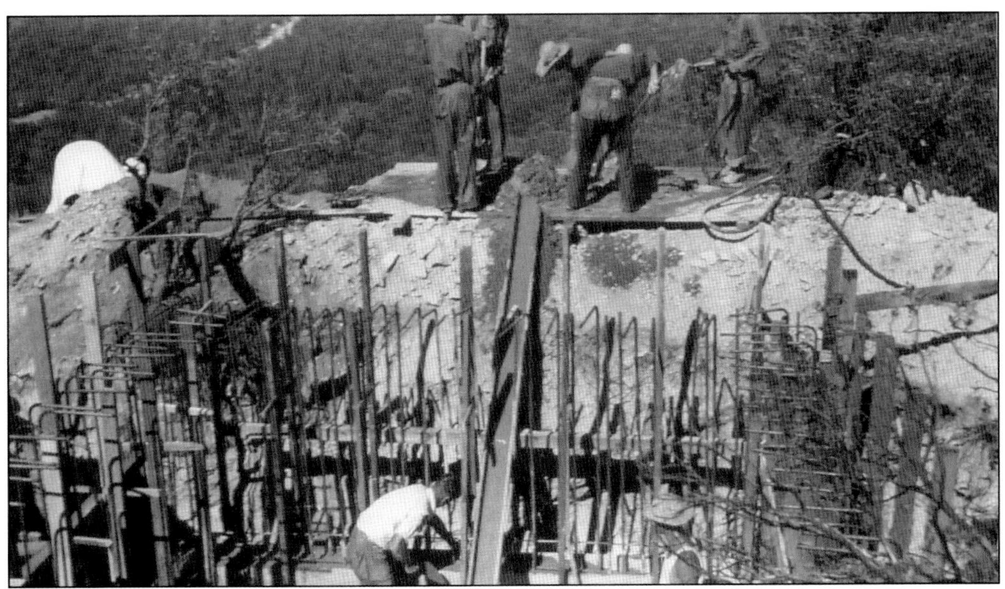

The CCCers who built the Massai Point facilities also constructed a fire lookout on Sugarloaf Mountain. They began by excavating a basement and building a foundation. Above, they are mixing cement by hand on a platform using sand from the excavation (left) and water from 55-gallon drums (see previous page). The cement was shoveled down the sluice (center) to the waiting finishers. Plenty of CCC manpower also constructed a road on the side of Sugarloaf Mountain, below. The road begins at the Echo Canyon parking area and ends at a trailhead. The trail to the lookout is rated an easy one and is a popular hike with today's monument visitors.

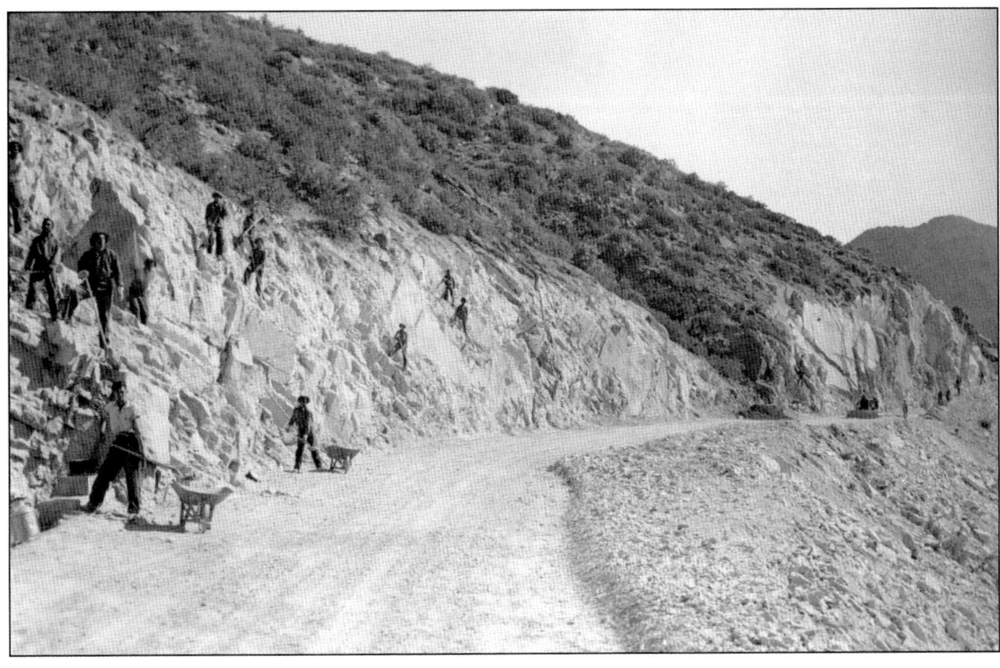

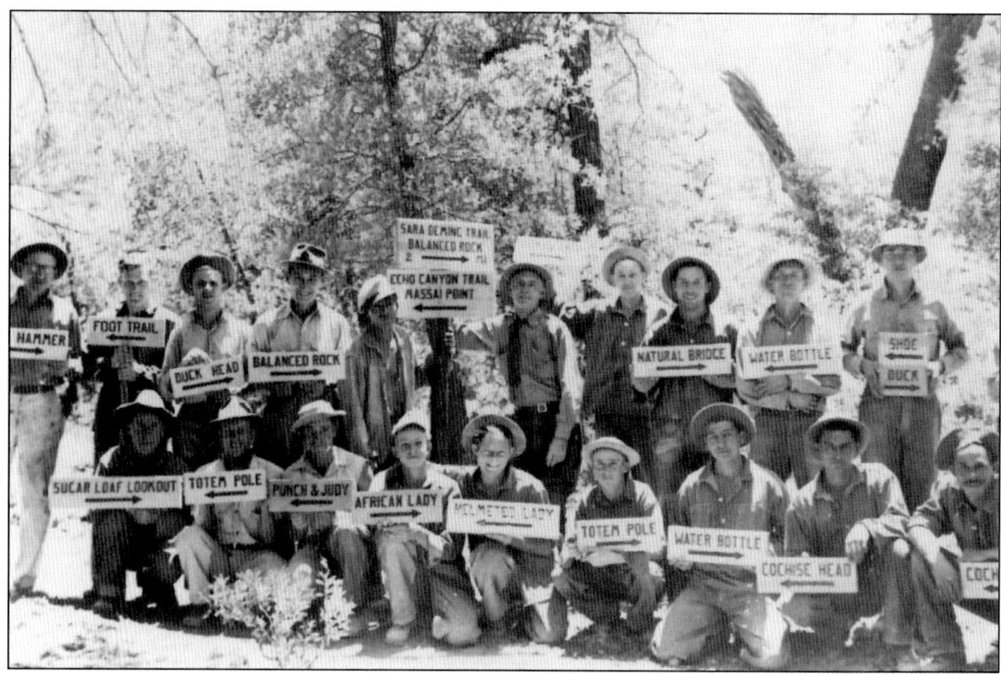

The CCC crews also constructed other monument trails. Above, they are holding directional signs. The highest sign in the middle points to the Sarah Deming Trail. Riggs family lore says that Deming was a Faraway guest who suffered an accident that ripped her pants. Martha Stark (page 80) rescued her by removing her apron and wrapping it around Sarah. A CCC crew poses in front of the rock formation known as China Boy below. China Boy is on the south side of the Bonita Canyon road about midway between the monument visitor center and Massai Point.

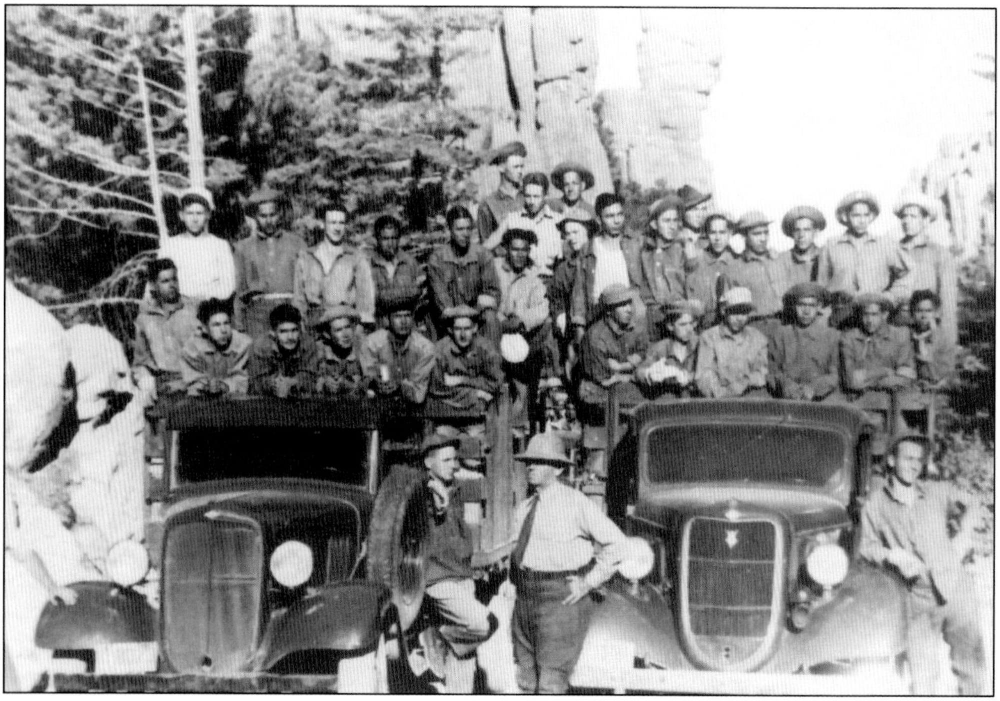

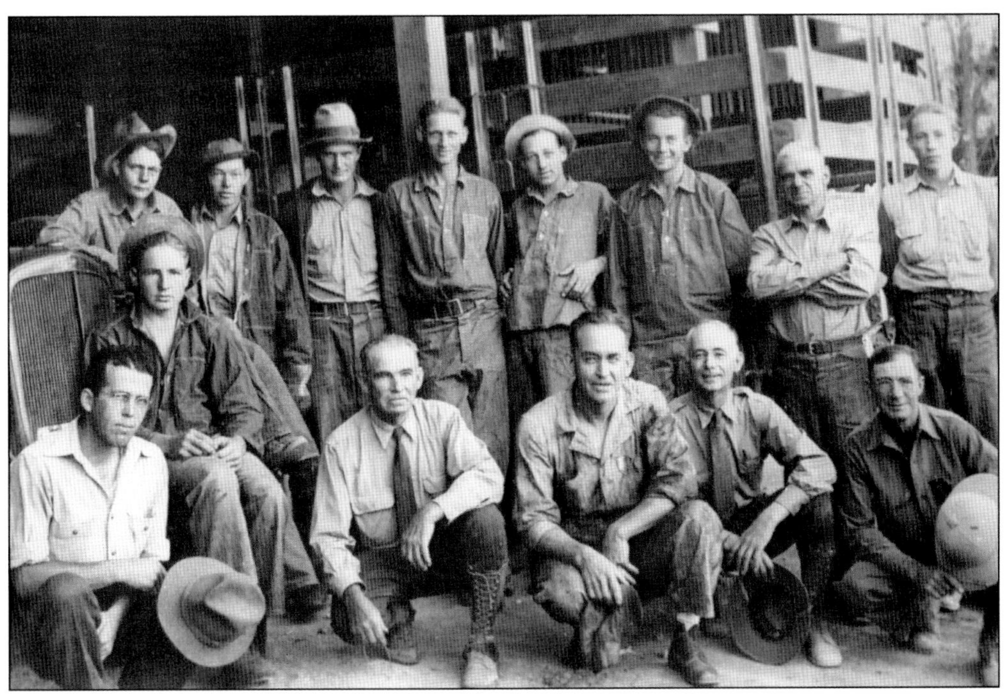

Managers and foremen gather for the photograph above, taken of CCC Camp NM-2-A's leadership in the mid-1930s. Ed Riggs is third from left in the front row. Barracks pictured below were built in 1934 to replace the tents in which the CCCers initially lived. The cost for constructing five barracks, a mess hall and kitchen, an infirmary, a rec hall, latrines, and a shower house was $14,000. The 175–200 members of Company 828 were from Arizona and Texas. They received regular weekend leaves, could take educational courses, and were under regular US Army officers. CCCers received $30 a week, of which $25 was sent to their families.

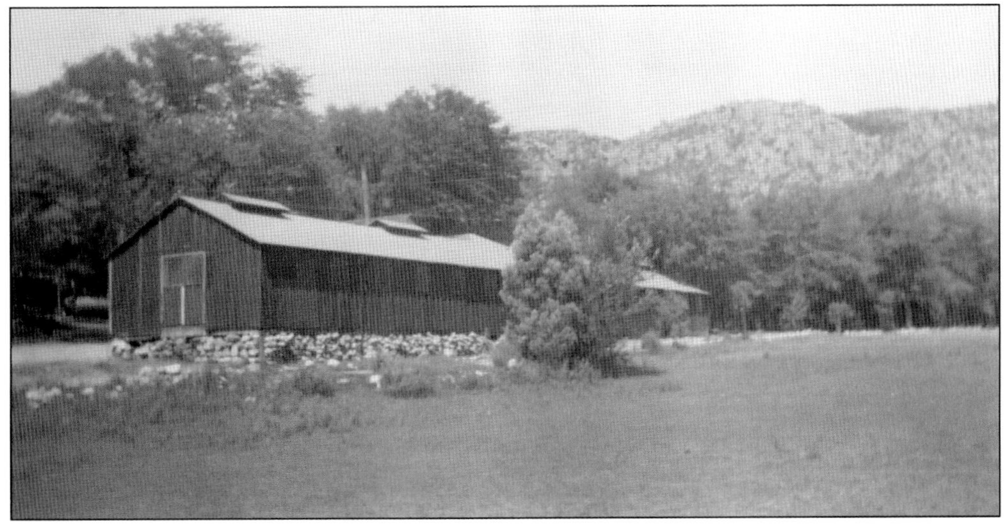

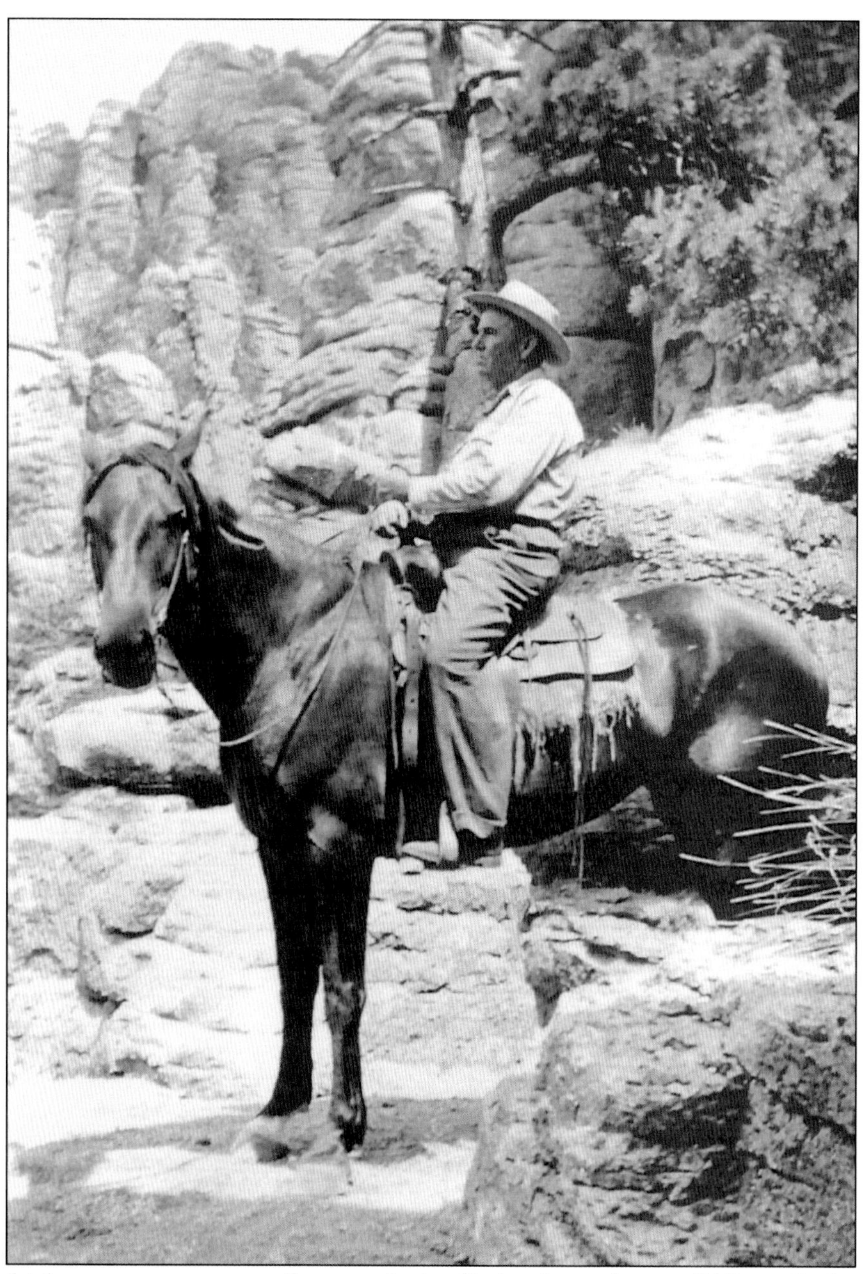

Riding his horse on monument trails was undoubtedly deeply satisfying to Ed Riggs. In the 1920s, he began establishing some of those trails. In the 1930s, he supervised CCCers as they constructed a trail up Sugarloaf Mountain. Ed then took on the challenge of designing a trail through Echo Canyon after several engineers declared it impossible. His design took 18 months to implement, partially because the CCC laborers, according to a National Park Service regional wildlife technician, took "great care . . . to avoid damage to vegetation and rock formations. . . . Rock supporting walls have been carefully laid so as to give a natural appearance." One quarter-mile section of the trail required 11 switchbacks on a grade averaging minus-11 percent. The photograph on page 31 shows part of the Echo Canyon Trail. The inscription on Ed's grave marker includes: "He engineered construction of Echo Trail. He wished this to be his monument."

Nine

Faraway and the Silver Spur

After the CCC camp closed in 1940, Ed and Lillian negotiated a deal with the federal government in which they received the site's five barracks, mess hall, and shops. They envisioned a facility for large groups of guests and leased operations to another couple as Faraway Lodge.

But World War II limited Americans' recreational time, and after the war, Ed and Lillian confronted changed expectations of what a guest ranch experience should involve. Participatory activities such as cattle roundups and drives were often ignored in favor of more symbolic events such as dinners out of chuck wagons resembling Hollywood movie props.

Faraway Lodge did not prosper and underwent several management adjustments and a name change to Silver Spur Guest Ranch before achieving stability in the 1950s with owners Ray and Martha Kent. They had a 10-year noncompetition deal with Ed and Lillian, signed in 1945, limiting Faraway to horseback rentals and some meals. One reason Ed and Lillian did this was Emma's declining health and Lillian's loss of eyesight in 1942. Combined with hearing difficulties, Lillian grappled with many lifestyle adjustments.

Matters did not get better in 1950, when 96-year-old Emma died as well as Ed. Lillian began a lengthy struggle with grief, depression, and in 1955, a debilitating decision of whether to recommence the guest ranch business when the noncompetition agreement expired.

Lillian did resume guest ranch operations but had to rely on hired help and lessees to run things. This included cottage and room rentals, meals, and horseback rides into the monument, since fewer guests opted to assist with cattle chores.

Helping was Ben, who, after the death of his first wife, married a Faraway guest and built a nearby home. Another assistant was Julius Porter "Andy" Anderson, who became Faraway manager in 1960. He saw Lillian and Faraway through their final years. Faraway closed in 1970, and Lillian died in 1977.

After her death, Ben and Hildegard approached the National Park Service about Faraway becoming part of the monument. That happened shortly after their 1978 deaths and after the NPS had bought and dismantled the Silver Spur, from 1967 to 1971.

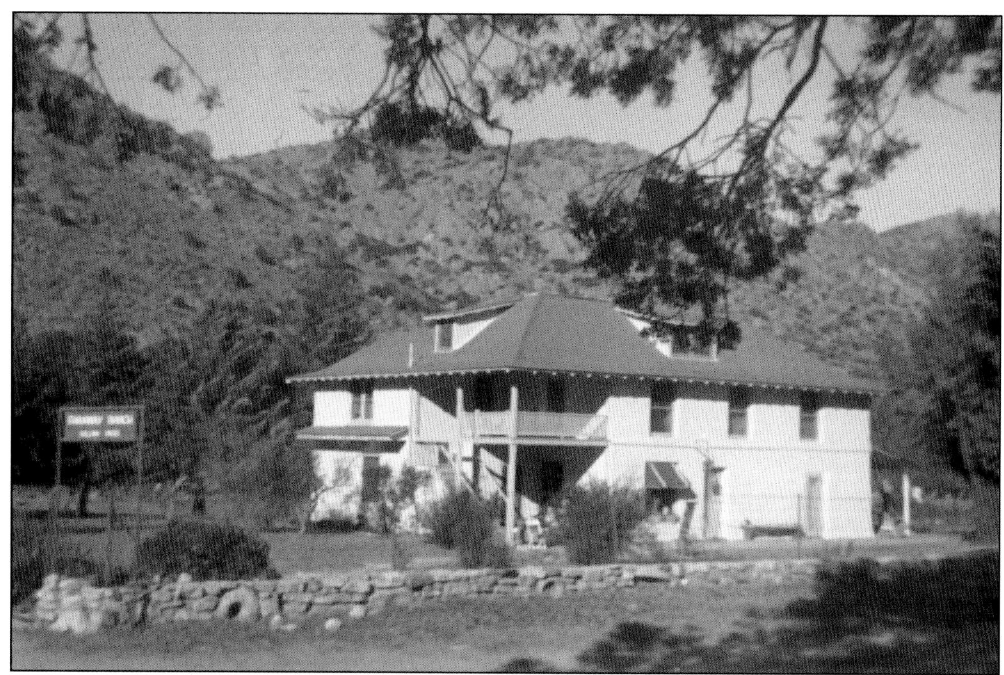

Depending upon the entryway they chose, visitors driving into Faraway Ranch during the 1950s and 1960s first saw either the main house (above) or the corrals (below). Both structures were facets of the Faraway experience that Lillian Riggs offered to guests. She presided over Faraway's main house and shared stories about the people who had lived in and visited the house. The corrals were the hub for 10 or so horses who, with steadiness and forbearance, carried visitors in Chiricahua National Monument to see the Wonderland of Rocks or out onto two pieces of ranchland Lillian owned. The Holderman, in the Sulphur Springs Valley, was winter pasture for Lillian's cattle herd. The Double Z, in Apache Pass, was summer pasture. Roundups and drives moving cattle back and forth between the two places happened twice a year. Faraway guests were welcome to help.

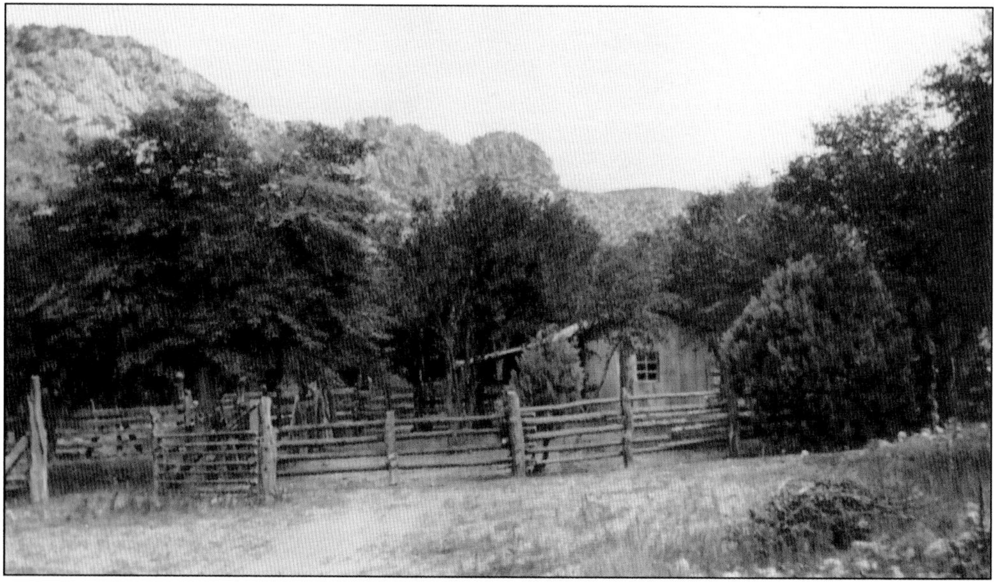

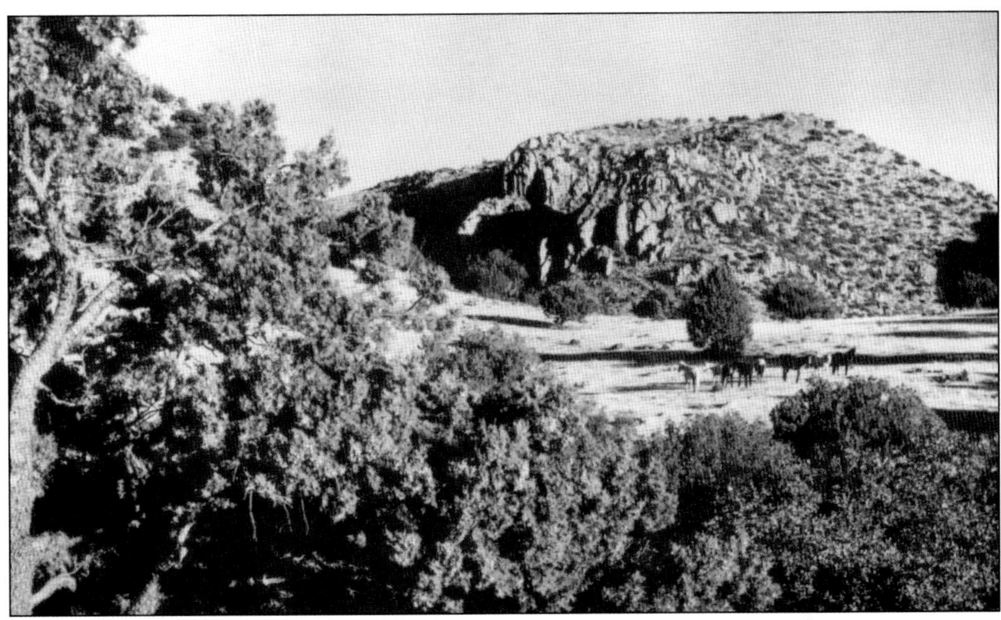

The ranching style used by Ed and Lillian Riggs is known as "the Texas system." It was strongly influenced by generations of northern Mexico ranchers, who generally handled their cattle only twice year, since this required minimal capital and labor outlay. Today, 50 years later, many ranchers manage their horses and cattle, such as the Faraway stock shown in these two photographs, in a holistic style. This requires meticulous monitoring, precise planning, and active administration, tasks successful ranchers carry out willingly because it is a hands-on way for them to care for their livestock and their land.

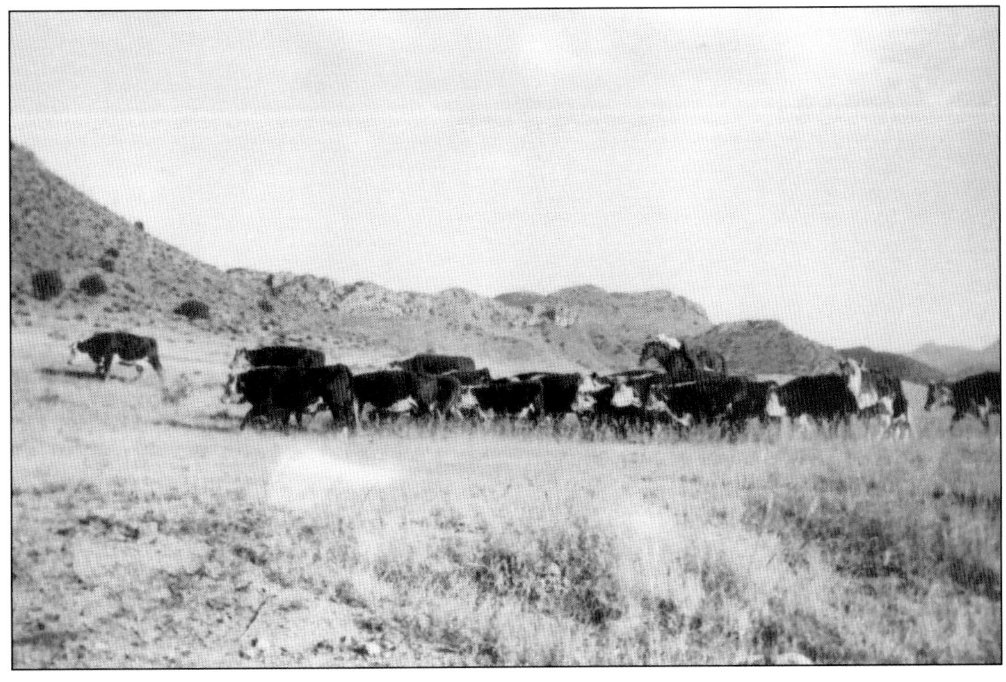

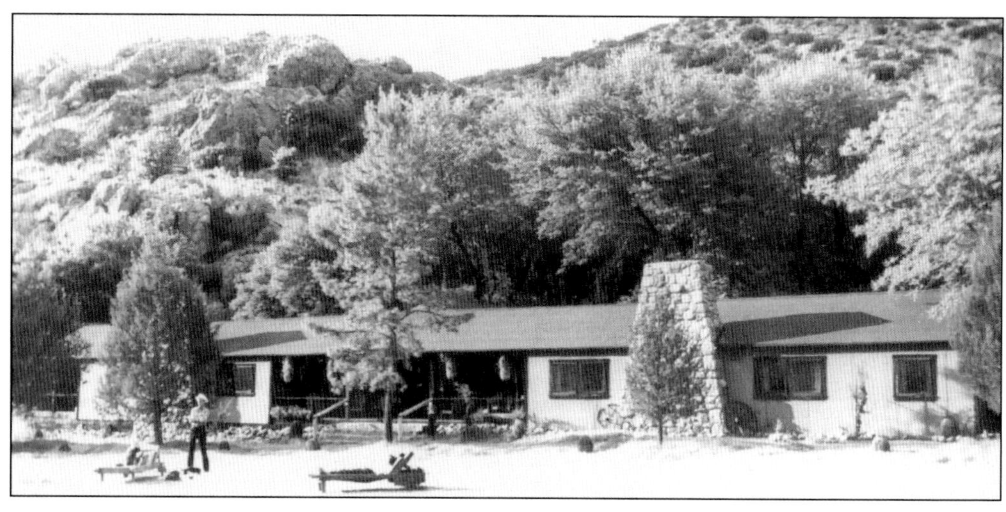

In 1940, after the CCC camp closed, Ed and Lillian regained control of the property and converted the buildings into Faraway Lodge, with an emphasis on group usage. They leased this operation, but it had limited success, mainly because World War II severely limited travel. In 1945, William Sprague purchased Faraway Lodge and transformed it into Silver Spur Ranch. The main house (above) was the remodeled CCC barracks seen on page 107. The Silver Spur experience could include riding (below).

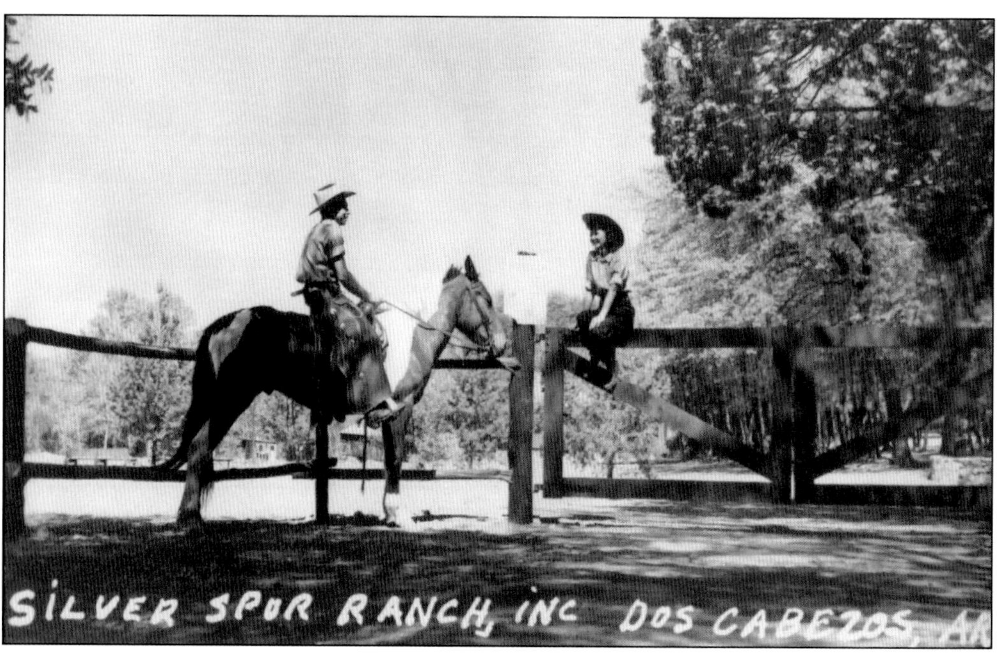

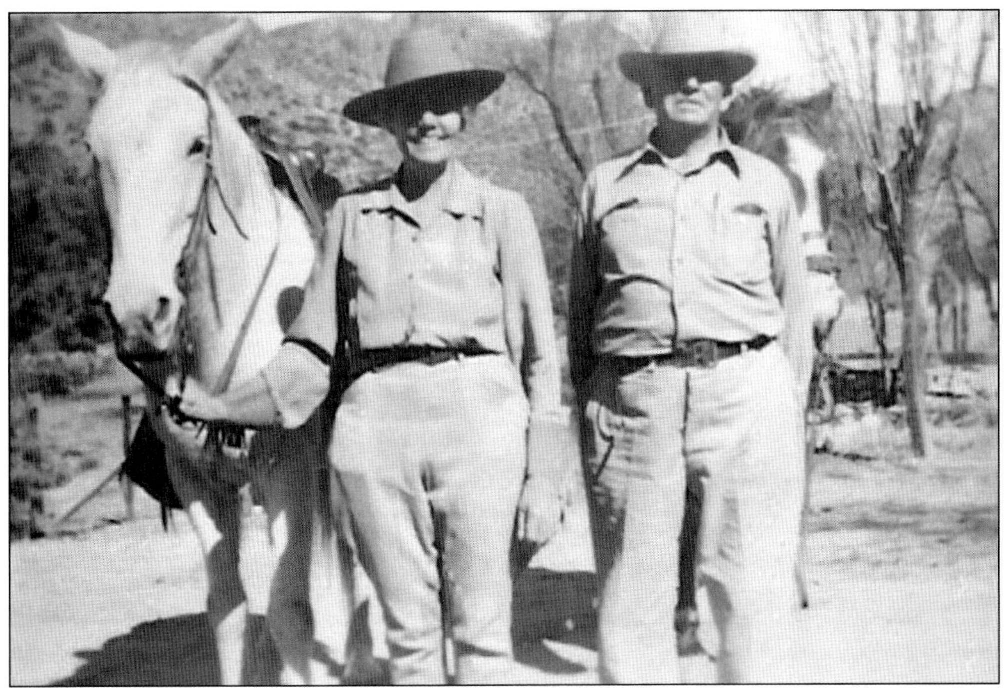

In 1942, Ed and Lillian gave up the guest ranch business, and three years later, they signed a noncompetition agreement with the Silver Spur. One reason they did this was that cattle prices were high. Another reason was Emma's reoccurring and Ed's incipient health issues, but the major reason was Lillian's blindness. Since 1900, she had endured a gradual loss of hearing. In the 1930s, she developed sight problems, which worsened despite a cataract operation. In 1942, at age 54, Lillian became totally blind. So she and Ed (above) let the Silver Spur host guests and hold impromptu rodeos (below). In 1950, both Ed and Emma died, and grief and depression almost overwhelmed Lillian. Nevertheless, she persisted.

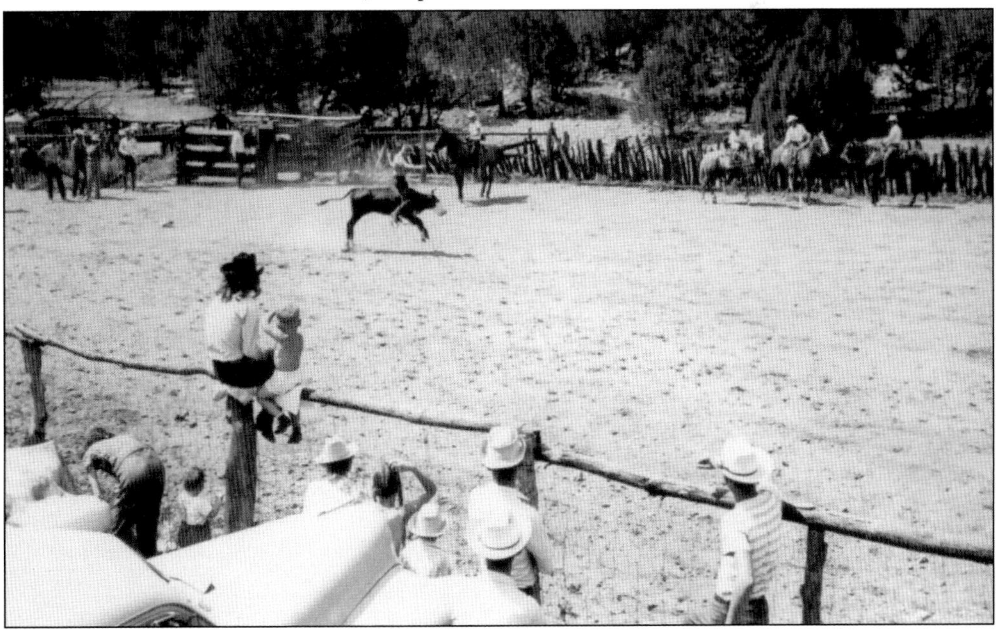

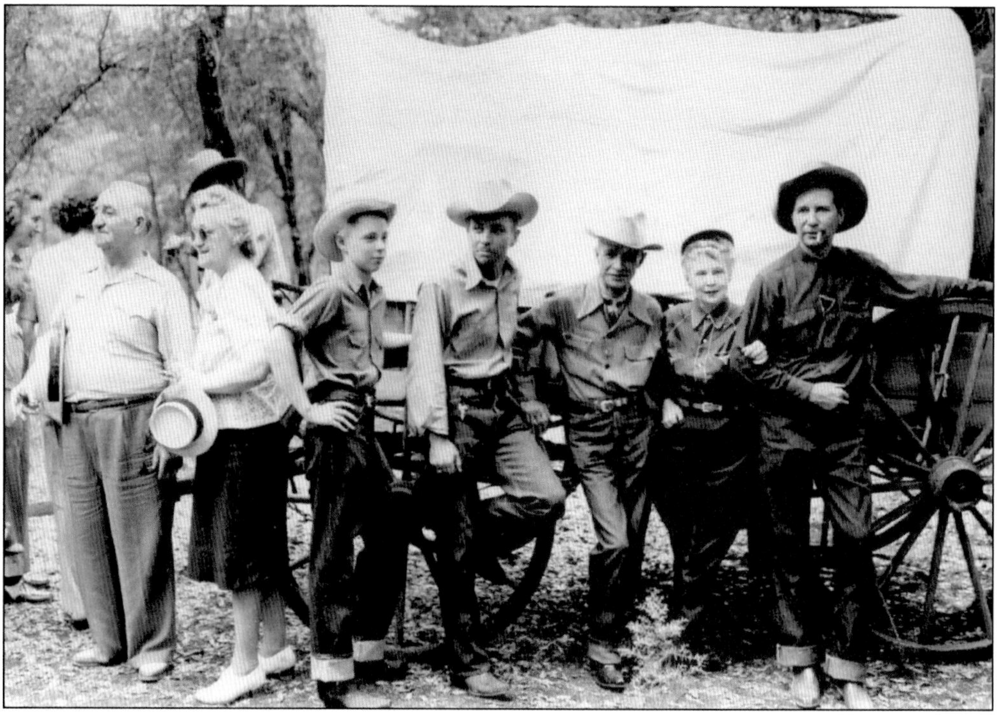

In 1955, when the noncompetition agreement expired, Lillian resumed guest ranch operations, but the business had changed greatly. Fewer guests in the 1950s and 1960s wanted hands-on experiences such as roundups and branding. Instead, influenced by television shows, guests wanted symbolic activities that represented what they thought was "real ranch life." Compare this Silver Spur chuck wagon and the 1950s guests gathered around it with the authentic chuck wagon on page 91. (Both, courtesy of Douglas Historical Society.)

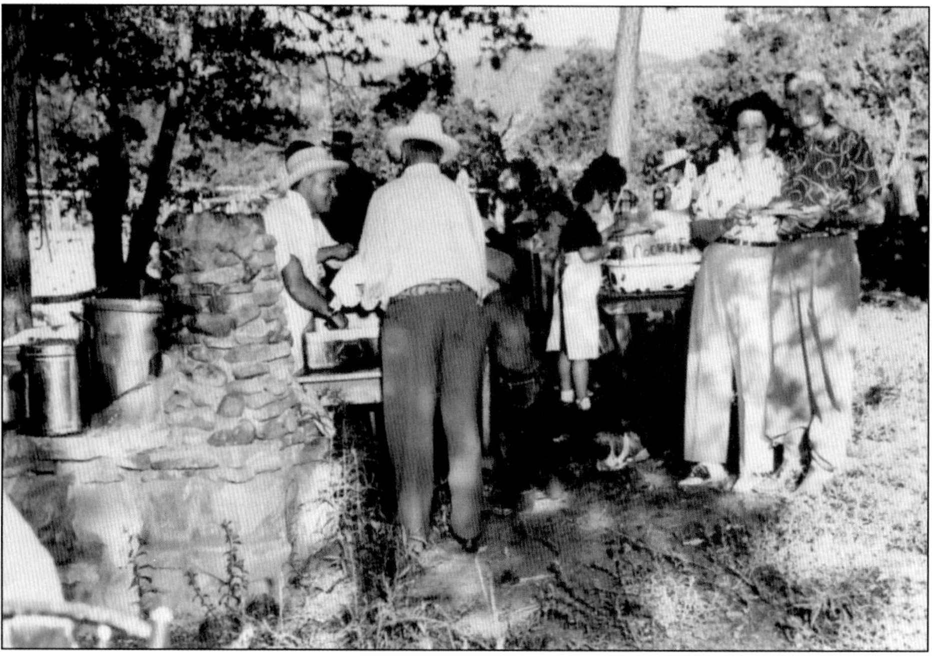

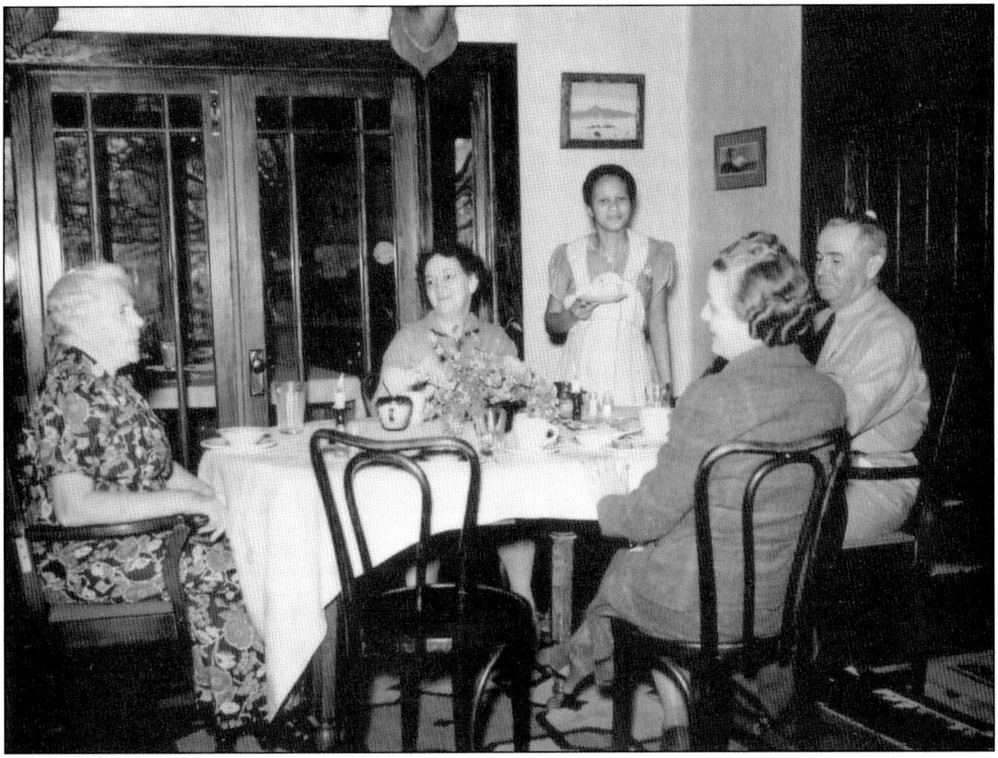

Lillian's physical difficulties forced her to rely on hired help to run Faraway. Leagatha Martin (standing above) serves, from left to right, Emma Erickson, guests Mrs. Stroem and Mrs. Weaver, and Ed Riggs in the main house's small dining room. Below, Lillian's employees Claude and Marion Noland pose in front of Faraway's entrance sign for Lillian's 1958 Christmas card. The Nolands were from Minnesota, and their clothing reflects their vision of Western wear.

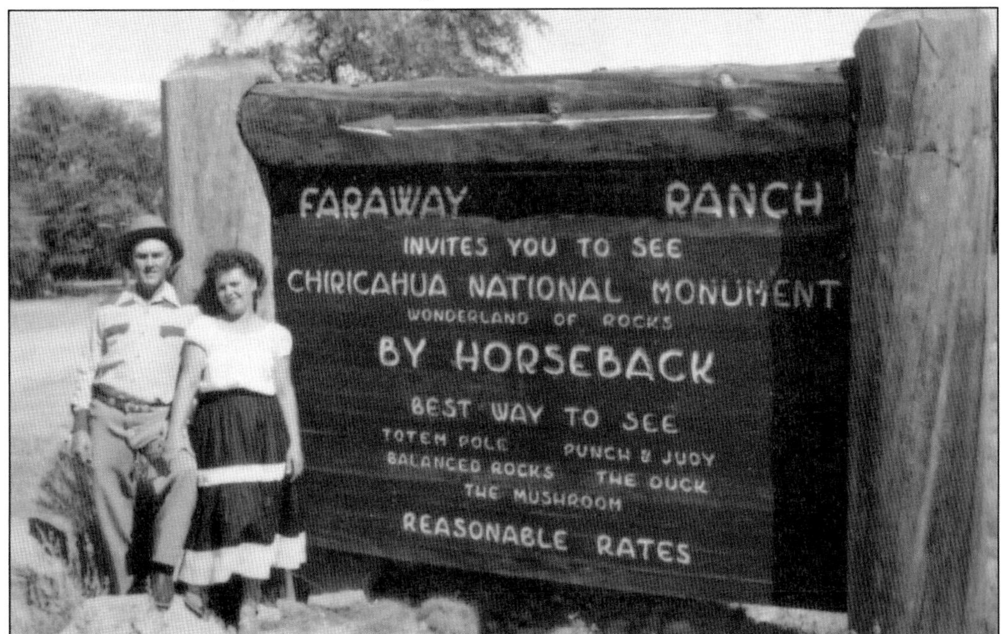

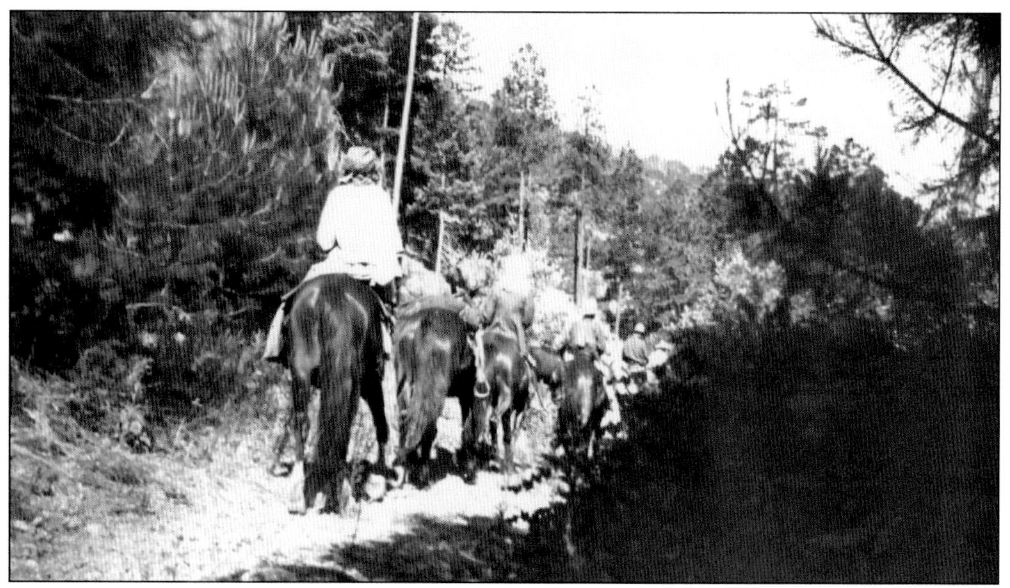

While some aspects of the guest ranch business changed between the 1940s and 1950s, others did not. A prime attraction for Faraway guests remained riding horses into the Wonderland of Rocks (above). A popular excursion was up the Rhyolite Canyon and Sarah Deming Trails to the entrance of the Heart of Rocks Loop. There, Faraway guests tied their horses and walked the loop to see Punch and Judy, Duck on a Rock, and the large balanced pinnacle rock. The height gained by being on the back of a horse (below) provided clear views of many formations, including Cochise's Head.

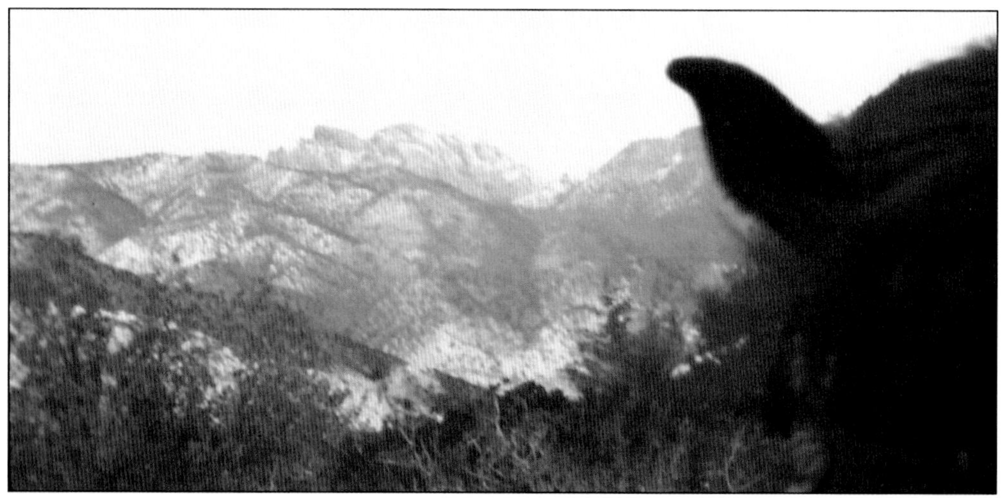

In the 1950s and 1960s, visitors could stay in Faraway's main house or set up housekeeping in one of three buildings. The Stafford cabin (top) usually accommodated long-term renters. The Alcor/Mizer guest quarters (middle) consisted of a moved Stafford cabin portion combined with a fieldstone section. In 1949, Ed and Lillian purchased Martha Stark's cabin (bottom) and transported it to Faraway. It hosted guests until it burned down in 1967. The cowboy house (not pictured) was another two buildings fused; one part came from Ben's homestead. The cowboy house was home for people such as Myrtle Westbrook, who leased Faraway's horse operations from 1959 to 1961.

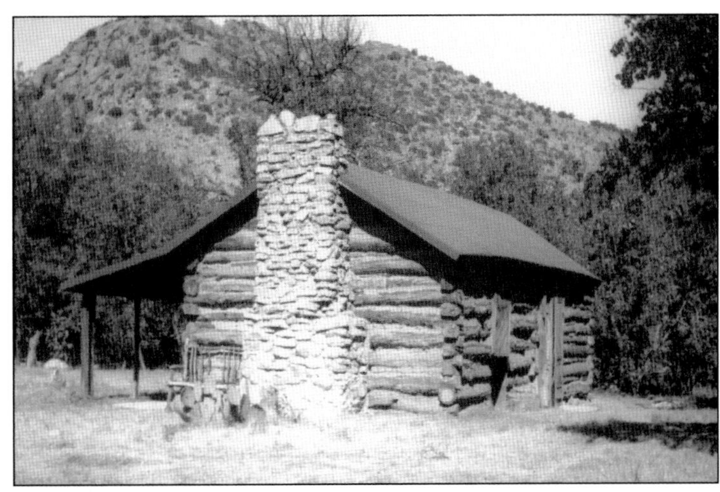

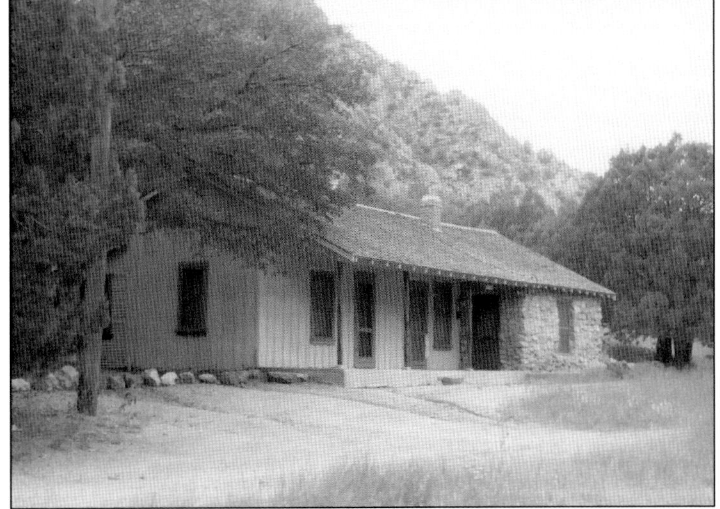

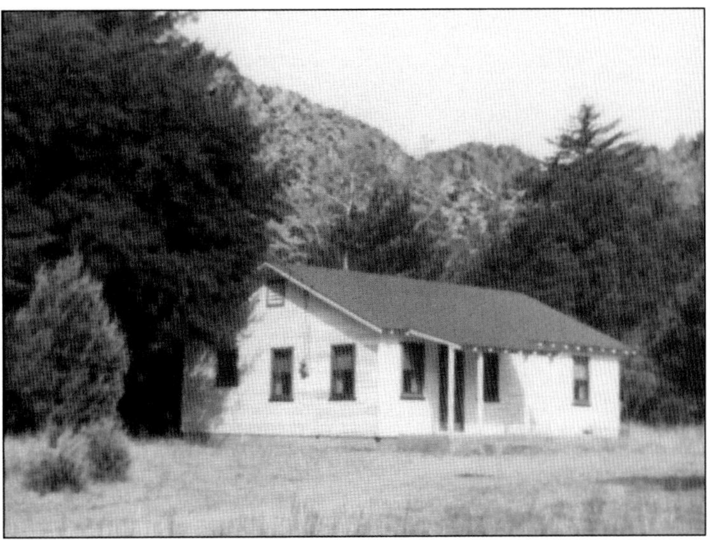

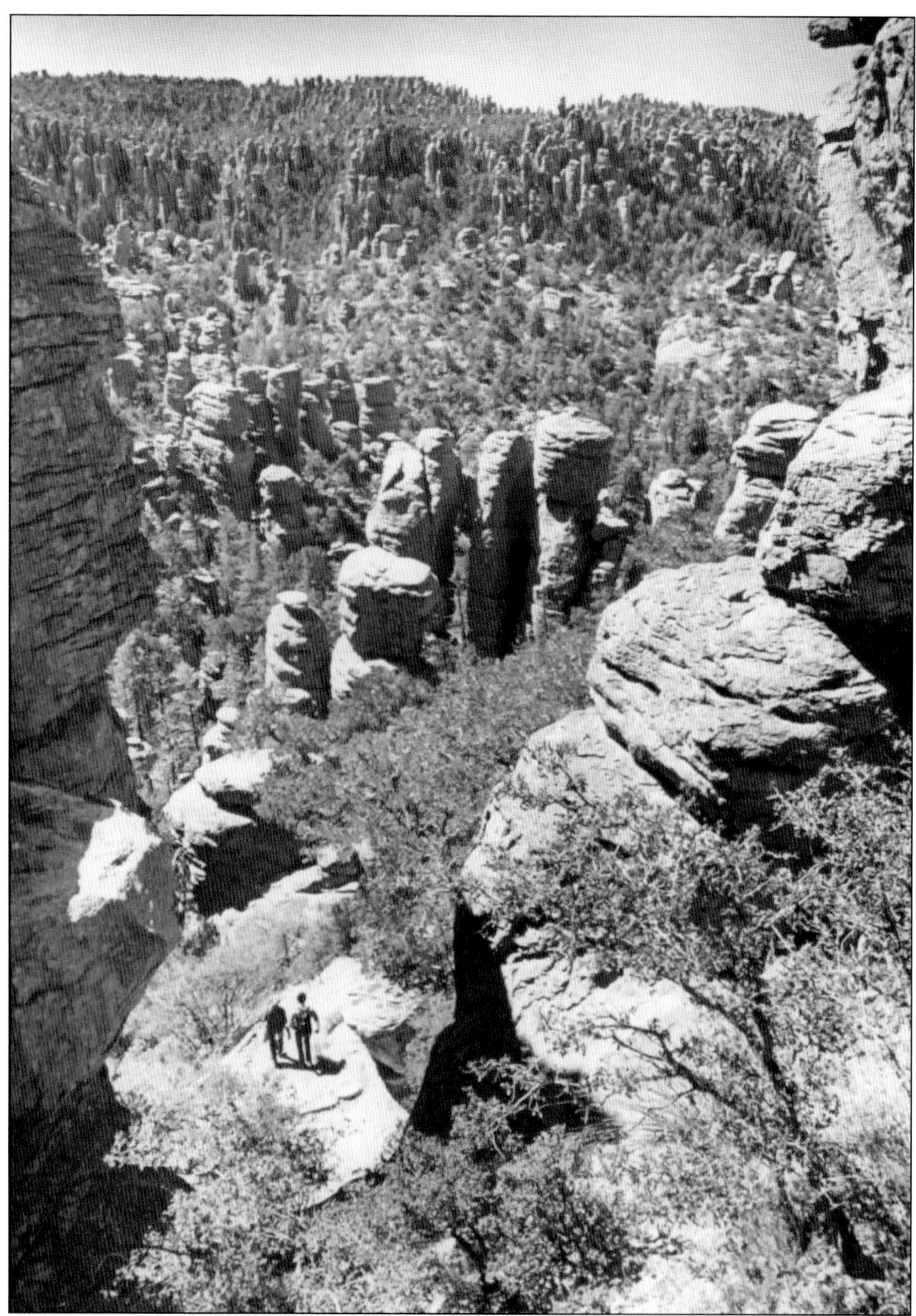

Toward the end of Faraway's life span, hiking became more and more popular. Fewer guests rode through the Wonderland of Rocks, and an increasing number walked. These included people who strolled along National Park Service pathways and enjoyed the variety of the monument's plant and wildlife as well as the sensation of being amongst the pinnacles.

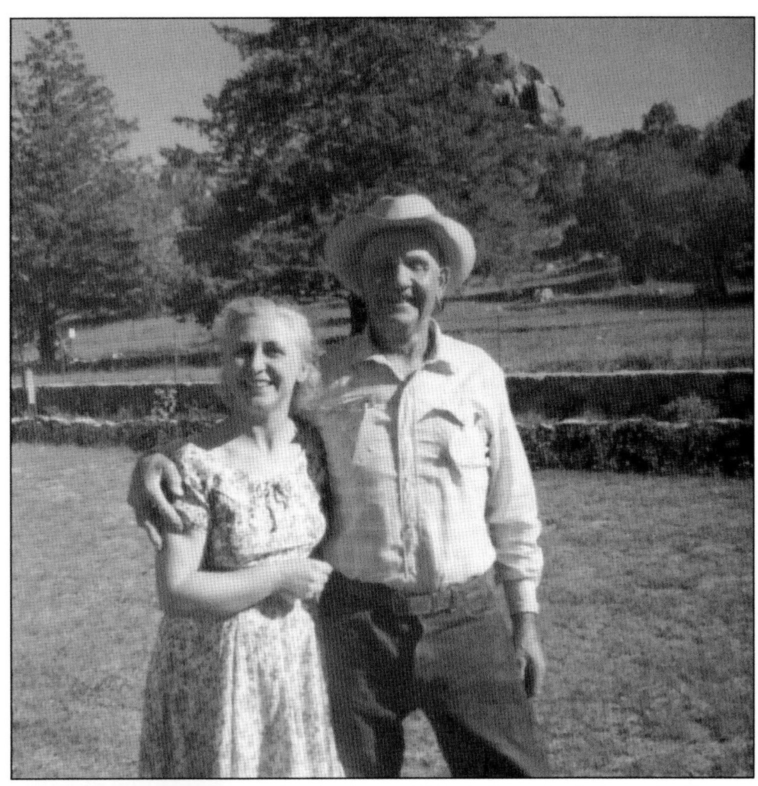

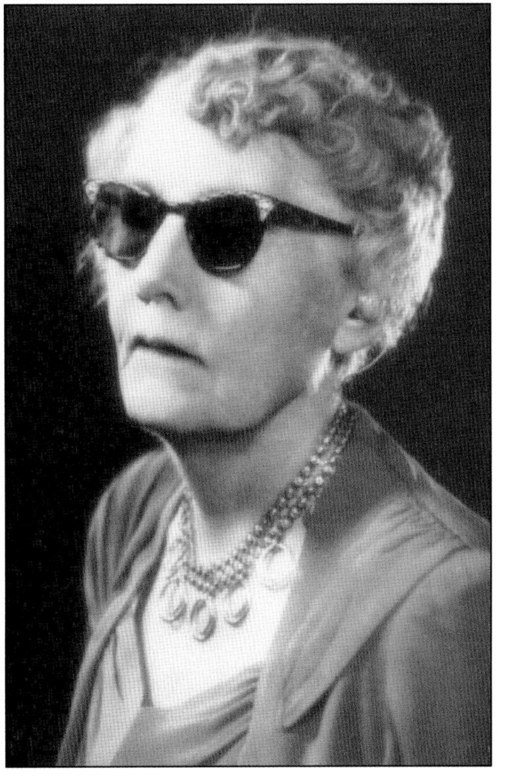

In the late 1950s, Lillian (right) gradually recovered her zest for life. She held forth in her living room, deriving pleasure from talking with the guests that Faraway still attracted. They ranged from local families to a disabled Canadian World War I veteran. Lillian's visitors admired her and the steadfast manner in which she ran Faraway. One thing reducing Lillian's depression was her brother Ben's second marriage. He and his first wife, Belle, were living in central Arizona where she died in 1955. Ben returned to Cochise County and met Ethel Keller while she was a Faraway guest. They married in 1959, living first at Faraway (above) and then building their own house nearby.

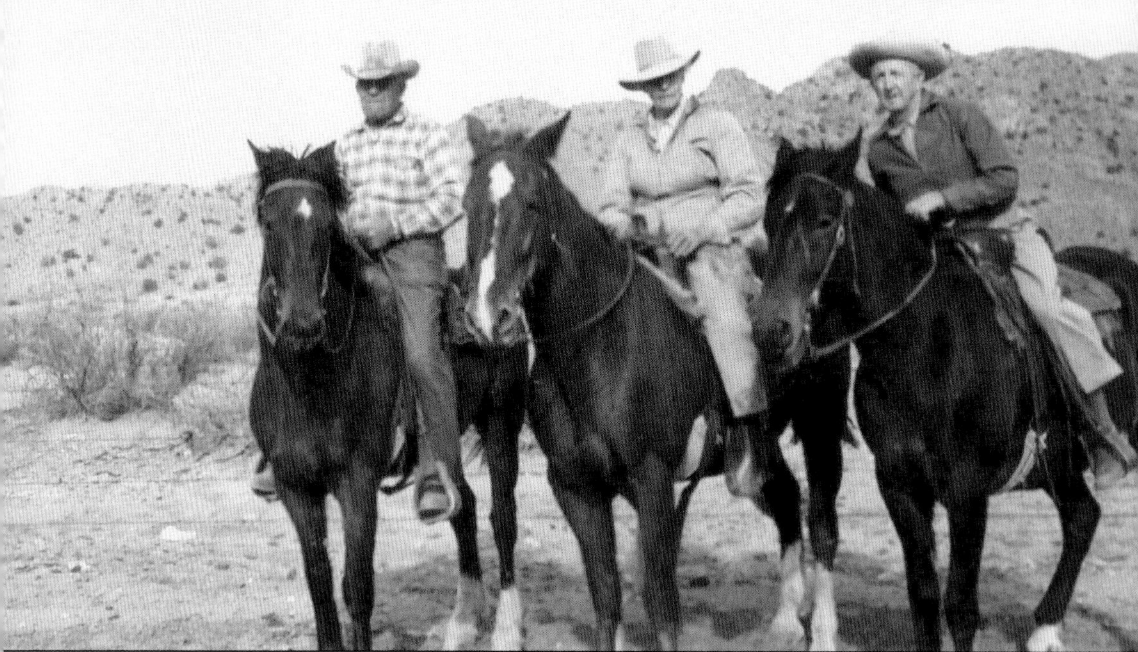

After returning to Cochise County, Ben helped Lillian with Faraway's cattle. But she had to rely upon others to maintain Faraway. After 1960, Lillian's main assistant was J.P. "Andy" Anderson, right. He is with Ben and Lillian in this photograph, taken at the Double Z. Andy proved to be a mixed blessing, for he alienated many of Lillian's family and friends and allowed Faraway to become run-down. But he also provided Lillian with the companionship she craved, and he faithfully looked after her, even during the two years she lived in long-term health-care facilities in Willcox. Lillian died on April 26, 1977, and Andy on December 23, 1978.

Ten

Chiricahua National Monument Now

In the 1930s, CCC members developed 12 miles of Chiricahua Monument trails and infrastructure, including a visitor center in Bonita Canyon. It is one way sightseers receive an introduction to the monument.

The visitor center has displays and is where reservations for nearby Bonita Canyon Campground can be made, along with www.recreation.gov. The visitor center is a starting point for the monument's main hiking trail, the place to arrange daily hikers' shuttle service, and where to sign up to "Rock the Rhyolite." Hikers who cover at least five miles document this with photographs or selfies and then show them to a ranger at the visitor center to receive a free commemorative pin.

Rangers offer programs and talks at the campground. Some are for Junior Rangers, who can check out backpacks filled with items such as binoculars to use during their visit. If a Junior Ranger fills out a workbook and turns it in, she receives a special badge and other recognition.

Another way visitors learn about the monument is during Faraway Ranch tours. That is because Erickson family members sold Faraway to the National Park Service in 1979. NPS conservators restored the buildings and their contents to their 1950s condition.

Yet another way people learn about Faraway happens when they stop to look at the cemetery in Bonita Canyon's entrance. The first person interred there was Louis Prue following an 1892 horse accident. He asked to be buried at Bonita Canyon's mouth so he could watch his cattle on their way to water in the canyon.

"I am sorry to hear of Mr. Prue's death," wrote Neil Erickson at the time, "that it should happen in such a way, but our journey's end in this world is soon reached and therefore we should all make the best of life while we do live."

In 1937, Neil was buried just west of Prue. Emma joined Neil in 1950; their children Ben and Hildegard, in 1978. Lillian, however, is buried with her husband, Ed, in the Riggs Family Cemetery, out in the vastness of the Sulphur Springs Valley.

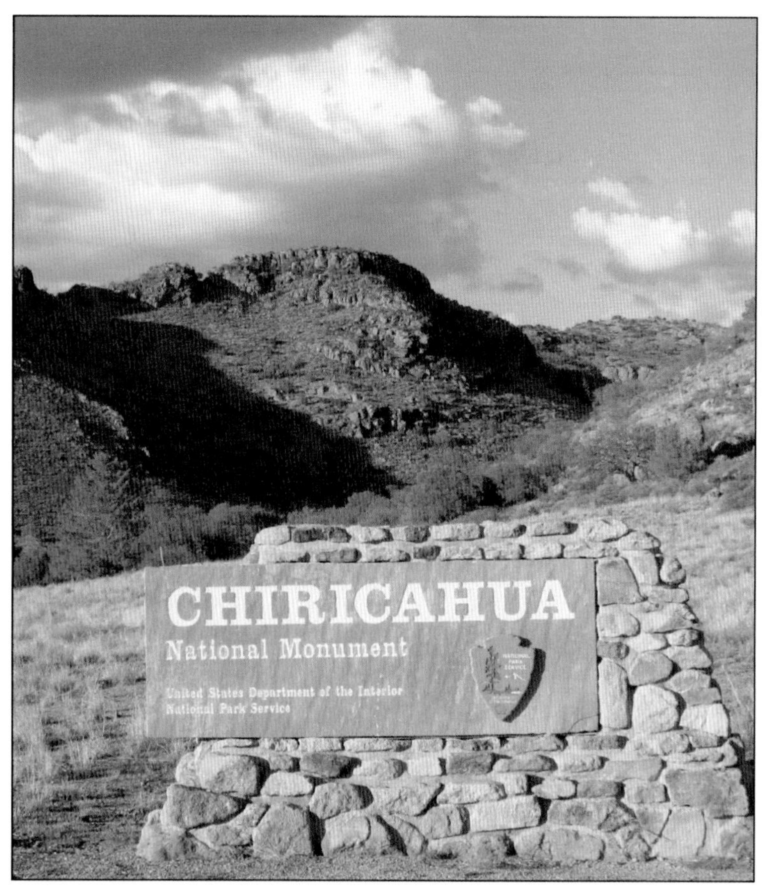

The entrance to Chiricahua National Monument (left) is always open. The visitor center (below), whose core was constructed by CCCers, is open every day except Christmas from 8:30 a.m. to 4:30 p.m. At the center, visitors can view a short orientation video, look at interpretive displays, obtain maps, learn about the hikers' shuttle service, browse the book and gift store, and make reservations for nearby Bonita Canyon Campground.

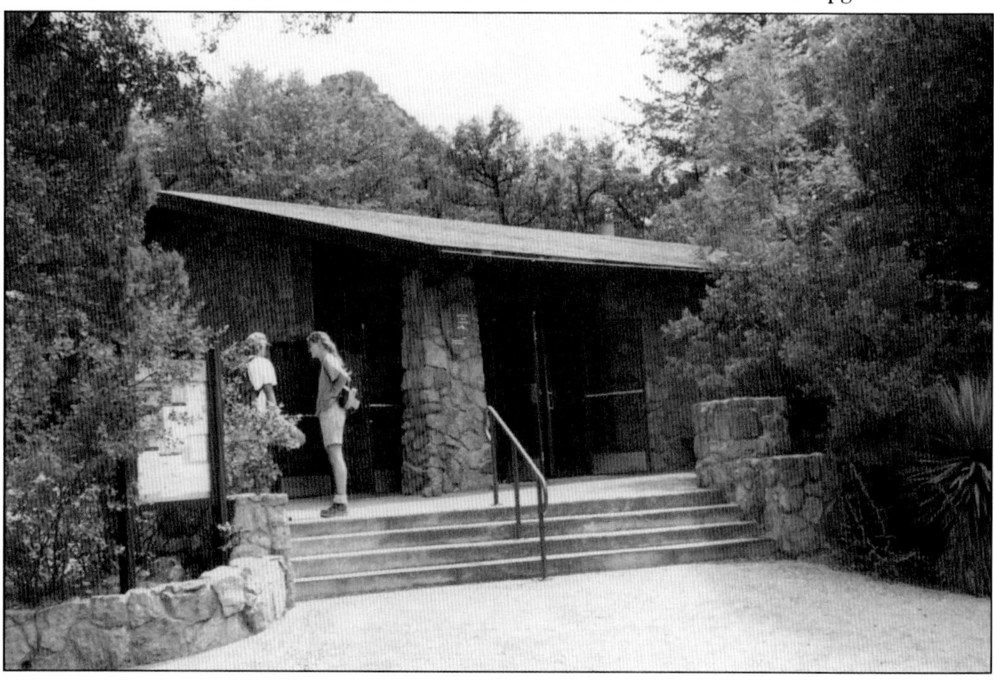

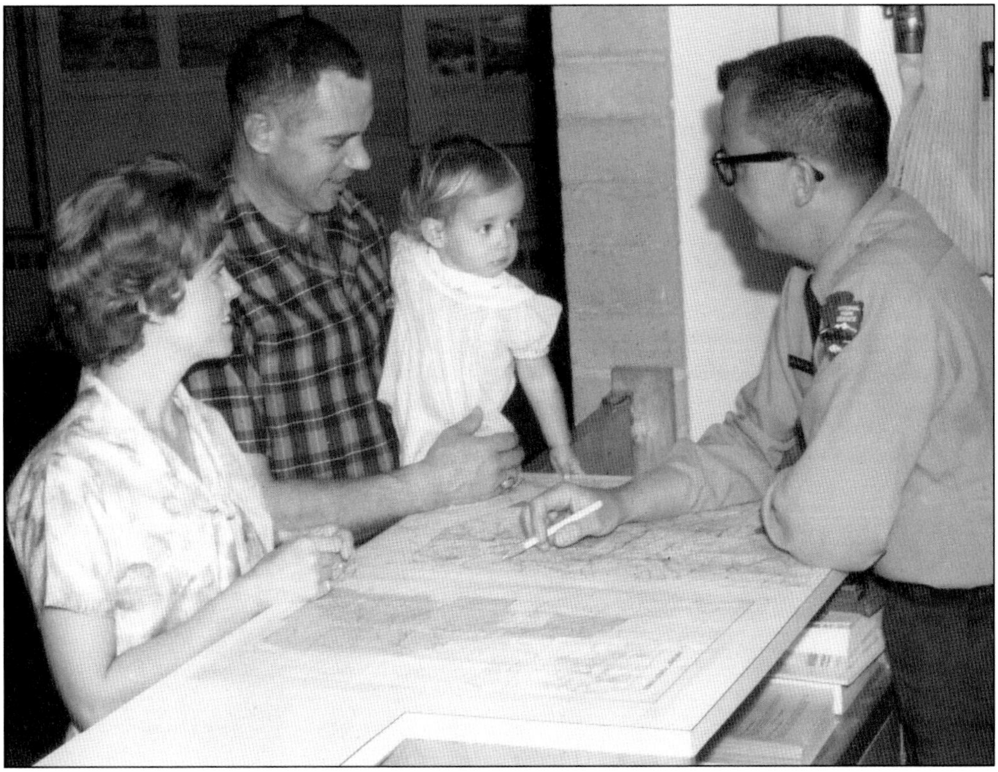

National Park Service rangers and volunteers have always been glad to help visitors learn about Chiricahua National Monument's geology, animals, plants, history, and people. Since NPS personnel believe the monument's future stewardship is most important, they encourage youngsters like the ones below to become Junior Rangers. Prospective Junior Rangers can pick up a free activity booklet at the visitors center and check out a free discovery daypack with items they can use during their monument visit. Upon completing the activity booklet and returning it, Junior Rangers receive a badge and certificate.

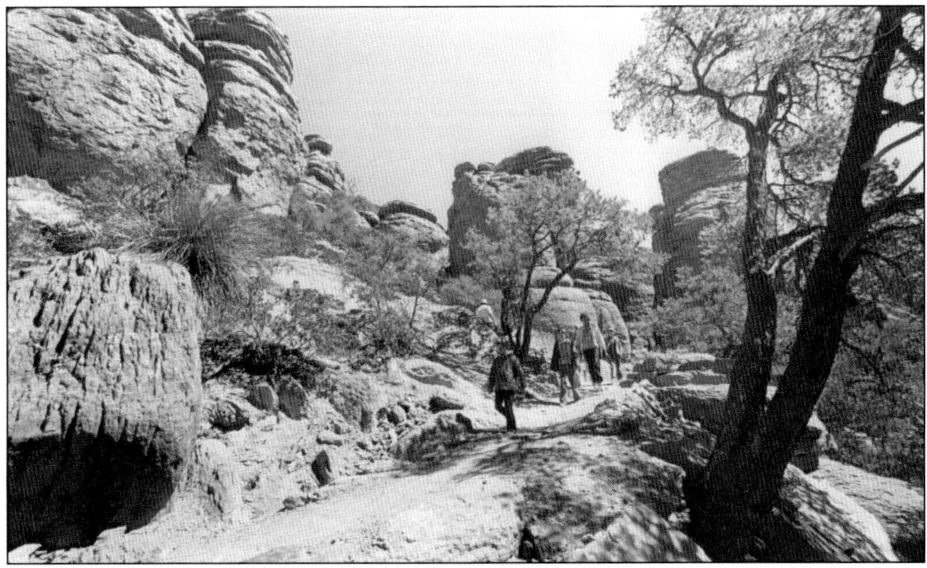

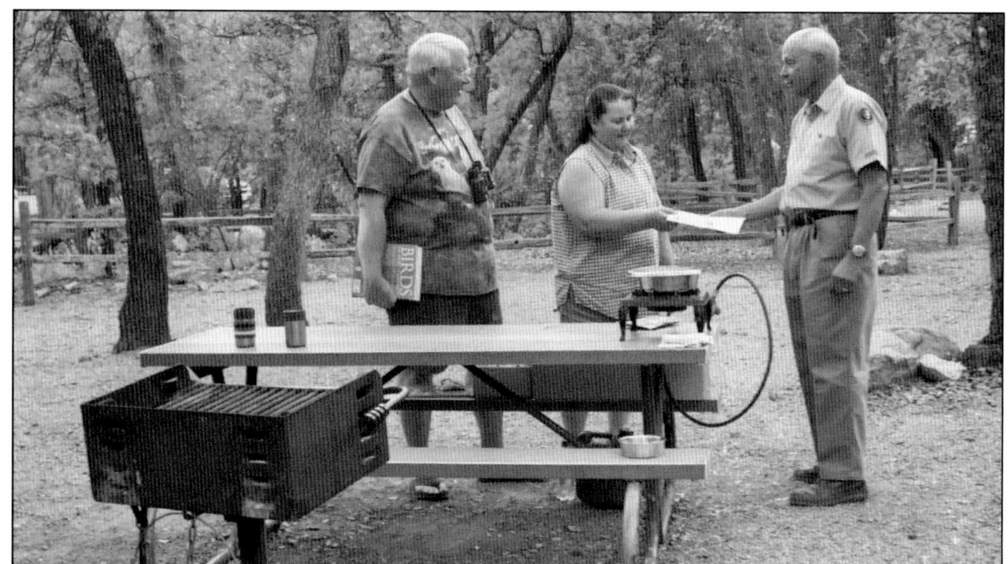

National Park Service campground hosts such as Pat Conway (right) can provide visitors staying in Chiricahua National Monument's Bonita Canyon Campground with birding data or info about programs given in the campground amphitheater. Bonita Canyon Campground reservations can be made at www.recreation.gov. Because the Bonita Canyon scenic drive is narrow and winding, recreational vehicles and trailers longer than 29 feet are not allowed beyond the visitor center. Utility hookups are not provided except at one site reserved for ADA access that has electricity available for medical usage. (Photograph by Suzanne Moody.)

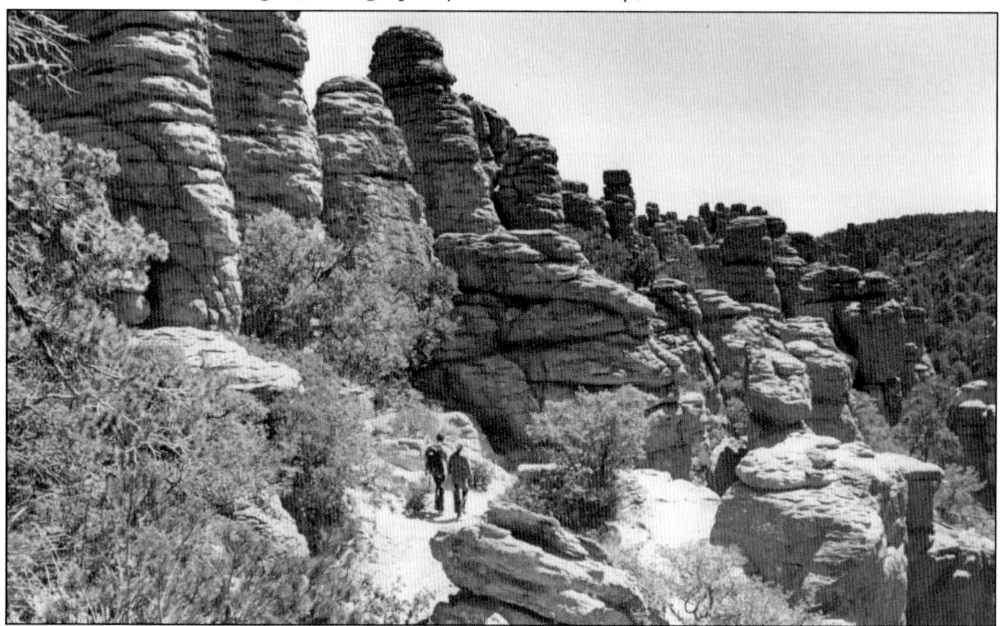

Hikers such as these two exploring some of the 17 miles of Chiricahua National Monument trails are encouraged to Rock the Rhyolite. It is a fun way for families and friends to earn "I Hike for Health" pins while exploring the scenery and history of Chiricahua National Monument. Each hiker must cover at least five miles within the monument. Show photographs or selfies taken on each trail hiked to monument staff at the visitors center to receive a pin.

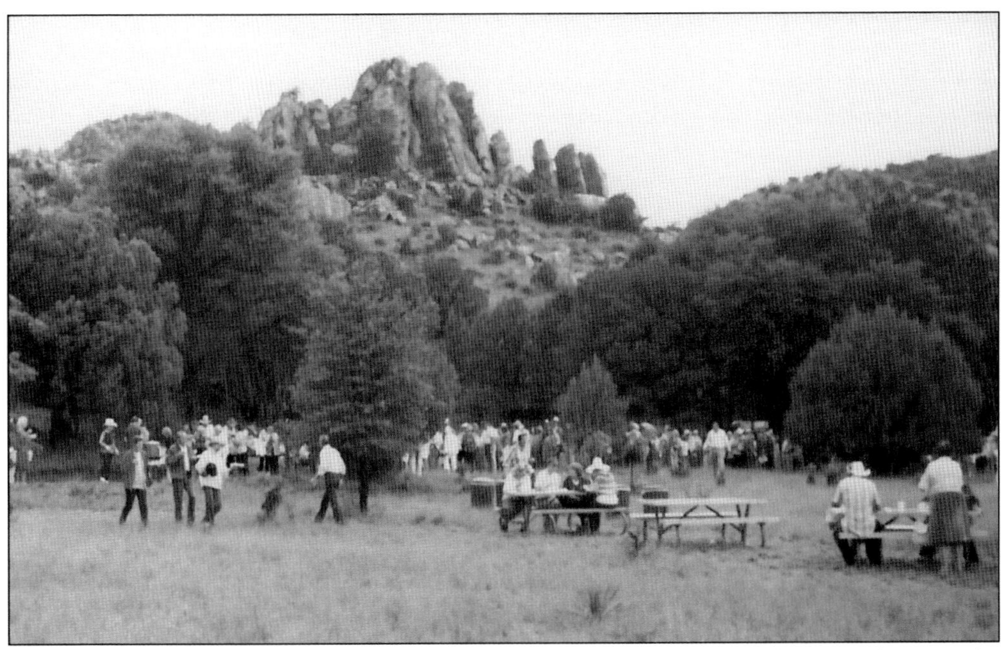

The National Park Service acquired Faraway Ranch in 1979 and carefully restored it over the next decade. On August 27, 1988, visitors flocked to Faraway (above) for a dedication ceremony. The details sightseers saw included Faraway's tack room, with its painted coffee cans that once held the bridles of the horses whose names were on the cans. A long line of people waited to enter the main house through the living room door (below). Once inside, they saw the couch where Lillian once sat, displayed with objects including her purse, white cane, and copies of the *Saturday Evening Post* issue she treasured because it contained an article about Faraway. Currently, National Park Service tours of the house are given on Saturdays and Sundays at 11:00 a.m. and 2:00 p.m. (Both, author's collection.)

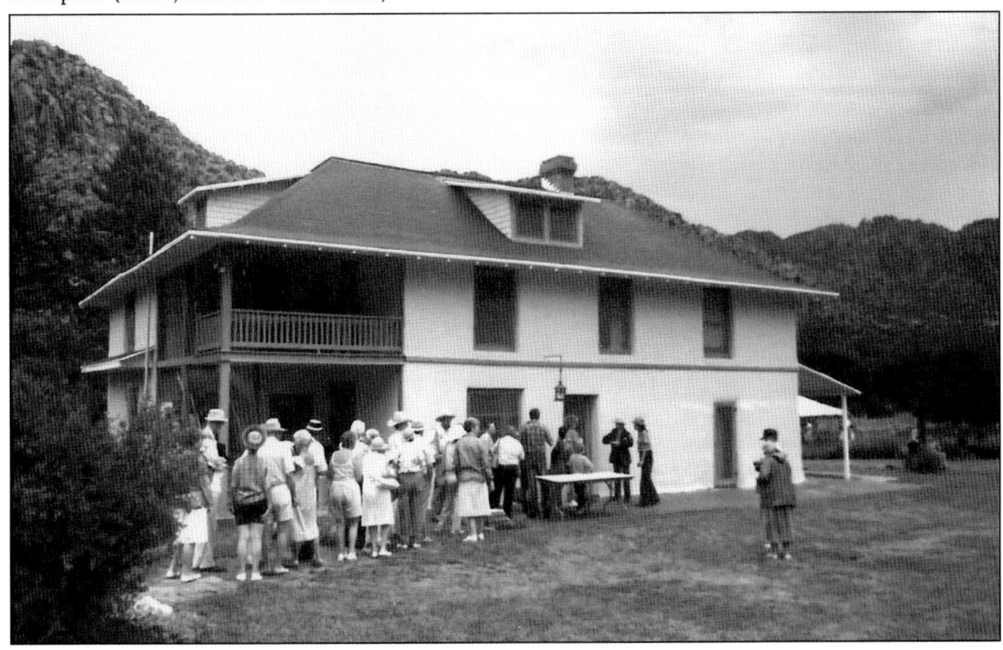

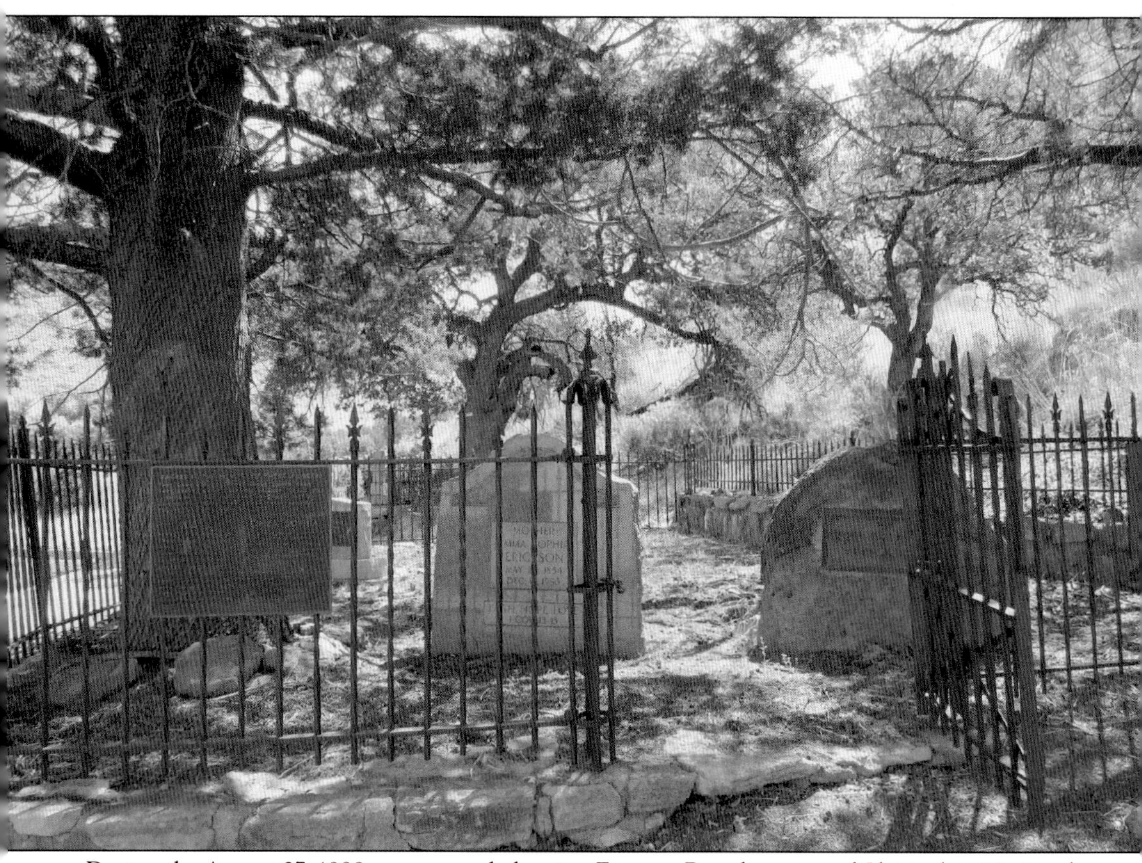

During the August 27, 1988, ceremony dedicating Faraway Ranch as part of Chiricahua National Monument, hundreds of people enjoyed a barbecue lunch and heard speeches by Congressman Jim Kolbe, various NPS officials, and Erickson family members. Without a doubt, the most moving speech was made by Bob Barrel. He met Emmajoy Hutchison, Hildegard's daughter, when she was visiting her aunt at Faraway and he was posted as an NPS ranger at Chiricahua National Monument. After marrying Emmajoy, Barrel spent much of his NPS career in Hawaii. He described the Hawaiian belief that an event is blessed by the gods if it rains on the event. Since it gently rained on Faraway during much of the dedication, Barrel expressed his great pleasure of ample blessings. Then he talked about his time working at the monument in the 1960s:

> As a young ranger here, before I knew the Ericksons, I'd be working at park headquarters and people would drive in. They would have tear streaks on their faces. They would still be as emotional as, goodness, I am now. And it didn't take me long to know why this was. They had stopped at the Erickson Cemetery and read the words that Lillian wrote and put on the cemetery, which are the words which to me describe in a nutshell Neil and Emma. And I think they deserve a reading: "Sacred to the memory of these pioneers. They came when only the brave dared come. They stayed where only the valiant would stay. Born in Sweden, Americans by choice—not by accident of birth—they loved their adopted country and served her well. They carved a home from the wilderness with the warp of labor and the woof of dreams. They wove a pattern of life as beautiful as the sunsets and as enduring as the mountains they loved so well."

(Photograph by Suzanne Moody.)

Bibliography

Heald, Weldon. *Sky Island*. Princeton, NJ: D. Van Nostrand Co., 1967.

Livingston, Dewey. *A Pioneer Log Cabin in Bonita Canyon*. San Francisco: National Park Service, 1994.

Pallister, John S., Edward A. de Bray, and Douglas B. Hall. *Guide to the Volcanic Geology of Chiricahua National Monument and Vicinity, Cochise County, Arizona*. No place: US Geological Survey, 1997.

Tagg, Martyn D. *The Camp at Bonita Cañon*. Tucson: Western Archeological and Conservation Center, 1987.

Taylor, Rick. *Hiking Trails and Wilderness Routes, Chiricahua Mountains of Arizona*. Tucson: Rainbow Expeditions, 1977.

Torres, Louis, and Mark Baumler. *Historic Structure Report: A History of the Buildings and Structures of Faraway Ranch*. Denver: National Park Service, 1984.

Wehman-French, Lisa. *Faraway Ranch Special History Study*. Santa Fe: National Park Service, no date.

DISCOVER THOUSANDS OF LOCAL HISTORY BOOKS FEATURING MILLIONS OF VINTAGE IMAGES

Arcadia Publishing, the leading local history publisher in the United States, is committed to making history accessible and meaningful through publishing books that celebrate and preserve the heritage of America's people and places.

Find more books like this at
www.arcadiapublishing.com

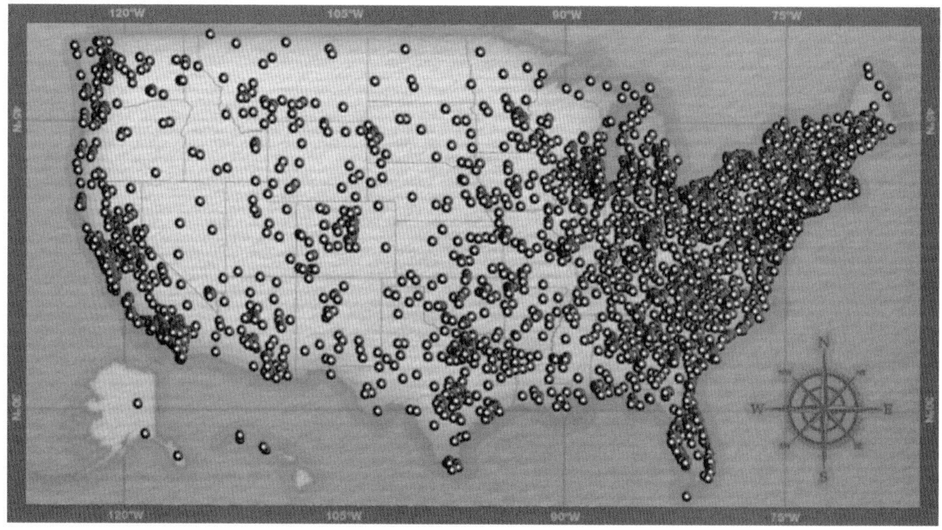

Search for your hometown history, your old stomping grounds, and even your favorite sports team.

Consistent with our mission to preserve history on a local level, this book was printed in South Carolina on American-made paper and manufactured entirely in the United States. Products carrying the accredited Forest Stewardship Council (FSC) label are printed on 100 percent FSC-certified paper.

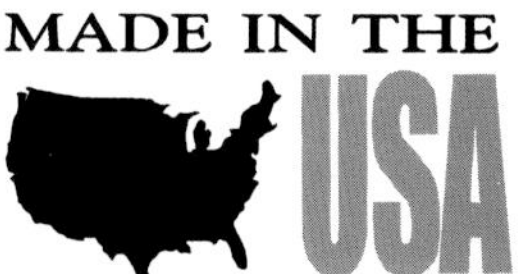